The Codetermination
Movement in the West

The Codetermination Movement in the West.

Labor Participation in the Management of Business Firms

Edited by

Svetozar Pejovich
University of Dallas

Lexington Books
D.C. Heath and Company
Lexington, Massachusetts
Toronto

Library of Congress Cataloging in Publication Data
Main entry under title:

The Codetermination movement in the West.

Papers presented at a conference organized by the Liberty Fund, 1977.
Includes index.
1. Employees' representation in management—Europe—Congresses.
2. Employees' representation in management—Congresses. I. Pejovich,
Svetozar. II. Liberty Fund.
HD5660.E9C56   658.31'52   77-18480
ISBN 0-669-02112-1

Contents

Preface

In recent years, various European countries have initiated legislation providing for worker participation in the management of business firms. Those states are now actively promoting "industrial democracy" through the use of codetermination schemes. *Codetermination* means that labor representatives are being given seats on boards of directors of business firms. This movement in Western Europe is bound to eventually reach the United States. A number of articles in the *Wall Street Journal, Business Week,* and elsewhere suggest that the idea of labor participation in corporate management is beginning to be discussed here.

Cognizant of the effects that codetermination might have in social restructuring of the West, the Liberty Fund, a foundation established to encourage study of the ideal of a society of free and responsible individuals, organized a conference on codetermination in the winter of 1977. The conference was held in Dallas in cooperation with the University of Dallas and was attended by 30 invited scholars from the United States and Western Europe. The purpose of the conference was to enhance the understanding of the political and social as well as economic effects of the codetermination movement in the West.

This book contains the papers presented at the conference as well as a general background paper on codetermination. A somewhat shorter version of this paper was published in the *Modern Age* (Winter 1978). The other papers blend historical and descriptive observations on the one hand with theoretical analysis on the other.

The first part of the book contains five chapters. My background chapter deals with the concept of codetermination, its sources of support, and some possible consequences of codetermination on the allocation of resources. Chapters by Fisher, Monissen, Ryden, and Shenfield provide detailed historical background as well as information about the current status of the codetermination movement in Germany, Sweden, and Great Britain.

The second part of this volume has three chapters. North's chapter shows how property rights have developed in Europe in response to changes in the economic conditions of life. North demonstrates the existence of a strong mutual interdependence between law and economics which, in turn, provides a framework for the analysis of codetermination. Nonmarket forces inherent in the coercive power of government and unleashed by political and social pressures explain increasing attenuation of ownership rights in the West. Furubotn's and Gallaway's chapters discuss in some detail the effects of labor participation in the management of business firms on investment and employment.

In summary, this book is an early attempt to assess the consequences of codetermination. It has neither a rich body of theory nor a wealth of evidence to draw from. Thus the purpose of this book has to be a modest one. It is hoped that the book establishes a general framework for the analysis of codetermination—a framework that relies on behavioral consequences of the interdependence between the legal system and economic life.

The writing of Chapter 1 was facilitated by a grant from the Foundation for Research in Economics and Education. In preparing the manuscript for publication I received invaluable help from my colleague Eirik Furubotn. Finally, I am grateful to Karen Stickle for her unlimited patience, excellent editorial assistance, and prompt typing services.

Part I
The Concept of Codetermination, Its Historical Development, and Current Status in Western Europe

1

Codetermination: A New Perspective for the West

Svetozar Pejovich

The Concept of Codetermination

In recent years, various European countries such as Denmark, the Netherlands, Norway, and Sweden have joined Germany and France in actively promoting "industrial democracy" through the use of codetermination schemes. The British Parliament is, as of this writing, considering comparable legal changes. However, in Switzerland, a decisive majority of the Swiss people voted against codetermination.

Codetermination is a major postwar social experiment in Western Europe. It is being introduced into the social life of West European countries via a series of laws and regulations. The common trait of all codetermination laws in Western Europe is the same: labor representatives are being allowed to participate in decision-making processes of business firms. However, the number of employees as well as the process by which they are elected (or appointed) to the governing authority of the firm varies from one European country to another. Where the governing authority of firms is divided into two tiers, such as in Germany and the Netherlands, the labor representatives sit on the supervisory board. Where there is a single board of directors, the employees' representatives take their place in that body.

Codetermination laws (that is, the requirement to seat voting labor representatives on firms' boards) are usually accompanied by additional legal constraints on right of management and owners of firms. Restrictions on the right to layoff employees, to choose or modify production techniques, and to close plants are but a few examples of such constraints. The purpose of those legal constraints is to resolve problems and issues that codetermination laws generate. The economic effects of codetermination stem from the resulting reallocation of decision-making powers within business firms. The analysis of codetermination must then consider both the content of various laws and regulations, and the effects these legal constraints have on economic behavior as well.

Sources of Support for Codetermination

There is little evidence that workers are strong supporters of codetermination. Laws on codetermination were soundly defeated in Switzerland, the only country in which a referendum on that specific issue was held. I conjecture that workers' lack of strong interest in codetermination is due to the fact that those who support codetermination have done a bad marketing job—they emphasized a wrong issue. Proponents of codetermination have been emphasizing the psychological and sociological effects of labor participation on workers (participatory democracy, humanization of labor) rather than its potential for raising total labor compensation. However, workers have traditionally been more interested in the machinery for raising their real incomes than in participatory democracy. From the point of view of workers, the negotiation of collective agreements by labor unions is the most important, best understood, and most historically acceptable manner in which employees have sought to influence income transfers, employment policies, and total working environments of the firms in which they work. In other words, unless workers perceive codetermination to be an effective vehicle (like unions) for raising total compensation, their attitudes toward labor participation in the management of business firms is likely to remain somewhat lukewarm.

The major support for codetermination in Western Europe comes from intellectuals. They insist that codetermination is being promoted *on behalf of* labor. Whatever the facade of words, codetermination is a vehicle through which the intellectual community seeks to restructure Western societies in ways that conform to its own perceptions of justice and equality.

It is, however, important to distinguish between intellectuals who see codetermination as a vehicle for making capitalism a "just" system and those who look upon codetermination as a step toward destroying it.

The first group of intellectuals views the modern corporation as a political entity. This "political" conception of the firm is then relied upon to justify the insistence on democratic participation of owners, managers, and employees in the decision-making process. The Commission of the European Communities summarized this type of attitude as follows:

The increasing recognition [is] being given to the democratic imperative that those who will be substantially affected by decisions made by social and political institutions must be involved in the making of those decisions. Employees not only derive their income from enterprises which employ them, but they devote a large proportion of their daily lives to the enterprise. Decisions taken by or in the enterprise can have a substantial effect on their economic circumstances, both immediately and in the longer term; the satisfaction which they derive from work; their health and physical condition; the time and energy which they can devote to their families and to activities other than work; and even their sense of dignity of autonomy as human beings.[1]

Codetermination is then seen as a Pareto optimal move that bestows benefits on labor without any detrimental effects on stockholders. In 1973 Willy Brandt said that codetermination belongs to the substance of the process of democratization in the West.[2] In other words, labor representatives on the board of the firm should be expected to concern themselves with the wage bill, the hiring and firing of workers, and the work environment, while managers would have to educate labor representatives about tradeoffs between wages, job security, and working conditions—in ways similar to those used by politicians in a democracy.

Most research on codetermination has been done by organizational psychologists.[3] In fact, their work has dominated the reports of the various European commissions.[4] The organizational psychologists emphasize the effects of codetermination on decision processes. They focus their attention on issues such as whether labor representatives on the board are ineffective because they lack knowledge or because of inadequate legal provisions. The organizational psychologists are not concerned with the consequences of codetermination on the allocation of resources, capital formation, and the flow of innovation. The focus on organizational processes and legal resolutions needed to effectively bring codetermination about has led the organizational psychologists to rely on opinion surveys and informal discussions for evidence in support of labor participation in the management of business firms. They simply assert that codetermination is desirable and seek legal changes to bring it about.

The following quote summarizes the position that most organizational psychologists seem to hold. Moreover, the last sentence in the quote argues that codetermination is a Pareto optimal move; that is, it argues that codetermination bestows benefits on labor without, at the same time, endangering traditional business interests.

. . . The European experience of worker representation at board level suggests that, to be even marginally effective as a meaningful form of industrial democracy, workers require parity representation on a meaningful board, a formal recognition of their link with trade unions, and a less restricted notion of board secrecy. Without such conditions worker directors are trivial in democratic terms. Even with such conditions the European experience suggests that conventional business interests will not be endangered.[5]

The organizational psychologists face the problem of reconciling their argument that codetermination is a Pareto optimal move with the fact that we need laws to force owners of business firms to accept it. If codetermination is beneficial to both stockholders and labor, why must stockholders be forced by law to engage in it? Why do they not voluntarily negotiate a mutually beneficial institutional restructuring? Jensen and Meckling summarized this point as follows:

The fact that stockholders must be forced by law to accept codetermination is the best evidence we have that they are adversely affected by it. By itself, that evidence is more telling than the combined results of the opinion surveys. But, the evidence is not limited to this fact. The evidence suggests, for example, that firms in the "Montan" industries [mainly mining and steel] in Germany tried to escape the more extreme codetermination requirements which applied thereby changing their organizational structure and activities. The practice was widespread enough to induce the government to enact a series of special laws (the Codetermination Protection Acts) to prevent avoidance. There is also evidence that under less than parity [i.e., equal representation on the board of directors for both workers and stockholders] codetermination laws which prevailed outside the "Montan" industries in Germany prior to 1976, firms often created "executive" committees with review and decision-making responsibilities from which labor was deliberately excluded. All of this evidence suggests that those who argue that codetermination either benefits stockholders or is innocuous, have an uphill task in making their case.[6]

It has also been argued by economists who support codetermination that productivity of labor is not technologically determined; that is, the conventional concept of efficiency in production (the profit-maximizing set of inputs) fails to recognize that the effort expanded by inputs is a variable that is affected by changes in the values of other variables in the system.[7] The argument is that the *right to participate* in determining wage rates, employment policies, and working conditions in the firm tend to increase workers' utility. The productivity of labor would then increase as workers became more satisfied with their total working environment. Within the framework of the conventional theory, this chain reaction from labor participation via worker utility to productivity of labor is interpreted as an upward shift in the marginal productivity of labor schedule.[8]

Western economists who support codetermination do not always reject the market mechanism. H. Nutzinger wrote, " . . . the market mechanism is not merely the only feasible form of social coordination that is consistent with workers' management but it is also the only desirable form."[9] Clearly, the importance of the market mechanism in reducing the cost of identifying alternative uses for resources and in generating incentives to allocate resources to their highest valued uses is understood by Professor Nutzinger. However, what he and other intellectuals who support codetermination have failed to comprehend is that their advocacy of codetermination is based on purely personal preferences. There is no theoretical work that presents economic analysis of codetermination at a professionally acceptable level. Also, European experience with codetermination is too young to evaluate. All that we know is that codetermination has not emerged voluntarily in the West. Thus it is hard to accept the position that codetermination is a Pareto optimal move, and therein lies the true danger of this social experiment. Suppose that codetermination fails to generate behaviors that are consistent with a Pareto optimal allocation of resources. Then, given the prevailing political climate in the West, a failure of codetermination to generate favorable outcomes is not likely to result in the abandonment of labor participation. It is more likely to bring about additional legal changes whose purpose would be to *correct* the system. The intellectuals who believe that codetermination is a vehicle for making capitalism work better might then discover that they have caused its downfall. As Professor Furubotn said, "The predictable outcome of additional 'corrective' measures will be a cumulative movement away from traditional capitalist system and the relatively free system currently known in Western Europe and the United States."[10]

Another group of intellectuals that support codetermination are the Marxists. They have revived Marx's specific criticism of capitalism that centers on the concept of alienated labor.[11] Ideally, a nonalienated worker should be unable to distinguish between work and leisure. The right of ownership in nonhuman resources, however, alienates man from work activity and makes work and leisure distinguishable. Emphasis here is on the dehumanization of man. This dehumanization of man is a direct consequence of the right of ownership. Private-property capitalist economy forces people to perform unchallenging, repetitive, and often repulsive work, and to lead unfulfilling lives. It follows that Marxists will support any law that attenuates the right of ownership in resources. This includes codetermination, which they consider as a step in the right direction. The following quotes capture the essence of their position on codetermination:

. . . Capitalist development, through bureaucratic order and hierarchical authority in production, limits work activities to those that (a) permit an essential role for capitalists and their managerial representative; (b) facilitate supervision and discipline of workers; (c) allow for flexible control from the top; and (d) limit through the division of tasks, the initiative of workers to "safe" levels.[12]

. . . I would argue that in this historical period only an expansion of the degree of democratic and participatory control that individuals have over their lives is compatible with full personal development, rewarding social activity, the elimination of class, racial, and sexual antagonisms, and material equality. The contribution of political democracy to this end is vitiated by the totalitarian organization of production. Only democracy and participation in production, i.e., the replacement of the capitalist class by the working class (white collar and blue, black and white, male and female) as the architects of production, and the accountability of managers and technicians to the will of workers, is compatible with equality and full individual development.[13]

Codetermination in Western Europe

The development of codetermination in Germany, Great Britain, and Sweden is discussed in this book by Fisher, Monissen, Shenfield, and Ryden. The purpose of this section is to briefly summarize codetermination schemes used in some other West European countries.

The Commission of the European Communities has been very active in promoting codetermination laws in Europe. The argument of the Commission is that all member states stand to benefit from laws that make internal structues of business firms similar. According to the Commission, common legal standards can be relied upon to facilitate the flow of resources among member states. To this end, the Commission of the European Communities issued "Proposal for a Fifth Directive on the Structure of Societies Anonymes" in 1972. The relevant passages from the Directive are as follows:

The Member States shall make provisions so that the structure of the company takes the form . . . (a) the management organ responsible for managing and representing the company; (b) the supervisory organ responsible for controlling the management organ; (c) the general meeting of shareholders. . . .
No less than one-third of the members of the supervisory organ shall be appointed by the workers or their representatives or upon proposal by the workers or their representatives.[14]

Of course, the Commission of the European Communities cannot compel member states to pass codetermination laws. However, it seems reasonable to assert that its influence on member states contributed to the emergence of participatory laws and regulations.

Codetermination redefines the balance of power between the shareholders, management, employees, and labor unions. Labor unions in particular are fearful that codetermination might reduce their leading role as the exclusive bargaining agent for workers. Moreover, labor unions seem generally reluctant to get involved in the management of privately owned firms whose workers they represent. Thus a necessary condition for getting labor unions in Western Europe to accept codetermination is to give them some control over the appointments of labor representatives to firms' boards.

In Denmark, two laws on codetermination were enacted in June 1973.[15] They gave the employees of all companies employing at least 50 people the right to elect two members of the board of directors. They are elected for a two-year term and enjoy the same rights and obligations as other members of the board.

In France, privately owned companies with at least 50 employees must admit two labor representatives to their boards. However, labor representatives join the board in a consultative (nonvoting) capacity. Changes are now being contemplated in France whereby the number of labor representatives on the boards will be increased. They will also be granted a full voting privilege. In state-owned firms, labor representatives occupy one-third of the seats on the council of administration and enjoy the same rights and obligations as other members of the council.

In Ireland, firms are free to decide whether to admit labor representatives to their boards. The official policy of the Ministry of Labor is to encourage labor participation in the management of business firms. Labor unions in Ireland have gone along with the idea of labor participation, providing that they participate in the selection of the employees' representatives.

In Luxemburg, the law requires that all firms with more than 1000 employees have a council of administration on which one-third of the members represent the employees. The employee representatives are chosen in a secret ballot from among the company's employees. In coal mining and the steel industry, labor unions designate three members of the council directly. Moreover, those union-appointed members of the council of administration need not be employees of the firm in question.

In the Netherlands, employees participate in the appointment of the members of the supervisory council in firms employing at least 100 employees or having a capital including reserves of at least 10 million guilders. In these companies, a firm's council is formed. The members of the council are elected by the employees. The firm's council has the right to participate in some limited decisions of the firm's management, such as pensions, participation in profits, safety and health provisions, and the like. The firm's council also nominates individuals to serve on the supervisory council of the firm. However, no person can be recommended to serve on the supervisory council who is employed either by the company or a labor union representing the employees of that company. The firm's council can also object to the appointment of a new member to the supervisory council if, in opinion of the firm's council, that person is not qualified to serve on the governing authority of the firm or the composition of the supervisory council would not be appropriate if that person were appointed. In general, codetermination in the Netherlands has some unique features of its own. Employees participate—via their membership in the firm's council—in the selection of the members of the supervisory council of their respective firms, but they cannot elect representatives from their own ranks.

Codetermination in Eastern Europe: The Case of Yugoslavia

Yugoslavia is the only country in the world today that has been experimenting with various codetermination schemes since the early 1950s. Thus, any attempt to assess economic and social consequences of codetermination should not overlook the Yugoslav experience—even though Yugoslavia is a socialist country. Codetermination in Yugoslavia has taken on the extreme form of turning over complete control of the affairs of business firms to labor. This is why Yugoslav firms are being referred to as labor-managed firms. Unlike workers in firms under codetermination schemes whose representatives sit on boards of directors along with representatives of shareholders, in Yugoslavia firm collectives run the enterprises. Firms under codetermination schemes in the West lie between the private corporation on one side of the spectrum of potential organizational structures and the labor-managed firm on the other. A behavioral analysis of firms under codetermination requires an understanding of the performance of both private corporations in the West and labor-managed firms in Yugoslavia. The purpose of this section is to outline the organizational structure of the labor-managed firm and to identify the content of property relations between the firm and the state.

The concept of self-management by labor is a permanent and fundamental characteristic of the Yugoslav social system. Article 1 of the 1974 Constitution says, "The Socialist Federal Republic of Yugoslavia is a federal state . . . based on the power of and self-management by the working class and all working people." Article 10 defines the Yugoslav social and economic system as being "based on freely associated labor and socially owned means of production, and on self-management by the working people in production and in the distribution of the social product in basic and other organizations of associated labor."

The social substance of self-management in Yugoslavia lies in the state ownership of capital goods and the employee ownership of the returns to capital (i.e., profits). The content of property relations in Yugoslavia is the essential and distinguishing feature of its economic system. In capitalism, the mode of entry into decision making (concerning the allocation and use of nonhuman resources) is the prerogative of ownership, either directly or through hired representatives. In centrally planned socialist states, the mode of entry into decision making is the prerogative of the Party leadership, either directly or through the state bureaucracy. In Yugoslavia, the mode of entry into decision making is the prerogative of those who work with capital assets directly (associated labor). This is the trademark of the Yugoslav concept of self-management.

In Yugoslavia, capital goods cannot be privately owned. Individual investment alternatives in that country are restricted to monetary assets, human capital, and some very limited types of physical assets, such as small shops, restaurants, taxi businesses, jewelry, and the like, where private property rights do not necessarily and obviously violate the principle of social ownership of capital goods. Generally, the term *social ownership* means property that is exclusively controlled by the state authority. The term *social* is usually used for political and ideological reasons.

The principle of self-management in Yugoslavia has attenuated the state's right of ownership in capital goods. The Yugoslav government had to develop new property rights capable of reconciling the constitutional principle of self-management on the one hand with the constitutional requirement that capital goods be socially owned on the other. That was accomplished by transferring some specific property rights from the state to business firms. Firms are free to choose how to use capital goods in their possession. They are allowed to rent or sell their capital goods to other firms (not to private citizens, though), to buy capital goods from other organizations, and to produce them for their own use. Firms can freely change the composition of their capital goods; that is, they can substitute one type of asset for another (cash for machines). These rights are the constitutional rights of employees in business enterprises. An implication is that the state cannot take capital goods away from these organizations.

Firms do not own the capital goods in their possession, however. Thus their rights in capital goods must be subject to some constraints. The basic organizations of associated labor must maintain the book value of their assets via depreciation or other means; for example, if they sold assets for less than book value, the difference had to be deducted from the earnings and reinvested. Periodically, an organization's assets are revalued to take into account the effects of inflation. The basic organizations of associated labor must also purchase insurance policies in amounts equal to the total value of their assets.

According to the Yugoslav law, capital assets owned by the state and held by business firms are set up in three funds:

1. Business Fund
   a. *Fixed capital:* land, forests and plantations, buildings, mines, tools, machines, means of transportation, installations, livestock, others
   b. *Working capital:* liquid assets (cash, demand deposits, foreign currency), accounts receivable, inventures, small tools, others
   c. *External investments:* joint investments with other organizations of associated labor, time deposits, investments in a bank, credits to other organizations of associated labor, others
   d. *Building fund*
   e. *Reduction in the business fund:* all sorts of bad debts, uncollectable claims, others
2. Reserve Fund
3. Collective Consumption Fund

The purpose of the Business Fund is to maintain and expand the scope of business operations. The Reserve Fund and the Collective Consumption Fund are earmarked for specific purposes. These funds are kept on separate accounts so that they are not used by firms to carry out regular activities.

The most unique feature of the Yugoslav economic system is that the employees have the right of ownership in the net product of their respective firms. This particular right captures the essence of self-management in Yugoslavia. The working collective does not own nonhuman assets of its organization (it has some well-specified rights in capital goods, though), but it does own the returns from these assets. The worker's right to share in the earnings has replaced the work for a contractual wage in Yugoslavia.

The analysis of the legal norms and institutional constraints that affect the formation and distribution of net product yield significant insights into the behavior of the basic organization of associated labor. It identifies the link between the system of rewards and productivity responses in Yugoslavia. Moreover, the analysis of net product permits deeper understanding of the range of objectives pursued by business firms, their behavioral patterns, and the possible causes of some economic problems in Yugoslavia.[16]

The law recognizes three major sources of total revenue: sales of goods and services, value of internal transactions, and returns on external investments. The term *internal transactions* refers to the value of transactions between various departments within a firm (e.g., shipping department in a department store). These transactions are valued at the prevailing market prices.

External investments are joint projects undertaken by two or more firms, e.g., time deposits, investments in a bank, and credits to other firms. Since the right of ownership in the returns from capital goods in Yugoslavia belongs only to those who work with those assets, the Yugoslav government made an ideological concession when it agreed that the collective can lend funds (or physical assets) to other collectives and capture returns. Importantly, the firm can make external investments only from its Business Fund and Collective Consumption Fund, and must deposit the returns into the same two funds.

The total revenue of the business firms are divided into three categories: expenditures for goods and services, amortization, and net product. Expenditures for goods and services are all business expenses that have to do with the formation of the total revenue. Turnover and custom taxes are included in this category. Turnover taxes are paid on the sale of final goods. They vary from one product to another, and from one region of the country to another; the average tax rate is about 13 percent. According to the law, business firms should consider the obligatory depreciation rates as minimal; that is, the collective may choose to depreciate assets at a higher rate. The asset that has been fully depreciated but is still productive must be reappraised (at its market price). If a fully depreciated asset is sold to another collective, the proceeds from the sale must be allocated to the Business Fund.

The net product, or *dohodak,* is the most important category in the distribution of a firm's total revenue. It is divided between legal obligations from *dohodak* and the residual that belongs to the collective. The law enumerates 11 legal obligations that must be met from *dohodak* (insurance premiums, social consumption tax, national defence tax, etc.). Legal obligations of firms in Yugoslavia are either fixed (fees) or proportional (taxes).

The residual (profit before wages) belongs to the business firms. According to the law, the residual must be divided between the Wage Fund, the Collective Consumption Fund, the Business Fund, and the Reserve Fund. The allocation of the residual among these funds is determined by the collective, subject to some legal constraints.

The composition of the Business Fund was explained earlier. The allocation to the Business Fund together with depreciation allowances contribute the base for new investment activity of a firm. From the point of view of the firm's employees, every dollar of the residual that is allocated to the Business Fund reduces their current incomes and promises larger incomes in the future. The Reserve Fund is to cover losses, protect the firm against emergencies, and make payments to employees when their incomes fall below the legal minimum.

The Collective Consumption Fund has the general purpose of improving the standard of living of the firm's employees. The most common uses of the Collective Consumption Fund are subsidies for apartments, care centers, recreation halls, scholarships, resort homes, and the like. The allocations to the Collective Consumption Fund are subject to the same legal obligations as the allocations to the Wage Fund.

The Wage Fund is subject to the social security tax. The remainder is then allocated among the employees. The rules for the distribution of the Wage Fund are determined by the collective. However, these rules must be clearly defined and announced in advance by the Workers' Council. In most firms the distribution of the Wage Fund is as follows: a specified number of points is attached to each job in the firm. While the criteria for determining the number of points for each position differ among organizations of associated labor, the following factors are frequently stressed: required skills, education, health risks, and hardships. The Wage Fund is then divided by the total number of points in the firm. That procedure determines the value of a point per accounting period. Next, the value of a point is multiplied by the number of points associated with each job, and the result is the employee's income for that period. The average range between the job with the largest and the job with the smallest number of points tends to be almost 5:1 in Yugoslavia. Also, the employees' incomes tend to vary from one accounting period to another in accordance with the profitability of business operations.

The most recent development in Yugoslavia is deeply rooted in the idea of self-management by labor. It is also a totally unique and perhaps dangerous experiment. I refer to the Law of Associated Labor of 1976. This law allows the employees of any department in a firm to form their own *basic organization of associated labor.* In conventional language, *basic organizations of associated labor* are work units, plants, departments within firms, and the like. The only requirement for forming a basic organization of associated labor is the identifiability and separability of the flow of receipts. That is, a group of workers must be able to show that the results of their joint work within a firm can be independently expressed. Each firm can then have one or more basic organizations of associated labor. A basic organization of associated labor controls its own business activities and owns its net product. The law of 1976 specifies broad outlines of the relationship between basic organizations in the same enterprises. Within these constraints of law, basic organizations must draw up contracts that specify in detail their mutual rights and obligations. A. major emphasis in these contracts, according to law, must be placed on the market forces of demand and supply. Moreover, the employees of a basic organization of associated labor have the right to decide to leave a firm (and take capital assets with them). However, they have to demonstrate that their gains from leaving the firm exceed the cost borne by the firm.

The right to govern a basic organization is vested in all employees of the basic organization, while the right to operate it is granted to the director (*poslovodni* organ). The employees exercise their right of governing the basic organization in two ways: directly and indirectly.

The forms of direct controls are *general meetings and referenda*. The employees govern a basic organization indirectly through a Workers' Council. The Workers' Council is the highest organ of management in a basic organization. Members of the Workers' Council are elected by all the employees for a two-year term. They can be reelected only once—the purpose of this constraint is to prevent the development of a closed governing group within the enterprise.

The director is the chief executive officer. He is appointed (and fired) by the Workers' Council. The Workers' Council must announce the position in the media and fill it by way of public contest. The director is responsible for the development, search and formulation of profitable policies, investment alternatives, and business strategies. The Workers' Council makes the final choices from among the alternatives presented by the director. However, the director's evaluation as well as his method of presentation of the available alternatives must influence the Workers' Council's choices.

If a firm has more than one basic organization of associated labor, its governing structure is as follows: Each basic organization sends its own representatives to the Workers' Council fo the firm. The Workers' Council of the firm elects the director. The relationship between basic organizations themselves and their rights and duties with respect to the firm must be regulated by contracts.

Yugoslavia has its own conglomerates as well. Firms may join together in what the Yugoslavs call the joint organization of associated labor. The Workers' Council of a joint organization consists of delegates nominated by business firms. It elects the director who, in turn, must cooperate with member enterprises. The rights and duties of working organizations in a joint organization are regulated by contractual agreements among themselves.

Legal and Economic Consequences
of Codetermination

Economic activity involves social interaction at two levels. The first level involves the development, specification, and modification of institutions by which the community seeks to resolve problems that have their source in economic scarcity. *Institutions* are defined here as legal and conventional arrangements that arise from the existence and pertain to the use of scarce goods. They specify the prevailing property rights in resources and define the general character of economic life in the community.[17]

The second level of economic activity involves decision making, individual choices, and contracts (exchange). These activities reflect man's search for more utility within a given set of institutional constraints. People seek contracts and negotiate terms of exchange expecting to reach higher levels of satisfaction. Importantly, exchange is more than a transfer of goods between contracting parties. Exchange is a transfer of some specific rights to do things with the goods that are being traded. A contract with a car rental agency as well as one with a car dealer are about the same physical object, the car. Yet the bundle of rights the consumer acquires in these two contractual arrangements are not the same. The consumer cannot receive the same increment in his total utility from renting a car as he gets from buying it. The bundle of rights to do things with goods that are being traded affects terms of exchange.

No person can transfer to other people more rights in a good than he himself possesses. Thus the prevailing institutional structure determines the scope and content of contractual activities. The analysis of exchange is then concerned with utility-maximizing behavior of individuals and the resulting allocation and use of resources, given the prevailing property rights structures.

The prevailing social structure is far from rigid. Social institutions change in response to forces that could be either endogenous to the system or imposed upon it from without.[18] In either case, changes in the prevailing institutional structures generate behavioral patterns that disrupt the existing equilibrium and take the economy *away* from it. This is so because institutional restructuring means a change in the constraints within which people seek and negotiate mutually preferred contracts.

Codetermination is likely to affect both levels of economic activity. Thus the effects of codetermination are not limited to marginal adjustments within the system. Labor participation in the management of business firms changes the prevailing relationship between the shareholders, managers, employees, and labor unions; it affects the social structure. Eventually, contractual activities of utility-seeking individuals (within the new set of institutional constraints) identify new equilibrium relationships. The analysis of codetermination must then identify changes in property rights structures, establish their effects on penalty-reward structures, and infer the expected behavioral patterns before it could turn to the question of new equilibrium relationships.

Legal Consequences of Codetermination

Laws on codetermination affect the prevailing set of relationships between the shareholders, managers, employees, and labor unions concerning a number of issues, such as wage negotiations, vector of labor compensation (fringe benefits, share of profit, contractual wate, etc.), employment policies, work environment, role of unions as the employees' exclusive bargaining agents, equity financing, and the like. These issues arise from uncertainties concerning the location of decision-making powers, appropriability of rewards, and the relationship between risk taking and bearing of costs in labor participatory firms. And these uncertainties then threaten the level and character of economic activity. In other words, codetermination laws initially affect the prevailing property rights structures without specifying new ones.

A major effect of codetermination is therefore to generate problems that require legal resolutions. The new social structure will then emerge via political negotiations that result in new laws. Therein lies a major danger of codetermination. It triggers institutional restructuring that is exogenous to the system; changes in property relations do not emerge from voluntary interactions of utility-seeking individuals. Thus codetermination cannot be presumed to be a Pareto optimal move; that is, the benefits received cannot be presumed to exceed the cost borne by other members of the community. Moreover, exogenous changes in the law have effects that go beyond redistribution of wealth. Instability of the existing legal system tends to affect the character of economic life in a country. Why?

The major function of law is to provide for the predictability of behavior.[19] The legal system defines the "rules of the game." From the point of view of a decision maker, the prevailing system yields a flow of benefits—the predictability of other people's behavior. The flow of benefits from law depends on its stability. As time goes by we learn how to adjust the system, identify exchange opportunities, and exploit the most beneficial ones. In addition, most business decisions have long-run consequences. A stable legal order encourages people to exploit exchange opportunities that have long-run consequences.

Frequent and unpredictable changes in the legal system or expectations about frequent changes in the legal system reduce incentives to exploit exchange opportunities that have long-run consequences. Legal instability raises the cost of exploiting these alternatives. The resulting increase in both the rate of interest and uncertainties about the future must affect the rate of capital formation, the pattern of investment activity, and the flow of innovation.

To secure the flow of benefits from law, the legal system must be maintained and changed only infrequently and in response to a broad consensus of all citizens. However, the legal system is a public capital good. The individual who incurs the cost of maintaining it confers benefits on others. The lack of appropriability of benefits reduces incentives to any person to bear the cost of maintaining the prevailing legal system. A textile manufacturer who supports free trade confers benefits on the consumers. In fact, people have incentives to seek changes in the existing rules whenever those changes promise to increase their wealth. The textile manufacturer has incentives to seek a change in law that would protect him from foreign competition. In other words, changes in the "rules of the game" in response to the efforts by individuals or organized groups should be recognized for what they are: conversion of a public capital asset into a source of private benefits. The resulting instability of the existing legal system must affect the allocation of resources, economic efficiency, and the character of economic life in the country.

Codetermination laws in Western Europe are bound to generate a flow of legal changes. The resulting institutional restructuring could then be expected to introduce a degree of instability in West European legal systems, with all the accompanying effects previously mentioned.

Economic Consequences of Codetermination

Economic analysis of codetermination presupposes a political theory capable of explaining the development of the new institutional structure. We do not have such a theory. Moreover, we do not have a theory that would tell us how the board of directors will behave when labor representatives join it. It follows that economic analysis of codetermination faces a serious problem just getting off the ground. Predictably, there are very few theoretical works on the consequences of codetermination written at a professionally acceptable level of quality.[20] Even these works are tentative in their conclusions. All that one finds in the literature is either a description of codetermination laws in Western Europe or results of various opinion surveys or naive attempts to provide a theoretical justification for labor participation in the management of business firms. In the meantime, West European countries are being pushed into a major social experiment with little if any understanding of its eventual effects on the level and character of economic life.

Until political developments in Western Europe provide more evidence on institutional changes accompanying codetermination laws, economic analysis of codetermination must be limited to our *perception* of the behavior effects of labor participation in some key institutions in a private property free-market economy. In other words, the best we can do at this time is to identify social institutions that codetermination tends to affect and perceive some possible behavioral effects of labor participation on the allocation of resources, employment, capital formation, and the rate of innovation. Those perceptions provide a tentative framework for a theory of codetermination.

The *freedom of contract* and the *right of ownership* are two fundamental institutions in a free-market, private property community. Contractual freedom means that people are free to seek contracts and negotiate terms of exchange. Freedom of contract serves an important social function of identifying alternative uses for resources. The right of ownership ensures that the highest-valued alternative is chosen. Thus contractual freedom and ownership generate specific and predictable behavioral patterns that are consistent with both individual liberty and economic efficiency. Instead of prescribing solutions for social problems that find their source in economic scarcity (e.g., planning), contractual freedom and ownership define the *procedure* for human interactions and *generate incentives* for each individual to seek the most preferred solutions for himself, given other people's right to do likewise.

Codetermination endangers both the freedom of contract and the right of ownership. By prescribing the nature of economic arrangements within a firm, codetermination laws restrict individuals' freedom to seek and negotiate the most beneficial organizational forms. It is important to understand that the freedom of contract means that labor participation in corporate management could emerge out of *voluntary* contractual arrangements, as have many other organizational forms (corporations, cooperatives, partnerships, nonproprietory firms, etc.). Indeed, there are cases in which codetermination has emerged voluntarily. If codetermination bestows benefits on labor in excess of stockholders' costs, why do we need laws that force stockholders and labor to engage in such contractual arrangements? Clearly, if the benefits captured by labor exceed the cost borne by stockholders, they would find it in their mutual self-interest to voluntarily negotiate a form of codetermination. The fact that codetermination has not emerged on a nationwide scale out of voluntary contractual arrangements means that it is a costly (inefficient) form of economic organization, that it could not survive competition against other contractual arrangements, and that it could be brought into existence only by government "fiat." When codetermination is imposed by the state, it restricts contractual freedom and, in a behavioral sense, interferes with identification of the value that people attach to different alternatives.

Codetermination also interferes with the right of ownership. Labor participation in the management of business firms implies the political action of granting labor a voice in areas of decision making that have traditionally been the prerogative of ownership, either directly or through hired representatives. In essence, codetermination means a change in the mode of entry into decision making. When the mode of entry into decision making through ownership is circumvented by law, the result must be a significant institutional restructuring. Public acceptance of the idea that it is legitimate and proper for the state to limit the decision-making power of those who supply investable funds and assume the risks of production suggests that the extent of institutional reorganization depends on the political process.

Moreover, it is reasonable to conjecture that codetermination questions the owner's right to claim and dispose of profits. Clearly, the role of profits in directing resources is ignored. The institutional arrangements of codetermination reflect the view that profits emerge from the exploitation of labor and are the legitimate object of redistribution.

Business decisions entail risk. Risk arises from the fact that current decisions about the use of resources have future consequences (measured by changes in the value of the resources). These future consequences can only be anticipated. Different property relations imply different assignments of benefits and losses from current decisions. Under the regime of private property rights, the owner bears *all* the future changes in the value of his assets. This marriage of decision-making power and the bearing of future consequences generates incentives for the decision maker to continuously seek the most valuable alternatives for his resources.

A possible effect of codetermination comes via a divorce between decision making and risk bearing. In a codetermination firm, labor representatives do not bear *all* changes in the value of the firm's assets. Codetermination attenuates the right of ownership. Attenuation of ownership implies a change in the quality of decisions. It is so because labor representatives in a participatory firm have fewer (I did not say *no*) incentives to seek the most profitable outlays. Given workers' time horizon, which is limited to their expected employment by the firm, labor-participatory firms have more incentives to choose investment alternatives and business policies that shift incomes forward and postpone costs (e.g., faculty in charge of the university's endowment fund). For example, consider two investment alternatives of equal costs. The expected present value of one alternative is $1000, while the other yields only $750. However, if the returns from the first alternative are discounted over a period of 20 years and those of the second over only 5 years, workers would tend to push the management in the direction of choosing the less profitable one. Even in the absence of sharing in the firm's profits, wage negotiations and their perception of job security would provide workers with incentives to perfer business policies that promise larger annual earnings over a limited time period (i.e., the expected length of employment by *that* firm) to those policies that maximize the firm's present worth.

As we have seen already,[21] codetermination is also defined on the ground that productivity of labor will increase in response to changes in workers' total compensation (pecuniary and nonpecuniary). However, there is no theory showing that gains from improvements in labor productivity will offset the resulting increase in labor costs. Actually, if such were the case, an optimal codetermination arrangement would have emerged contractually. It simply is not enough to claim that work effort is positively related to worker's utility.

Finally, codetermination means a transfer of wealth from the shareholders to labor. We can conjecture the following chain of events: the rate of return from capital invested in labor-participatory firms (mostly corporations) will fall; the resulting flight of capital into the other (nonparticipatory) alternatives such as small firms, human capital, bonds, and foreign investment will change investment patterns in the economy; the rate of capital formations in the corporate sector will be less and in other areas greater than it would otherwise; the rate of return in nonparticipatory investments will fall, while the marginal productivity of labor will rise. In the corporate (participatory) sector the rate of return from investment will rise, while the marginal productivity of labor will fall. In equilibrium, corporate firms will produce smaller outputs and charge higher prices than they would otherwise. Conversely, prices will be lower and outputs greater in nonparticipatory sectors of the economy.

If this simple scenario is predictive of the general effects of codetermination, labor participation in the management of business firms will result in the reallocation of resources away from the most efficient, technically advanced, and productive sector of the economy and toward less-efficient, technically less-capable and less-productive alternatives. A general decline of the level and character of the economy could then be predicted.

In summary, the idea of codetermination is being pushed in the West without much knowledge concerning its effects on the character of economic and social life. In effect, we are being asked to accept, on faith, that codetermination will yield net social benefits. Indeed, it is possible but does not seem likely. The proponents of codetermination must offer a theory that is not emotional in tone and poor in logic; that is, they must offer a theory that yields refutable propositions concerning economic effects of labor participation in corporate management. Until this is done, the following points imply that codetermination is likely to be a costly social experiment: (1) codetermination has failed to emerge out of voluntary contracts, as have many other organizational forms; and (2) forced codetermination *restricts* individuals' freedom to seek and negotiate mutually preferred contractual arrangements and *attenuates* the right of ownership in capital goods.

Notes

1. "Employee Participation and Company Structure in the European Community," *Bulletin of the European Communities,* Supplement (August 1975): 9.

2. See Chapter 4 of this book.

3. M. Jensen and W. Meckling, "On the Labor Managed Firm and the Codetermination Movement," paper presented at the Interlaken Conference on Analysis and Ideology, June 1977.

4. E. Batstone, "Industrial Democracy and Worker Representation at Board Level: A Review of the European Experience," *Industrial Democracy: European Experience,* Industrial Democracy Committee Research Report, London, 1976; P. Davies, "European Experience with Worker Representation on the Board," *Industrial Democracy: European Experience,* Industrial Democracy Committee Research Report, London, 1976; A. Martin, "From Joint Consultation to Joint Decision-Making: The Redistribution of Workplace Power in Sweden," *Viewpoint,* June 1976; Mitbestimmung in Unternehmen, Mitbestimmungs Kommission, Stuttgart 1970.

5. E. Batstone, "Industrial Democracy and Worker Representation," p. 43.

6. M. Jensen and W. Meckling, "On the Labor Managed Firm," p. 7.

7. D.W. Rasmussen, "Worker Owned Firms in a Free Enterprise Economy," paper presented at the Southwestern Social Sciences Meeting, Dallas, April 1977.

8. H. Leibenstien, "Allocative vs. X Efficiency," *American Economic Review* 56 (June 1966): 392-215, H. Leibenstein, *Beyond Economic Man* (Cambridge, Mass.: Harvard Univ. Press, 1976); and P. Blumberg, *Industrial Democracy: The Sociology of Participation* (New York: Schocken Books, 1968).

9. H. Nutzinger, "Self-Management in the Public Sector," paper presented at the Interlaken Conference on Analysis and Ideology, June 1977.

10. See Chapter 7 of this book.

11. For a discussion of the concept of alienated labor, see S. Pejovich, "The Relevance of Marx and the Irrelevance of Marxian Revivals," *Modern Age* 21 (Winter 1977): 30-38.

12. H. Gintis, "A Radical Analysis of Welfare Economics and Individual Development," *Quarterly Journal of Economics* 86 (November 1972): 591.

13. H. Gintis, "Welfare Economics and Individual Development: A Reply to Talcott Parsons," *Quarterly Journal of Economics* 89 (May 1975): 301-302.

14. "Proposal for a Fifth Directive on the Structure of Societies Anonymes," *Bulletin of the European Communities,* Supplement (October 1972): 8-9.

15. For detailed descriptions of codetermination schemes in Western Europe upon which the rest of this section is based, see "Employee Participation and Company Structure in the European Community," *Bulletin of the European Communities,* Supplement (August 1975).

16. For a detailed analysis of the behavior of the Yugoslav firm, see S. Pejovich, "The Banking System and the Investment Behavior of the Yugoslav Firm," in *Plan and Market,* M. Bernstein, ed. (New Haven: Yale Univ. Press, 1973); and S. Pejovich, "The Labor Managed Firm and Bank Credit," in *Economic Analysis of the Soviet-Type System,* J. Thornton, ed. (Cambridge: Cambridge Univ. Press, 1976).

17. See E. Furubotn and S. Pejovich, "Property Rights and Economic Theory: A Survey of Recent Literature," *Journal of Economic Literature* 10 (December 1972): 1137-1162.

18. See H. Demsetz, "Toward a Theory of Property Rights," *American Economic Review* 57 (May 1967): (347-1373; D. North and R. Thomas, *The Rise of the Western World* (Cambridge, Eng.: Cambridge Univ. Press 1973); and S. Pejovich, "Towards a Theory of the Creation and Specification of Property Rights," *Review of Social Economy* 30 (September 1972): 309-325.

19. For an original discussion of law as a public capital good, see J. Buchanan, *The Limits of Liberty* (Chicago: Univ. of Chicago Press, 1975), pp. 123-129.

20. Examples are M. Jensen and W. Meckling. "On the Labor Managed Firm"; and Chapters 7 and 8 of this book.

21. See note 8.

2 Labor Participation in Great Britain

Arthur Shenfield

Definitions

Labor participation may assume a variety of forms. We shall define the principal forms as follows.

Codetermination

In codetermination, representatives of employees are appointed or elected to the governing authority of an enterprise. Where, the governing authorities of companies are divided into two tiers, the supervisory board and the board of management, such as in Germany and the Netherlands, the employee representatives sit on the supervisory board. In most other countries there is normally a single board of directors, and employee representatives take their place in that body.

The employee-directors may be elected by all the employees of the enterprise or by selected groups of employees, or they may be in some way nominated, possibly by the trade unions of which the employees, or some of them, are members.

Copartnership

In copartnership, employees or selected groups of employees are entitled to receive shares in the ownership of the enterprise. The shares may be of a special character, distinct from those of the general shareholding body, or they may be the same as the latter. In the former case they may or may not carry voting rights, or their voting rights may be subordinate to those of the general shares; and their transferability, by sale or otherwise, may be limited, the most common limitation being a requirement that on leaving the enterprise employees must dispose of their shares at a valuation to a trust set up for this purpose. Since it confers a share of ownership upon employees, copartnership also implies an entitlement to a share of profits.

Profit-Sharing

Profit-sharing without copartnership amounts to an employee entitlement to a share in profits (in addition to wages or salaries) without a share in ownership. Normally it requires a formal arrangement specifying the entitlement and identifying those (all employees or selected groups of them) in whom it is vested. However, where it is the established practice of an employer to distribute a share of profits to employees without a formal arrangement, the practice is sometimes included in lists of profit-sharing schemes.

Consultation

Consultation implies formal arrangements for regular contact between management and other employees. It will normally vest the power or right of consultation in a works councils, on which managements and other employees will be represented. Less often the consultation may extend to companywide councils, where enterprises are of a multiplant character. Consultation may also extend to a whole industry, where representatives of managements and other employees from numerous enterprises meet each other. In these cases the employee representatives will most often be trade union officials or nominees.

Collective Bargaining

Agreements between employers and trade unions often include provisions that limit the decision-making powers of employers in ways that are additional to the constraints normally imposed by settlements on wages or conditions of work. In these cases there may be a very effective form of employee participation in managerial decisions, but through the agency of a trade union whose aims and policies may well not accord with the desires of a particular firm's employees.

In this chapter I shall be principally concerned with codetermination, copartnership, and profit-sharing, and in lesser measure with consultation. I shall not be concerned with collective bargaining, since it mainly raises questions which, though of great and perhaps paramount importance in labor relations, are at most peripheral to problems of labor participation.

History

As the original home of the industrial revolution, Britain displays a long history of attempts at labor participation in various forms. Nevertheless, with the relatively unimportant exceptions of some forms of consultation and the appointment of employees or trade union representatives to some of the nationalized industries' main or subsidiary boards, the whole system has remained to this day voluntary in character. There have never been (and to this day there are not) any laws in Britain requiring codetermination, copartnership, or profit-sharing in private industry. It is very likely, as we shall see later, that laws may very soon be passed requiring various forms of participation, but this stage has not yet been reached.

Before the fourth quarter of the nineteenth century, there was no persistent, widespread, or successful movement toward labor participation (e.g., the ultimately abortive schemes of Robert Owen).[1] The fourth quarter of the century saw a change, partly because of the challenge presented by the rise of well-organized trade unionism (mainly among the skilled up to 1881,[2] but thereafter also among the semiskilled and unskilled), and partly because of the emergence among employers themselves of some reaction against the rugged individualism of the early industrial revolution. The motives which then induced a number of firms in various industries to experiment with schemes of copartnership or profit-sharing (but not codetermination) were thus mixed. Partly they were aimed at the improvement of worker productivity; partly they were intended to engender a worker loyalty to the firm to stand against the pretensions of the unions; and partly they arose from the spreading notion that workers were morally entitled to at least a share in profits and perhaps also a share in ownership.

I must hasten to make clear here that the reaction among employers against the rugged individualism of the early industrial revolution is in no way to be assumed to indicate intellectual or moral elevation among them. All that it meant was that the doubts about the virtue or efficiency of the free enterprise system that spread among the intellectual classes from the 1880s onward in Britain began to influence the minds of businessmen themselves, although the doubts were often based on egregious intellectual error.

In 1884 a group of employers and men active in public life formed an association with the cumbersome title, The Labor Association for Promoting Cooperative Production Based on Copartnership of Workers. Though it referred to copartnership, it made no clear distinction between copartnership and profit-sharing, and in fact most of the schemes initiated under the umbrella of the association were schemes of profit-sharing. In 1902 it changed its name to The Labor Copartnership Association, and later to The Industrial Copartnership Association. Very recently it changed its name to The Industrial Participation Association, which is the title under which it operates today.

The champions of the movement were always in a small minority among employers, but from time to time they numbered some of the most prominent industrialists of their day (e.g., William Lever, later Lord Leverhulme, the founder of the great firm of Lever Brothers, now Unilever Ltd.; and Seebohm Rowntree of the famous Rowntree cocoa and chocolate company). They tended to be supported by politicians and other public men who considered themselves to be of a "progressive" character, by which was indicated a belief in the partial virtue of the free enterprise system combined with a belief in the need to soften the alleged harshness of its treatment of the worker. Such supporters tended to be associated with the Liberal Party, especially in the early years of the twentieth century when that party commanded the greater part of the working class vote; and to this day Liberal Party policy has tended to give prominence to the principle of copartnership as a means of reconciling the industrial interests of capital and labor.

With two exceptions, of which only one bore special significance, schemes of copartnership and profit-sharing displayed no special concentration in particular industries. They were most numerous in textiles and engineering because until the interwar years these were, with coal mining, the leading British industries (in coal mining until the interwar years wages were always linked in one way or another to coal prices and hence to profits, so that explicit profit-sharing schemes could not easily get a foothold),[3] but they never arose in more than a small or smallish minority of firms in these industries.

The two exceptions were the gas industry and retail cooperatives. In the gas industry (i.e., the industry producing gas from coal, and coke as the residual) prices were subject to public regulation, labor was largely unskilled, but employment was steady, so there were many long-service employees. In such circumstances profit-sharing and copartnership were attractive to employers for the generation of worker loyalty, which was at least part of the reason why for many years the General and Municipal Workers Union, which organized gas workers, was one of the least militant of unions.[4] In addition, the equities of the gas companies were regarded as exceptionally safe investments and were therefore attractive to the workers. After the nationalization of the gas industry by the first post-World War II Labor government, these schemes were terminated.

Retail cooperatives, though mainly concerned with cooperative ownership by customers and the distribution of trading surpluses to them, tended in numerous cases to extend the idea of surplus sharing to employees. However, as the cooperatives grew to maturity, the tendency was to move away from sharing with employees to limit sharing to "members" (i.e., customers).

With the rise to high importance since World War I of the chemical industry, a number of schemes of copartnership and profit-sharing became prominent in this industry. The largest of all British industrial companies, Imperial Chemical Industries, operates a copartnership scheme under which its employees receive an allotment of ordinary shares in the company that are not subject to any limitations on voting rights or disposal.

Throughout the history of copartnership and profit-sharing, the majority of employers have been indifferent to the movement. Since there has been no compulsion, they have been free to judge these schemes on their prospective merits. No scheme has ever produced so clear and compelling a case of improved productivity or harmonious labor relations as to be a completely persuasive example to industry. On the contrary, numerous firms have over the years experimented with such schemes and found improvement insufficient to justify persistence, if existent at all. But also because there has been no compulsion, there has been no opposition to the scheme as such from industrial owners or managers. Those who were not convinced of their virtue simply did not adopt them.

Opposition to the movement has come in the past, widely and persistently, from British trade unions. They have always regarded profit-sharing as a device to deceive the workers into thinking that they were getting something over and above their normal entitlement—and, to make it worse, deferred until the annual distribution of profits. They have always held the view that the workers' remuneration should take the form of wages, which should encompass all sums which of course they, the unions, would negotiate. Since profit-sharing is also in some measure designed to produce worker loyalty to the firm, it obviously runs counter to the union desire for maximum loyalty to itself.

Insofar as copartnership implies profit-sharing, it has similarly met with persistent opposition from the trade unions. So too with its effect, if any, on company loyalty and trade union loyalty. Yet union opposition, both to profit-sharing and to copartnership, has normally fallen far short in intensity and vigor from that mounted against employers in wage disputes. This is not because there is some element of appeal in the case of copartnership to any open or latent syndicalism in the unions. In its whole history since its modern beginnings in the 1850s, British trade unionism has been almost wholly free from syndicalist influences.[5] The reason why union opposition to these schemes, though ingrained and persistent, has not normally been heated or violent is simply the fact that they have never appeared to be numerous enough or important enough either to drive a significant wedge between the favored and the nonfavored workers or to make serious inroads into trade union power or influence.

The last available survey of profit-sharing and copartnership schemes was published in 1956 by the Ministry of Labor and related to 1954.[6] Though more than 20 years have elapsed since then, it is known that in that period the number and coverage of these schemes have fallen moderately. At the same time, the civilian labor force has risen by about 8 percent, but the employed labor force has remained roughly constant. The 1954 figures, showing that only about 1½ percent of the employed labor force was then covered by profit-sharing or copartnership schemes, are thus above the ceiling of any reasonable estimate of the present percentage coverage. We are thus enabled to say with some confidence that the number of participants is now below 1½ percent and above 1 percent of the employed labor force. Whatever the precise figure may be, it is clearly a small percentage of the employed labor force. The relevant 1954 figures are shown in Table 2-1.

The relatively high coverage in chemicals (about 20 percent participation) arose from the dominance of the scheme operated by Imperial Chemical Indus-

Table 2–1
Profit-sharing and Copartnership Schemes, 1954

Industry Group	Number of Schemes	Number of Persons Employed	Number of Participants	Employed Labor Force
Agriculture, Forestry, Fishing	4	191	180	1.0 mn.
Mining, Quarrying, Treatment of Nonmetal Mining Products Other than Coal	17	49,855	30,105	1.2 mn.
Chemicals and Allied Trades	26	141,330	105,577	0.5 mn.
Metal Manufacture	9	25,389	12,526	0.5 mn.
Engineering, Shipbuilding, and Electrical Goods	57	91,000	39,521	2.0 mn.
Vehicles	8	55,782	35,800	1.2 mn.
Metal Goods not Elsewhere Specified	6	3,178	2,164	0.5 mn.
Precision Instruments, Jewelry	4	9,555	9,316	0.1 mn.
Textiles	30	23,968	13,874	1.0 mn.
Leather, Leather Goods, and Fur Clothing	22	30,726	15,195	1.5 mn.
Food, Drink, and Tobacco	22	39,022	28,719	0.9 mn.
Manufacture of Wood and Cork Paper and Printing	33	21,406	9,944	0.8 mn.
Other Manufacturing Industries	9	6,880	3,522	0.3 mn.
Building and Contracting	7	3,124	982	1.4 mn.
Gas, Electricity, and Water Supply	4	599	491	0.4 mn.
Transport and Communications Distributive Trades	19	28,717	21,047	4.4 mn.
Insurance, Banking, and Finance	10	29,672	13,308	0.5 mn.
Miscellaneous Services	6	3,232	1,932	1.9 mn.
National Government	0	0	0	0.6 mn.
Local Government	0	0	0	0.7 mn.
Professional Services	7	820	589	1.7 mn.
Total	310	564,446	344,792	22.6 mn.

tries, which is by far the largest employer in that industry. A similarly high coverage in chemicals would undoubtedly be displayed in 1976 if the figures were available.

The tendency of schemes to be started but later to be wound up is illustrated by the 1954 figures in Table 2-2. The figures show that although the movement is now at least a hundred years old, only 31 schemes (10 percent of the total) started before 1919 were still extant in 1954. In numerous cases termination was due to the winding up of the businesses concerned, or to their amalgamation with other businesses. Undoubtedly, however, disapointment with results, or the failure of results to inspire enthusiasm, was often a dominant factor.

Table 2-2
Longevity of Schemes, 1954

Date of Commence- ment of Schemes	Number of Schemes Existing at End of 1954
Before 1900	7
1900-1913	19
1914-1918	5
1919-1938	104
1939-1945	30
1946-1953	126
1954	9
Date Unknown	10
Total	310

The 1956 survey happened to view the movement somewhere near its apogee. There had been two previous official surveys, one in 1912[7] and one in 1920.[8] The former found 133 schemes in existence (plus a few for which figures were not available), covering upwards of 106,000 workers; the latter found 164 schemes extant, covering 243,000 workers. Thus there was a fair degree of progression up to the 1954 figure of 310 schemes, covering 344,792 workers. Though no further official survey has been made, it is certain that figures for 1976 would show a decline from the 1954 levels.

In the history of labor participation in Britain, copartnership and profit-sharing have occupied much the greater part of the stage. Of codetermination there has been almost nothing in private industry.[9] Of course very many employees who have started their careers as workers have been appointed to company boards, but only after graduating through management and not as representatives of the workers. Occasionally a trade union official has found his way to a company board, but only after leaving the trade union side and becoming transformed into a company man. In some of the nationalized industries, as I have previously noted, employees or trade union representatives have been appointed to main or subsidiary boards, but few would contest the opinion that they have usually had singularly little influence on major policy; and in any case, not being elected by the workers, they have not been seen by them as their representatives. These appointments have tended to be regarded as rewards for trade union officials or representatives of long service records, and thus a means of eking out their superannuation provision.

Consultation between management and workers of some ad hoc or informal character is as old as industry itself. However, formal arrangements more or less binding on managements until formally terminated did not arise until World War I. That war produced many new and unfamiliar problems of shopfloor and industrial management that stimulated ideas and proposals for formal consultation between management and workers. Labor was in short supply and prices tended to run ahead of wages, so discontent became rife in many factories. It was in this period that the shop steward movement took its rise. Before 1914 the shop steward, who is now in many workshops almost an all-powerful figure, was hardly in existence. At the same time, the intervention in industry by government inevitably caused by the needs of war set up pressures for consultation that could not have arisen before 1914.

In 1917 a high-level government committee (the Whitley Committee) recommended the establishment of Joint Industrial Councils, on a national, district, and works basis for a series of important industries. The councils were to be formed by representatives of management and workers, with governmental participation in the case of the national councils. High hopes were raised by this initiative for industrial peace and improved productivity, and 20 national and district Whitley councils were set up in 1918, and 32 in 1919. By 1921, there were 74.

The end of the war and the onset of the problems of readjustment exposed the flimsy character of these hopes. By 1923, the number of national and district councils had fallen to 62, 17 having been disbanded and 12 new ones created. Effectively the Whitley Council movement then began to peter out, and soon ceased to have any substantial influence. In 1939 about 1.85 million workers were nominally covered by the councils, but in practice there was only one group whose councils had a really weighty influence on employer-employee relations, namely the Civil Service. For by far the greater part of the employed labor force, the Whitley attempt at the establishment of formal consultation machinery proved a failure.

However, since World War I and more especially since World War II there has been a slow but steady development of voluntary consulation machinery within factories and firms. It is impossible to quantify this because in many cases it is of an informal character, and further, the effectiveness of the machinery varies very widely from case to case.

Though labor participation in any form has been so far almost wholly voluntary in character, legislation has in recent years progressively expanded and entrenched the rights of workers in ways that have severely limited the freedom of management (e.g., compensation for redundancy, protection against and compensation for unfair dismissal, protection against sex or race discrimination, extension of health and safety controls, etc.). However, these developments did not directly involve participation until the passage of the Employment Protection Act of 1975, the main provisions of which came into force in the early months of 1976. Under this act it has become obligatory for employers to consult trade unions about indended redundancies, and to provide them with a great deal of information concerning their businesses that may be considered to be relevant to the process of collective bargaining. To this extent, labor consultation has become statutory.

Prospects for the Near Future

Whereas in the long British industrial history participation has so far been almost wholly voluntary, it is extremely likely that Britain now stands on the brink of changes that will make participation compulsory. At the same time, the emphasis appears certain to shift from copartnership and profit-sharing to codetermination and consultation. The essential reason for this prospective shift is the great growth in the power of the trade unions. As we have seen, they have no liking for copartnership or profit-sharing, but they do have a very strong desire for consultation (provided that they, not merely the employees of a firm or firms, are the consulted); and though there are dissidents among them on this point, they have recently taken a liking to codetermination (provided that the appointment of worker-directors is in their hands).

When Britain entered the European Economic Community (EEC) in January 1973, it was widely anticipated that within a short time large companies (defined as large by the size of their labor force) would be required to appoint worker-directors to a supervisory board within a two-tier system. The EEC's "Fifth Directive" (settled before the UK, Ireland, and Denmark had joined the EEC) had laid down such a system for all EEC member countries.[10] However, the EEC Commission later modified its position in a Green Paper entitled "Employee Participation and Company Structure in the European Community."[11] The Green Paper recognized that the original proposals of the "Fifth Directive" were impracticable because (1) there was wide variation in current practice both between and within different countries; (2) some countries were unwilling and unable immediately to adopt the principle of employee representation; and (3) the proposals ran into opposition not only from industry but also in trade union circles.

However the Commission remained committed to the principle, if not the detail, of the "Fifth Directive." It stated that "for the Commission the overall objective, if not the specific approaches, of the proposal for a Fifth Directive remain valid and reasonably realistic, namely employee representation, not merely presence in a consultative capacity, on the supervisory boards of public companies." But "Member States must be free to adopt these principles with the maximum degree of flexibility possible . . . and certain Member States must be permitted to allow their public companies to approach the objectives in stages." It therefore proposed a transitional period in which companies could choose between:

1. Employee representation on a supervisory board
2. Employee representation on a single-tier board
3. A company level institution to "enable the employees' representatives to be

informed about and influence the conduct of the company's affairs, including major decisions of economic policy," without being directly involved in either a single-tier or supervisory board.

Further, the Commission conceded that "It should be possible to adopt Community legislation which obliged a Member State to enact a regime applying generally to public companies, but which also left it free to enact that the system could be modified by agreement between the company and the employees' representatives." Nevertheless, despite this concession to flexibility, the Commission argued strongly for the following:

1. Regulation at EEC level to establish a uniform structure for public companies throughout the Community
2. That this should be based on the two-tier board system
3. That there should be employee representation on the supervisory board (i.e., upper tier).

In view of its own commitments to EEC regulations, the British Government of 1973 (then Conservative) promised its own Green Paper on the "Fifth Directive," to be ready by the spring of 1973. It never appeared. It was strongly rumored that the Cabinet was unable to agree on the various drafts that were presented by its officials. In February 1974 the Conservatives lost the General Election and were succeeded by a Labour Government. Since the new government had many other preoccupations and in any case intended to put the whole question of EEC membership to a public referendum, it did not regard legislation for "industrial democracy" as urgently required.

However, early in 1975 a Labor backbencher introduced a Private Member's Industrial Democracy Bill, which received its First Reading by a large majority. It is certain that the government did not intend to let it go further; but by a mistake of Parliamentary management, the bill received a Second Reading in an almost empty House of Commons. The government was thus spurred into action and promised to introduce "industrial democracy" legislation in the 1976–1977 session of Parliament. On this understanding, the Private Member's Bill was withdrawn. Essentially the bill would have provided for supervisory boards on the German or EEC Commission's model, with 50 percent workers' representatives in a list of 20 nationalized industries, and in private enterprises with 2000 or more employees if demanded by any trade union recognized by the company concerned for the purpose of collective bargaining. Thus it paid obeisance to the principle of codetermination but took account of the well-known doubts among some trade unions about its desirability.

No further action came from the government until August 1975, when it announced its intention to set up a Committee of Inquiry into Industrial Democracy before embarking on legislation. The committee was to be headed by Lord

Bullock, lately Vice Chancellor of Oxford University. But the names of the members of the committee were not announced until December, and so its labors could not commence until then. It was urgently requested to report to the government by December 1976, which indicated that speed was to be as important a feature of its work as accuracy or wisdom. Its terms of reference were as follows:

Accepting the need for a radical extension of industrial democracy in the control of companies by means of representation on boards of directors and accepting the essential role of trade union organization in this process, to consider how such an extension can best be achieved, taking into account in particular the proposals of the Trades Union Congress Report on Industrial Democracy as well as experience in Britain, the EEC and other countries. Having regard to the interests of the national economy, employees, investors and consumers, to analyse the implications of such representation for the efficient management of companies and for company law.

It was obvious from these terms of reference that the Government had already approved a definite move toward codetermination, subject only to the always overriding importance in a Labour Government's policies of respect for possible trade union objections.

It was also obvious that the membership of the committee was such as to ensure that its report would favor not merely a measure of codetermination (for that was already settled by the terms of reference) but also a type of codetermination attuned to the growing pretensions and claims to power of the trade unions in modern Britain. Even the minority group of those who might oppose a great extension of union power (three leading industrialists) could be expected to endorse a moderate extension of that power.[12] Indeed their acceptance of the terms of reference implied as much.

The Trades Union Congress (TUC) Report on Industrial Democracy[13] referred to in the terms of reference was issued in 1974 and *inter alia* advocated a two-tier system with 50 percent employee representation on the upper tier. However, when it was debated at the 1974 congress, certain unions objected to the mandatory introduction of two-tier boards and employee-directors and called for a more flexible approach. Hence the final resolution on this subject:

1. Underlined the central importance of collective bargaining
2. Called for increasing union "control over the elements of management including dismissals, discipline, introduction of new techniques, forward planning of manpower, rationalization, etc."
3. Rejected the "mandatory imposition of supervisory boards with worker directors"
4. Called for "a more flexible approach giving statutory backing to the right to negotiate on these major issues but relating the control more directly to collective bargaining machinery"[14]

It is obvious that what matters most to the unions is their own power. If two-tier boards and worker-directors are at all likely to dilute their power or divert power from their officials or appointees to workers less subject to their control, the unions will be hostile to them. But if these arrangements can be made subservient to, or at least not damaging to, their power systems, they will accept and promote them.

Numerous employers' organizations and professional bodies issued reports or statements of policy on the matters to be considered by the Bullock Committee, though the evidence presented by them to the committee has not yet been published. Without exception they were opposed to a mandatory two-tier board system and, as is to be expected, to a mandatory 50 percent worker representation, though not absolutely clearly to any lesser representation. The views of the Confederation of British Industry (CBI), the Institute of Directors, and the Association of British Chambers of Commerce cover the great majority of the points to be considered.

The CBI declared itself to be anxious to see increased participation, and especially growth of worker involvement at the operating level. But if law came, it had to be flexible to meet the needs of diverse companies; and the mandatory imposition of a single system would create immense difficulties for industry. In particular the CBI made the following points:[15]

1. A two-tier board was likely to weaken shareholder control and decision making within companies. Any company might establish a two-tier structure now if it wished. To make it mandatory would be highly objectionable.

2. Taking into account the known views of the TUC on this matter, it had little confidence that union members of a board would acknowledge responsibility for board decisions or the responsibility implicit in board membership to act in the company's interests as a whole.

3. Board membership as advocated in the TUC report would simply mean an extension of negotiation by other means.

4. The objectives of the EEC's "Fifth Directive" were not without merit, but there was a need to consider alternative ways of meeting them.

5. Though current proposals for codetermination on the Continental model should be rejected, the communication, consultation, and negotiation arrangements in enterprises should give employees confidence that their views were taken into account by boards before decisions were reached.

6. Consultative machinery should be established in every company above a certain size, at both plant and company level.

7. Such machinery should not be a legal requirement, but should conform to a voluntary code of practice for employee participation.

8. Each enterprise needed to be able to decide for itself in consultation with its employees how to develop participation and where to strike a balance

in establishing procedures for communication, consultation, and collective bargaining.

The Company Law Committee of the Institute of Directors summarised views widely held among its members as follows:[16]

1. It preferred the unitary board to the two-tier system. The latter's disadvantages, delay in decisions and division of responsibility, outweighed any possible advantages.

2. It was not in favor of direct employee representation on boards, and especially if rights of representation were limited to trade union members; but it did favor the appointment to boards of people with employee backgrounds to ensure adequate representation of employee views.

3. It was attracted by the concept of an advisory board or council that would serve the purpose of communication without changing the present legal form of the company or causing an upheaval in shareholder-manager relationships.

4. It would favor legislation to give boards the power to recognize other interests as well as those of the shareholders. In brief, some specific responsibility to employees, customers, creditors, and the public interest generally might be spelled out in company law.

5. It urged the greater use of nonexecutive directors, the establishment of a code of best boardroom practice, and the establishment of a panel to comment publicly on the conduct of boards and to resolve disputes.

The Association of British Chambers of Commerce, in a report published in November 1975,[17] stated that greater employee participation was both inevitable and desirable. However, it was concerned that participation not interfere with the requirements of managers to manage or the rights of owners to own. The report made the following particular points:

1. The case for mandatory two-tier boards and employee-directors had not been made out.

2. Collective bargaining should be kept separate from any employee participation system.

3. The most important element in participation should be viewed as consultation. There should be a formal but flexible system of consultation by company councils on four main areas: finance, including plans for future investment and growth, sales, profit, and cash forecasts; changes in ownership, redundancy and plant closures; and operating and social considerations, such as welfare, safety, pensions, work patterns, corporate organization, training, and recruitment.

4. A code of practice for company councils should be embodied in company law, with a tripartite appeal body consisting of representatives of employers and employees and independent persons. Employees dissatisfied with consulta-

tion arrangements could appeal to this body, which would have powers of arbitration and conciliation but not of enforcement. However, where there was an intended change of ownership or there were intended redundancies of plant closures, there should be statutory requirements for consultation going further than a code of practice.

5. To confine employee representation on the councils of the unions would be objectionable. Councils should represent all groups of employees.

The position taken by the employers' bodies was obviously a defensive one, with an attempt to shift emphasis from codetermination to consultation. It also displayed the acceptance by employers to some extent of the fashionable views about labor relations of our day (note especially the Institute of Directors' acceptance of the popular but hopelessly indefinable concept of social responsibility, i.e., responsibility to employees, customers, creditors, and the public interest generally over and above the responsibility that arises under existing law and in conditions of free enterprise).

The principal questions the Bullock Committee was expected to answer were the following:

1. Should the appointment of employee-directors be mandatory for companies above a certain level in size? If so, what should that size be? If not, should some system of tax or other inducement be elaborated to make the appointment of employee-directors attractive?

2. Should the proportion of employee-directors, if appointment is mandatory, be 50 percent or less?

3. Should a two-tier system for companies above a certain size be mandatory?

4. Should the employee-directors be elected by the employees in each company, or should some part in their election be reserved for trade unions?

5. Should managerial employees below board level have a right of representation on the board with the other employees? If so, should they elect a representative or representatives as a separate group?

6. Should the responsibilities of the employee-directors be the same as those of the other directors, or should they be responsible in some measure to those who elected them or to the outside power of trade unions?

7. What forms of organized consultation between employees and employers, if any, should become mandatory, and what should be the place of trade unions, if any, in the system of consultation?

The committee's report was published on January 26, 1977. It embodied a majority report (that of all the members except the three industrialists) and a minority report (that of the three industrialists). The findings of the majority were widely leaked to the press well before publication. In particular it had been credibly rumored that the three industrialists had been ready to go far on the same road as the majority, but that in the event that the majority was uncompromising, the industrialists would screw their courage to the sticking point and issue a dissenting report.

In summary form, the majority's findings and recommendations were as follows:

1. Codetermination (i.e., the appointment of worker-directors) was a necessary and progressive development in the organization of industry; it was a right of the worker that should be recognized; and company law should be changed in order to take account of the interests of employees as well as those of stockholders.

2. The beneficial character of codetermination was borne out by the experience of the countries that had adopted it, particularly Germany.

3. The power to appoint the worker-directors should rest with the trade unions.

4. The two-tier board was undesirable on the ground that it would impose an inflexibility on company operations that would be detrimental to efficient management.

5. There was no danger of breaches of confidentiality arising from the links between the worker-directors and those appointing them, though a trend toward openness in the government of companies would be desirable.

Accordingly, the majority made the following recommendations:

1. Codetermination on a single-tier board should be applied in all public companies with 2000 or more employees in the United Kingdom, if the employees voted in favor of it according to the trigger mechanism described in recommendation 2. In the case of a holding company with 2000 or more employees, codetermination should be applied both for it and also, separately, for every subsidiary company with 2000 or more employees.

2. The trigger mechanism should be the following. By secret ballot, held at company expense, in company time, and on company property, all full-time employees (including those on short time or temporarily laid off) should vote to decide for or against codetermination. A simple majority should decide the issue, but the majority should represent at least one third of the eligible employees. A suggested question might be "Do you want employee representation on the company board through the trade unions recognized by your employer?"

A union or a group of unions should have the right to demand a ballot only if recognized on behalf of grades constituting at least one fifth of the company's employees.

If a ballot produced a vote against codetermination, there should be an interval of two years before another ballot could be taken.

If a ballot produced an affirmative vote, then after five years any union or group of unions representing at least one fifth of the employees should be entitled to ask for a ballot to see whether the employees wished to continue with the system. A simple majority, representing at least one third of the eligible employees, should be able to decide to discontinue the system.

There should be no separate voting constituency for managerial employees.

3. There should be an equal number of stockholder-appointed and union-appointed directors, plus a third group to be appointed by agreement between these two groups, which thus might be styled the $2x + y$ system. The y directors should be of an odd number greater than one but less than one third of the total board, save that where the employees numbered less than 10,000; the x's should be four each and the y should be three.

4. The chairman of the board should continue to be appointed as at present by the directors, who should continue to decide what his powers and functions should be.

5. The worker-directors should be appointed by the unions recognized by the company for bargaining purposes. The machinery for selection should be left entirely to their discretion. It was to be expected that those chosen would normally be employees (probably often chosen from the shop stewards), but it would be permissible to appoint full-time union officials.

6. The worker-directors should be appointed for a reasonable period, normally three years, and be eligible for reelection. They should be removable at any time by the unions holding the power of appointment.

7. The legal duties and liabilities of the worker-directors should be the same as those of the other directors.

8. The worker-directors should not be paid any director's fees in addition to their wages or salaries, but their directorial expenses should be met and they should be compensated for loss of earnings arising out of the performance of their directorial duties.

9. An Industrial Democracy Commission should be set up by the government to monitor the new system, and to provide advice and conciliation where needed. The Council of the Commission should consist of employers, trade union officials or nominees, and independent people.

10. In order to provide training for the worker-directors, a residential training course of about two to six weeks should be organized under the auspices of the Commission.

The dissenting minority reported as follows:

1. Those who worked in industry, whether managerial or nonmanagerial employees, were not ready for the changes proposed by the majority. Management, and, in particular, middle management, was against them.

2. The thrust of evidence from Germany was that successful industrial relations in German companies were mainly due to works councils, not to the appointment of worker-directors.

3. If there were to be worker-directors, they should sit on a supervisory board in a two-tier system, as in Germany. One third of the supervisory board

in such a system should be appointed by the stockholders, one third by the employees, and one third should be independent. Of the worker-directors, at least one should come from the shop floor, one from the salaried staff, and one from management.

4. No candidate should be eligible for appointment to the supervisory board unless he had been employed by the company for at least 10 years, had been a member of a council or committee below board level for at least 3 years, and had undergone adequate training.

5. Elections to the supervisory board from the employees should be valid only if there were at least three candidates for each office and if not less than 60 percent of the electorate voted. Candidates should be nominated in writing by 10 employees or by an independent trade union recognized by the company for negotiating purposes.

6. The supervisory board should have the power to approve appointments to the (lower) executive board, to dismiss members of that board if unanimous, to approve the remuneration of the members of that board, to require regular reports on the state of the company's business, to receive information on all matters substantially affecting the profitability or liquidity of the company, and to submit to the stockholders fundamental matters required by law or by Stock Exchange rules (e.g., winding up, amending the Memorandum or Articles of Association, changing the capital structure, or disposing of basic assets).

The public reaction to the majority report appears to have been prevailingly hostile or skeptical. In particular, its advocacy of the expansion of union power has induced hostility in broad sections of the public (including many union members), among whom union unpopularity runs more or less in parallel with union power. To quote the *London Times* (January 27, 1977), "Perhaps 100 men are making a claim to run the country. . . . The British abhor the monopoly of power. . . . The lack of concern for the interests of managers below board level is one of the most insulting characteristics of the report."

The hostility and skepticism have been intensified by the disclosure that the presentation of evidence to the committee was so maneuvered as to exclude the views of those unions or union representatives who did not want codetermination.

Even the most sober and impartial judgement on the majority report cannot avoid concluding that it is market by an extraordinary degree of incompetence, naiveté, and prejudice.

First, the notion of industrial democracy in the sense of workers' control or share of control of companies is accepted uncritically as if it were desirable on the face of things. If industrial democracy has any meaning at all, does it mean workers' control? If so, why? Is any kind of democracy suited to the organization of industry? If so, why should it be workers' democracy rather than or together with stockholder democracy? Can the tasks of management be successfully carried out under any kind of democratic control? By analogy, could an army be organized on the basis of democratic control in the sense of control by the private soldiers? If not, what is the difference between an army and an industrial organization? Above all what is the similarity to justify parallel arrangements between a political organization in which democratic control is clearly possible and workable and an industrial organization? These questions are hardly considered in the report.

The only argument of apparent consequence that is advanced for an element of workers' control is the familiar one that an employee has an interest in the employing company of a kind comparable with that of the stockholder, and that it should be recognized accordingly. This interest arises, it is thought, because the employee invests his life or career in the company. But why does not the employee's wage take account of this supposed "investment"? And if the employee "invests" in the company in a manner embodying something over and above what his wage is intended to cover, why is there not a similar "investment" by the company's suppliers and customers, representing something over and above the value of their transactions with the company? These questions are neither asked nor answered. The reason is obvious. The notion of the employee's "investment" in the company cannot survive scrutiny.

There is one particular observation in the report that is understood to be Lord Bullock's own individual contribution to the argument. It runs as follows. In the nineteenth century even liberal statesmen and political philosophers viewed the prospect of democracy, which was appearing on the horizon, with misgiving. Events have shown that nevertheless democracy was able to establish itself peacefully and successfully. So now the misgivings of those who fear that industrial democracy may produce industrial turmoil or economic inefficiency should be stilled. The historical parallel with political democracy indicates that their fears are unjustified.

Lord Bullock has the reputation of an academic historian of some standing, but the validity of such a reputation is called into question by the almost unbelievable naiveté of this alleged historical parallel. In the first place, the nineteenth-century misgivings about democracy have not proved to be unfounded. On the contrary, twentieth-century democracy has increasingly displayed the very defects the scholarly and liberal nineteenth-century friends of the people feared might arise. In the second place, the parallel equates a political society with an industrial organization as if such an equation required no demonstration, exposition, or analysis.

Second, the references in the report to the success of codetermination in other countries, especially Germany, display a willful disregard for the evidence. As the minority report says, the German evidence shows (and it comes from both employers and employees) that the works councils are the main source of success in industrial relations. But there is more to the German evidence than this. In Germany the closed shop is illegal, and the attitudes and forms of organization of the labor unions are far better attuned to industrial success than those of the British unions. All this is ignored by the majority report. Furthermore, codetermination in Germany was made possible and acceptable only because of the existence of the two-tier board system. It would not have been adopted, or if adopted it would soon have been discarded as unworkable, if German companies had operated under a single-tier system. This too was ignored in the report.

Third, whatever the merits of "worker democracy," this was not what the majority proposed. Except for the limited element of the trigger mechanism, the new power was to devolve not upon the companies' employees but upon the labor unions. A more blatant approval of empire building by a movement already invested with inordinate power could hardly be imagined. Not only were the unions to have the power of appointment of the worker-directors (who might in some cases be full-time union officials, not company employees), they were also to be entitled to exercise their power in any manner they pleased. In all other aspects of the proposed machinery the majority was ready, even eager, to go into details. But when it came to the exercise of union power, they clearly believed that they would be on holy ground where no outsider should be bold enough to tread. Thus it was that they were unable to consider the possibility of interunion disputes and rivalries in the exercise of the power, although conflict between unions is one of the most obvious features of union history.

Fourth, the obvious possibility of a conflict of loyalties among the worker-directors was disposed of without any satisfactory argument or scrutiny. Whose interests should these directors serve, those of the company (however they are construed), of the employees, or of the union or unions? This question goes to the heart of the whole notion of industrial democracy, and the report gives it a cavalier treatment. What happens when there is a dispute between the company and a union? We are asked to believe that the role of the union-appointed worker-directors would then raise no questions of particular consequence.

Fifth, the rejection of the two-tier board is a further example of the majority's evasion of the realities of the problems before them. Suppose that there were indeed a case for codetermination by legal requirement (codetermination by voluntary agreement is of course not in issue). Then it is conceivably workable only in a two-tier system, in which the supervisory board (on which the worker-directors would sit) would not be concerned with executive functions. In a single-tier system the board is concerned both with questions of high policy and with day-to-day executive matters, and most of its members (e.g., the managing director, the finance director, etc.) are charged with executive functions. A conflict of loyalties on a single board would hamper the discharge of executive functions exceedingly, whereas on a supervisory board it is conceivable that the effects of such a conflict would be resolved before instructions on high policy were passed down to the executive board.

If it is asked why it has been possible in the few cases of voluntary codetermination for worker-directors to sit on boards in the present British single-tier system, the answer is first that these directors are always in a minority in relation to the stockholder-appointed directors, and second, it is precisely because the arrangement is voluntary that conflicts of loyalties tend not to be decisive.

The report of the Bullock Committee minority was obviously defensive in character. It provided neither a clear endorsement of the case for codetermination nor a refutation of that case (in any case a refutation would have been inconsistent with the committee's terms of reference). However, it did offer some mitigation of the more obviously harmful elements in a codetermination system.

Immediately after the publication of the Bullock Committee's reports, the government announced that it accepted in broad principle the recommendations of the majority, and that legislation would soon be initiated accordingly. However, the precariousness of the government's Parliamentary majority, its difficulties with an already overloaded legislative program, and the less than enthusiastic reception of the report even among labor union members (emphasized by open opposition by a few union leaders, notably those of the Electrical, Electronic, Telecommunications and Plumbing Union), together suggest that legislation on the lines of the majority report is neither an early nor a likely prospect. The debate on codetermination will surely continue.

Notes

1. The first known profit-sharing scheme in the United Kingdom was devised in 1829 by Lord Wallscourt for workers on his farm. Subsequently, a few other landowners and substantial farmers operated such schemes, but they were never numerous or important.

2. In the 1880s there was an upsurge of discontent among various groups of unskilled and semiskilled workers, marked especially by two famous strikes, that of the match girls and that of the London dock workers. A great opportunity thus arose for trade union promoters to persuade these workers to copy the practices, already well-established, of the skilled workers. They did not understand that the predominant purpose of the skilled workers' unions was to keep out the competition of less-skilled men and women who might seek to enter their trades. Thus a basic cause of the low earnings of the unskilled was the power of the unions of the skilled.

3. From 1865 to 1874, a substantial coal-owning firm in the Yorkshire coalfield did operate a profit-sharing scheme. It was abandoned after a bitter strike by the workers. Tying wages to coal prices was a rough and ready, but more understandable and therefore more acceptable, way of linking wages to profits.

4. In two cases gas companies went further and provided for the appointment of employee-directors, elected by the employees. These were unique cases of codetermination and arose long before codetermination became a popular word or concept. However, the example did not spread. The adoption of profit-sharing and copartnership in the gas industry was in large measure a reaction to the famous London dock strike of 1889. The gas workers were of the same social and economic class as the dock workers, and in London they tended to live in the same neighborhoods. The great difference was that their employment was stable, not casual.

5. Before the engineers and the carpenters set the new model for skilled unions in the 1850s, there had been a good deal of syndicalist thinking in the unstable and erratically led unions of the first half of the century.

6. *Ministry of Labour Gazette,* May 1956.

7. Labour Department of the Board of Trade," Report on Profit-Sharing and Labour Copartnership in the UK," Cd. 6496, H.M.S.O., 1912.

8. Ministry of Labour, "Report on Profit-Sharing and Labour Copartnership in the UK," Cmd. 544, H.M.S.O., 1920.

9. See the previous reference to the two gas companies applying codetermination. These companies are no longer in existence, owing to the nationalization of the industry. A recent case of nascent codetermination was the appointment of a worker-director, chosen by the workers, at Bonser Engineering Ltd. (a manufacturer of fork lift trucks and mechanical handling equipment, with about 300 employees). There are a few cases of firms that have been wholly turned over to the employees, who have thus become the owners. Such cases, of course, go beyond any normal system of profit-sharing, copartnership, or codetermination. Two notable cases are the John Lewis Partnership (engaged in retail trade) and the Scott Bader Commonwealth (engaged in the chemical industry). In the John Lewis Partnership there are no "employees." All those who work in the enterprise are "partners," who own the enterprise and share its profits. In the Scott Bader Commonwealth the workers are styled "members," but the formal ownership of the enterprise is vested in the Commonwealth itself. By the charter of the Commonwealth, 60 percent of the profits must be ploughed back into the enterprise, 20 percent must be donated to charities, and 20 percent must be distributed to the members.

10. "Proposal for a Fifth Directive on the Structure of Societies Anonymes," *Bulletin of the European Communities,* Supplement (October 1972).

11. *Bulletin of the European Communities,* Supplement (August 1975).

12. Apart from Lord Bullock, the members were two academics, two very important trade union leaders, the Secretary of the TUC's Economic Department, a City solicitor, the Director of the Government's Office of Fair Trading, and the three leading industrialists referred to in our text. The Director of the Office of Fair Trading, who had formerly held a senior managerial position in industry and who probably would have sided with the industrialists in any

division of opinion, resigned before the committee's work was well under way, on appointment to the post of Director-General of the Confederation of British Industry. The views of the academics were well known to be likely to be favorable to the maximum possible pretensions of the unions, while Lord Bullock himself is almost a caricature of the modern highly placed academic administrator, of faded scholarly potential, who is looked to by governments for the apparently impartial chairmanship of commissions and committees, but who has neither the character nor the understanding needed to stand against the *Zeitgeist*. Thus, even with the City solicitor, whose support was uncertain and in the event proved nonexistent, the industrialists were sure to be in a minority.

13. "Industrial Democracy," report by the TUC General Council to the 1974 Trades Union Congress.

14. "Composite Resolution Number 17," Trades Union Congress, 1974.

15. See "Employee Participation: The CBI's Contribution to the Debate," and "The Responsibilities of the British Public Company," 1973.

16. "Employee Participation and Two-tier Boards," April 1973. See also "Submission to the Industrial Democracy Committee," April 1976.

17. "Employee Participation," November 1975.

Bibliography

Association of British Chambers of Commerce. *Employee Participation.* November 1975.

Balfour, C., ed. *Participation in Industry.* London: Croom Helm, 1973.

Brannen, Batstone, Fatchett, and White. "The Worker Directors." London: Hutchinson, 1976.

Brown, G. "Participation in Industry," Industrial Participation Association. London 1972.

Carpenter, C. *Industrial Copartnership.* London: Copartnership Publishers Ltd., 1912.

Cole, G.D.H. *The Case for Industrial Partnership.* New York: Macmillan, 1957.

Confederation of British Industry. "The Responsibilities of the British Public Company." 1973.

Copeman, G. *The Challenge of Employee Shareholding.* London: Business Publications Ltd., 1958.

"Employee Participation and Company Structure," *Bulletin of the European Communities,* Supplement (August 1975).

Fay, C.R. *Copartnership in Industry.* Cambridge: Cambridge Univ. Press, 1913.

"Industrial Democracy." Report by the TUC General Council to the 1974 Trades Union Congress.

Industrial Participation Association. "Participation by Legislation." London, 1974.

——. "Works Councils, Employee Directors, Supervisory Boards—A Guide to the Debate. London, April 1974.

Innis Macbeath. *Power Sharing in Industry.* London: Gower Press, 1975.

Institute of Directors. "Employee Participation and Two-Tier Boards," April 1973.

Lewis, J.S. *Partnership for All.* London: John Lewis Partnership, 1948.

"Profit-sharing and Copartnership Schemes." Report to the TUC, 1957.

"Profit-sharing and Copartnership Schemes." *Ministry of Labor Gazette,* May 1956.

"Proposal for a Fifth Directive on the Structure of Societes Anonymes." *Bulletin of the European Communities,* Supplement (October 1972).

"Report on Profit-sharing and Labour Copartnership in the UK" (Cd 6496). Labour Department of the Board of Trade, 1912.

"Report on Profit-sharing and Labour Copartnership in the UK" (Cmd 544). Ministry of Labour, 1920.

Thomason, G.F. *Experiments in Participation.* London: Institute of Personnel Management, 1971.

Wallace, W. *Prescription for Partnership.* London: Pitmans, 1959.

3 Labor Participation in the Management of Business Firms in Great Britain

Malcolm R. Fisher

This chapter falls into three parts. First, I wish to examine what some of the more detached British economists had to say about labor participation over the period under review. Second, because in a sense we discover that we have all been here before, I want to ask what his triggered the fresh interest in these forms of institutional arrangement. Finally, I want to assess the viability of a participation drive when its components have to be grafted onto a complicated institutional structure of production and distribution that we already possess.

Early Economic Thinkers

The review of the economic thinkers of earlier times must perforce be very selective. It will embrace John Stuart Mill in his writings of 1868, Alfred Marshall at various dates from 1890 to 1920, and A.C. Pigou from 1920 to about 1940. None of these men would be thought of as campaigners for worker participation, but rather as dispassionate thinkers and discerning economists of their day. The thinking of their times might be rounded off by a study of the many writings of C.R. Fay, the economic historian, on this subject.[1]

Of course, Mill was strongly committed in the sense that in his time he attached more importance to the rightful distribution of wealth than to its creation. Besides, he was concerned with the reduction if not the elimination of the class of nonlaborers who he considered controlled the lives of the laborers. In general, he preferred self-dependence for the laboring classes to dependence on other classes for protection. Mill distinguishes new countries such as America and Australia by the fact that in them those who begin life as hired laborers have the probability later on of becoming self-employed or employers, whereas in older countries a man's lot as hired laborer becomes a persistent one—something that he finds repugnant and something with which, as education and communication spread, labor will not be willing to tolerate. He cites with approval various cases of copartnership, including those of American ships trading to China where every sailor tends to share in the profits of the voyage. This encouraged good conduct by seamen and the comparative rarity of collision between them and the people or government of the country. He also highlights the case of the Cornish miners who each participate in the profits secured from a vein, even though these returns may be at times spasmodic and necessitate men living on credit for a period. Yet despite the costs thereby imposed, the men acquired independence and displayed an intelligence that surpassed other laborers, hence on balance securing a net benefit overall. The miner's accumulating savings bore witness to this.

Mill quotes with enthusiasm the participation arrangements introduced by H. Leclaire in Paris but points out that such could not have happened in Britain until the passage of the Limited Liability Act, which protected workers under copartnership arrangements from being responsible for the entire losses of a firm.[2] A natural development of this form of association would be for the workforce to acquire a voice in management itself. Mill details the development of the English cooperative movement, first in retailing and then in its embryo state in wholesaling at the time of his writing. From these he expects great things. Cooperation in distribution he views especially favorably, for he believes that it cuts down the excessive costs of distribution and releases resources for productive endeavor, thereby subscribing to the view that distribution costs too much. The overwhelming case for cooperative endeavor comes from the release of energies such that people will do the utmost rather than the least possible in exchange for their production.

Against these plusses, Mill notes some minuses:[3] "Unity of authority makes many things possible which could not, or would not, be undertaken, subject to the chance of divided councils, or changes in the management." A private capitalist, exempt from the control of a body, if he is a person of capacity, is considerably more likely than almost any association to run judicious risks and originate costly improvements. Cooperative societies may be depended upon for adopting improvements after they have been tested by success; but individuals are more likely to commence things previously untried. Mill recognizes that individual enterprise and companies of the joint stock pattern will over a period coexist with cooperatives, but he sees the eventual spread of knowledge and experience leading to the disappearance of the former and their absorbence in the latter. Old-style capitalists would find it to their advantage to lend to such institutions, and at diminishing rates of interest, and ultimately they might be willing to accept terminable annuities in exchange for their capital.

Finally Mill states that he agrees with socialist writers who support these cooperative conceptions, but he disassociates himself from those who argue against competition—and this is the most conspicuous and vehement part of their teaching.

They forget that wherever competition is not, monopoly is . . . they forget too, that with the exception of competition among laborers, all other competition is for the benefit of the laborers, by cheapening the articles they consume; that competition even in the labor market is a source not of low but of high wages. . . .[4]

Alfred Marshall wrote his *Principles* in 1890 and produced his shorter *Economics of Industry* in 1919. In each he discusses cooperative societies and associations immediately after outlining the limitations of government under-takings—the inability of the taxpayer who bears the ultimate risks to exercise an efficient control over the business and the difficulty in securing officers who will do their work with as much energy and enterprise as is shown in private establishments.

Experience shows creative ideas and experiments in business techniques and in business organization, to be very rare in Government undertakings, and not very common in private enterprises which have drifted towards bureaucratic methods as the result of their great age and large size.[5]

Marshall sees cooperative association as enabling those who take risks in an enterprise to be also employed in it and to participate in decision making within it. In and through participation in profits and decision making they are able to judge the honesty and efficiency of the business, detecting any laxity and in-competence. Second, they are able to reduce the need for superintendence as their own pecuniary interest reduces the tendency toward shirking by them-selves and their coworkers.

But here are disadvantages. Workers may not appreciate the talents required of managers—the strains of their tasks are not always evident in contrast with the efforts of manual workers and so petty jealousies may arise. Managers of co-operatives rarely have the alertness, the inventiveness, and the ready versatility of those men who have been selected by the struggle for survival. Those at-tracted by cooperation are ones in whom the social element is stronger and who do not desire to separate themselves from their old comrades but to work among them as leaders.[6]

Marshall does not believe that capital is the hindrance to further coopera-tive endeavor; many societies had already accumulated considerable capital. The real difficulty is to select people of those rare, entrepreneurial abilities to whom such capital can be entrusted. Moreover, this is not eased by the growing complexity of modern business.

In 1919, in *Industry and Trade*, Marshall turned more directly to an assess-ment of cooperative and collective organization as it had developed, devoting one of his celebrated appendixes to the subject.[7] He notes the tendency for co-operative undertakings to be limited to those retail trades which market staples mainly for the working classes, but he thinks that copartnership possesses wider potential. However, even here there are difficulties, for giving workers a say on the direction of the enterprise through their chosen directors enables those individuals to gain access to special information on production methods or nature of markets which they may release to rival concerns, directly or indi-rectly. Moreover, if the worker-directors are reticent to release such informa-tion to fellow employees, they may be regarded as behaving antisocially—yet to release information is to widen the scope for the passage of such information to rival concerns.

To this he adds the remark that trade unionists, including nearly all who are of militant temper, look with suspicion on copartnership.

Other limitations arising from the institutional form are also adduced earlier in the book.[8] Prompt and incisive action based on intuition associated with reason are not likely to come from a committee. Again every successive step in the extension of the cooperative movement has tended to weaken the import of those in whom the faith in the cooperative principle is most strong. Diminishing returns set in with growth. Moreover, some of the special features resulting from the application of the principle become available to alert traders who can now compete more effectively against the cooperators.

J.A. Hobson in the 1926 edition of the *Evolution of Modern Capitalism*,[9] in surveying developments in the twentieth century, wrote, "The history of Productive Cooperation, in the strict sense of the term, does not encourage hopes of wide success."

In various editions of his *Economics of Welfare* running up to 1938, A.C. Pigou stresses that cooperative activities give opportunities for the skills of working men to be harnessed for training in management, and that learning on the job is worth many times more formal but distant preparation.[10] This leads him to advocate a degree of state subsidy for further advancement of the form, since marginal social net product, in his view, exceeds marginal private net product.

In assessing the performance of purchasing associations Pigou points out that undue weight should not be assigned to the success of the English cooperative stores, for it is doubtful if, at the time, given the imperfections of competition in retail trading, the potentials for efficient retailing without cooperation were being fully realized. This point may have some bearing on more recent experience with the arrival of multiple stores and supermarkets. Cooperative concerns seem to be able to economize on advertisement, perhaps because there is an element of loyalty among the membership that promotes a stability in their trade over time, even though from a social point of view it may cause the instability to be borne disproportionately by noncooperative members.

Pigou provides several important examples of monitoring that work in favor of cooperative enterprise. He notes Marshall's point that such bodies would have no interest in adulteration of their goods, since, in another guise, they are also consumers, and emphasizes that provision of insurance, and the retailing of loans, has similar implications. The element of moral hazard here referred to is not adequately kept in surveillance with the joint-stock setup, save through costly inspection, for no one buyer is damaged by the action of another buyer. However, in the cooperative purchasers' association each has an interest in the actions of other buyers, for he can be damaged by what they do. Hence each buyer will serve as an unpaid inspector. This has an obvious overlap with the burgeoning field of market signaling.[11] But over a wide area of productive enterprise these advantages may be outweighed by negative factors—the lower alertness of the cooperative trader or the fluid nature of the market served (since so much hangs on customer loyalty—they are also unsuited where risk and uncertainty are strong). "Nor will they work as regards commodities and services for which economy demands centralized production, but of which the purchasers are spread over wide areas, and make their purchases at irregular intervals."[12]

The New Interest in Participation

Mr. Shenfield's chapter in this book suggests some reasons for the resurgence of interest in worker participation, though not all, I think.

One institutional category must always be seen, and assessed, in relation to other institutional categories, experienced or considered. Since early in the century, British industry has become increasingly regulated, while quite a lot has been nationalized. Much of that which remains in the private sector has become concentrated in larger groupings, many of them multinational in character. In much of British industry today the alert initiating entrepreneur is the exception rather than the rule. Matching these changes in ownership structure there have been changes in labor organization, with relative growth in the political influence of the trade unions, organized typically in general or industrial unions. Industry by and large has become more impersonal.

This century has seen a relative decline in the strength of the British economy, with frustrating efforts at stabilization both before and after World War II. Increased emphasis on macroeconomic stabilization policies has tended to focus attention on acts of government, and hostility has grown with government failures, with much of the workforce erroneously putting the blame on the productive units directly served. There has been much talk of "the strike of capital" during the downswings in economic activity, especially when prolonged. Workers have demanded more say in the determination of policies by which these features were provoked. Likewise successive governments have overridden the pricing and investment policies of nationalized industries in pursuit of their economic objectives—keeping fuel prices down at times of rapid inflation so as to attempt to stabilize a representative consumer price index—and some of the unfortunate consequences of these decisions have also provoked resentment.

With the current institutional structure and its working as a base, the introduction of some form of participation may well seem to constitute an improvement—even though when viewed in a less constrained setting, a different verdict might be reached.

Britain's disappointing economic performance compared with her industrialized neighbors, such as Germany, has caused people to look for differences; and active worker participation in Germany and its absence in Britain is a potentially powerful discriminator upon which attention has been focused. This aspect has gained reinforcement through EEC directives and intentions.

Again the presumed need of governments to conclude pay deals with the unions as a means of tempering inflation has made them willing to offer indiscriminately all sorts of side benefits, some of which, such as the willingness to view the merits of alternative schemes for securing codetermination, might yet prove to be a heavy price to pay long term for supposed short-term incomes or other inflation-control policies. Worker participation may then have been less sought for its own sake than for the reason that other features of the institutional structure have proved so inefficient in practice that an overlay of participation may lead to improvement. If this view has substance, it follows that a more efficient means of securing sensible arrangements for worker participation may still be to concentrate national attention first on the need for improved economic decision making at the macro level, e.g., a reduction in discretionary decision making in favor of adherence to "rules."

Judgment in Context

The arguments advanced by the economists of earlier times seem balanced and fair. It does not seem possible to advance any general criteria that will determine whether worker participation in any form is good or bad. Judgment, even in terms of efficiency, must be offered in context.

One of the most rudimentary institutional arrangements—the family subsistence economy—exhibits an entanglement of consumer and production decisions,[13] so we cannot argue that producer and consumer interests should always be kept distinct. This aim, which Henry Simons[14] stressed, could be supported in the following way. Once firms as specialized production units become established, their social justification is as providers of more commodities at less combined cost in resources and disutility than could otherwise apply. Some of these effects will be external. To this end, the producer components should not be able to secure disproportionate benefits at the expense of consumer elements in society, something that would result if monopoly power were augmented.[15] Codetermination and organizations such as purchasing associations (referred to previously) could increase the benefits to selective groups at the expense of others. The disadvantage of this must be assessed against the advantages that may accrue through better monitoring within the firm, reduced "shirking" in Marshall's terms.

To be successful the firm must enjoy a degree of protection sufficient to accomplish the efficient delivery of product at reduced resource cost that is its *raison d'être*. The selection of which firms are to perform, and to what extent, will normally be set by market competition, competition that must offer time for effective production appropriate to the nature of the product desired. In other words, the economy should settle with a minimum of restraint the degree of competition, but in a number of cases time must be permitted to entrepreneurs to amortize the investment projects in which they engage. Along these lines a degree of insider trading in joint stock companies can be justified. Linked to such accruals to enterprise will be some returns to machinery, as well as some returns to highly specific labor employed. In such enterprises one can see some rationale for codetermination, if monitoring and other favorable effects of cooperation are to be secured. But this is at most an argument for selective, not general, worker representation on the board. Moreover, where the specific labor shoulders some of the risks, this argument is relevant; where it does not, participation should not extend beyond the supervisory tier.

If we start from the side of the worker, we may argue that workers may derive general benefits from forming associations with other workers, even though such associations may very easily tend to become organs operating in restraint of trade. An economist can in no sense describe voluntary associations of workers within trade unions as wholly bad.[16] Even their elimination should not necessarily encourage a free enterpriser to class this as beneficial for society at large. This is not to deny that many activities, if not most, associated with present-day unionism are in restraint of trade, and hence bad for society. If workers derive advantages from trade unions, and society were on balance to benefit, how can such trade union representation on boards of firms be adjudged harmful? Here comes the rub. The case for worker representation on boards has been made out for specific types of labor only, but claims for union representation on boards may not be argued on this basis. Unions, we should recall, are not made up of a homogeneous group of workers in aim, skill, age, or many other ways. Hence participatory groupings between employers and employees, including those which lead toward codetermination on boards, could arise voluntarily on one criterion; and groupings of workers with workers into unions could arise voluntarily on another criterion. Yet the combinations of the two types of groupings could prove inefficient, or even disastrous. This would be especially so when the loyalties built up within a trade union that straddle firms are different from the loyalties established between management and men within a firm. For in the latter, time is required for amortization of enterprise activity; and prior release of information, with the risks of premature exposure to strong competition, is prejudicial to this. Yet within a union, loyalty consists of mutual trust and full disclosure of information, which could imply release of knowledge of a firm's potential performance.

Where does this discussion get us? It suggests that codetermination, where it develops, should emerge voluntarily. It suggests that union membership as a criterion for board membership is inefficient or dangerous, unless such members are sworn to secrecy or the union is exclusive to the firm in question. To proceed otherwise is to run the risk of producing excess competition that will result in the discontinuance of production of the product or the transfer of production into more monopolistic units. Division of loyalties creates tensions, not concord. Hence trade union distrust of worker cooperation schemes has a certain rationale.

The development of the more advanced schemes for worker cooperation alters the mix of rewards for labor from the fixed wage: uncertain tenure relationship to the fixed wage plus equity element; less uncertain tenure arrangement. How the mix should be arranged in the production nexus is not clear, and may be left to competitive processes. What is clear is that the demarcation line should not be uniform or different groupings of workers, as I have emphasized with reference to generally trained as opposed to specifically trained workers.

But this way of looking at the matter gives undue weight to arrangements within a firm at any point of time. However, a firm is a transitory unit of enterprise, and a person has to plan his activities over a working lifetime, which could be longer than that appropriate to his relationship with a firm. Optimum patterns of mobility over a working lifetime cannot, it seems, be decreed; and successful use by some of monopoly or union power may result in benefits secured by shifting the adjustments required onto others—either by reducing undue mobility or increasing unduly more than adequate mobility for them. In the absence of clearcut social norms, there may be much to be said for allowing such matters to be voluntarily determined by competitive processes.

In general it has been assumed that the pattern of events has been largely determined by the voluntary formation over time of different institutional forms upon which further changes in structure have been grafted. But we must now formally recognize that through the legislative process, partly in the justifiable case of "public goods" and partly in other less clearcut ways, a range of regulated activities may induce changes in the institutional structure in a manner that would not have voluntarily been arrived at. Many of the present-day large enterprises may have emerged through this means, while the nationalized industries have done so unequivocally. The presence and persistence of these political constraints has altered the institutional structure from what it would otherwise be, and hence in economic jargon the case for cooperative schemes must be judged on second-best criteria if these structural features are to be taken as given. Of course, it may be wiser to question and seek to reform the institutions themselves rather than to qualify their working by cooperative schemes such as are so often advocated. In Marxian terms it may be better to take a step backward in order to take two steps forward. There is no obvious virtue in taking income policies as given and superimposing worker participation schemes over, abandoning the former and letting any of the latter develop naturally.

Finally, it is often the case that a committee structure hinders innovation and creativeness—a convoy cannot exceed the speed of the slowest ship. Worker codetermination schemes would tend to do this directly, and also indirectly, by making it more difficult for entrepreneurial talent to be replaced when it is exhausted by depreciation or death. Within the trade union movement we have only to point to the bitterness caused by employers' attempts to install new machinery to emphasize our argument.

Most of these points can be drawn directly from the writings we examined in the opening section. All I have done is embellish them, set them down in the contemporary social scene, and draw out some of the properties with reference to tools of modern analysis.

Much of the recent analytic literature relates to labor-managed economies as distinct from capital-managed economies and not to the hybrid case I have been discussing. Within the hybrid world the patterns of coexistence will depend on the selection processes that dominate the markets. In the hybrid world much will depend upon the willingness of lenders of capital to dispose of funds into copartnership or codetermination firms—their greater rigidity will tend to induce a premium on borrowing rates. In such a world workers themselves may elect to place savings in other firms or industries through bond or equity purchase rather than place all their "eggs in one basket."

Through worker participation schemes workers may enhance the possibility of securing more directly the fruits of economic progress for themselves *within* the firm, but the growth of such schemes could inhibit the pace of economic progress in general *across* firms, thereby ensuring that less will be available for the competent workers of each of the constituent firms.

Copartnership firms offer specific benefits but through more conservatively motivated organizations than the traditional joint stock company. Trade unions promote the interest of specific workers employed in a range of firms and in this way may even help the development of free entry that a labor-managed structure would fail to achieve. In the world of coalitions, trade unions in this form could serve as a balance to labor-managed firms in the order of things.

A viable theory of coalitions is not available. All I may note is that the variety of institutions that exists in a society may already be serving a desirable function in promoting a balance between progress and security.

Notes

1. Mill, J.S., *Principles of Political Economy* (London: Longsman 1866), esp. Book IV, Chap. VII; A. Marshall, *Principles of Economics,* first ed. (London: Macmillan 1890), ref. to 8th ed.; A Marshall, *Economics of Industry* (London: Macmillan 1916); A. Marshall, *Industry and Trade* (London: Macmillan 1919); A.C. Pigou, *Economics of Welfare,* first ed. (London: Macmillan 1920), ref. to 4th ed.; C.R. Fay, *Co-Partnership in Industry* (Cambridge: Cam-

bridge Univ. Press 1913); C.R. Fay, *Co-Operation at Home and Abroad,* 4th ed. (London: P.S. King & Sons 1936).

2. See Fay *Co-Partnership in Industry.*

3. Mill, *Principles of Political Economy,* p. 475.

4. Ibid., p. 477.

5. Marshall, *Principles of Economics,* p. 304.

6. Ibid., p. 306.

7. Marshall, *Industry and Trade,* Appendix P.

8. Ibid., p. 294.

9. J.A. Hobson, *Evolution of Modern Capitalism,* revised ed. (London: Allen & Unwin 1926).

10. Pigou, *Economics of Welfare,* p. 205.

11. Michael Spence, *Market Signalling* (Cambridge: Harvard Univ. Press 1974).

12. Pigou, *Economics of Welfare,* p. 326.

13. M.R. Fisher, *The Economic Analysis of Labor* (London: Weindenfeld and Nicolson 1971), Chap. 6.

14. H.C. Simons, *Economic Policy for a Free Society* (Chicago: University of Chicago Press 1948), Chap. VI.

15. J.E. Meade, "Labor-Managed Firms in Conditions of Imperfect Competition," *Economic Journal* (December 1974).

16. M.R. Fisher, *Measurement of Industrial Disputes and Their Economic Effects* (Paris: O.E.C.D., 1973), Chaps. I and III.

The Current Status of Labor Participation in the Management of Business Firms in Germany

Hans G. Monissen

Introduction

In his governmental declaration of 1973 former German *Bundeskanzler* Willy Brandt stated, "Codetermination belongs to the substance of the process of the democratization of our society."[1] This contention supplies at least two important pieces of information. The first one is the expressed strong preference for organizing society according to political criteria—or, to formulate it in the jargon of modern economics, the allocation of scarce resources among competing claimants and uses should be predominantly based on political processes. The second piece of information we can draw from the preceding political declaration is that all opponents to economic codetermination have to realize that their opinions stem from basically antidemocratic attitudes. Surprisingly, the political concept behind Brandt's statement is the ideal of a "free citizen in a free society," a rather perverse inversion of the classical liberal notion in which this ideal is inseparately related to the existence of a minimal state and the realization of competitive capitalism.[2] It seems rather simple to rationalize the preceding governmental view if we search for the underlying methodological principle and the connected theory of society (*theory* understood in a cognitive and not epistemological sense). Statements like the preceding show a holistic view of society that is tied in with the adoption of methodological collectivism or a societal approach as contrasted to methodological individualism, which is the dominant principle for organizing the scholarly efforts of the majority of the economics profession.[3]

Given the existence of two different and apparently noncompatible methodological principles to explain the workings of society, it is not surprising that the controversy over codetermination is centered almost exclusively on the justification and precise foundation of codetermination per se. The cost of this methodological polarization lies in the fact that the direct economic and social effects of codetermination remain to a large degree outside any systematic investigation. To the best of my knowledge, at least before the enactment of the

*The author is indebted to Hans Nutzinger for a critical discussion of an earlier draft.

Codetermination Act of 1976, there did not exist a single piece of empirical research focusing on the ultimate welfare effects of codetermination if we apply the analytical and methodological standards of modern economic theory. Recent advances in the theory of the firm, combined with a fruitful incorporation of the modern theory of property rights, have demonstrated that economic theory is able to analyze the effects of institutional changes on key economic variables in a systematic and predictable way and to assess and evaluate the workings of alternative socioeconomic arrangements. Thus the economic consequences of codetermination should, at least in principle, be open to a systematic theoretical analysis.

My task, however, is only a descriptive one; I try to take stock of the discussion, thereby preparing the ground for a theoretical and empirical investigation. To achieve this goal, I propose to continue as follows. First, I will give a short description of the historical development of the idea of codetermination, which includes a summary of the ideological background. This summary should only convey the empirical vagueness and theoretical emptiness of the ideological superstructure, and I therefore restrain myself from personal commentaries. The next part presents the existing legal framework. The last section describes the experiences with the Montan Act.

Historical Perspectives

The Development of Codetermination in Germany

The first essential legislative regulation of codetermination in the narrow sense of labor participation in management decision making was enacted in 1922. The Act on the Delegation of Works Council Members into the Supervisory Council (*Gesetz über die Entsendung von Betriebstratsmitgliedern in den Aufsichtsrat*)[4] took up a suggestion of the earlier Act on Works Councils (*Betriebsrätegesetz*) of 1920,[5] namely to delegate one or two members of the works council with seat and vote into the supervisory council of the respective business firms. For sure, social and political activities to regulate the employer-employee contract of the capitalistic firm by incorporating various degrees of employees' participation or codetermination can be dated back to the beginnings of the industrial revolution, but the only legal provision on managerial codetermination prior to the postwar legislation of the early 1950s was exactly that act of 1922.

During the first decades of the industrial revolution and the labor movement, the problem of organizing labor into collective action was brought into focus. If we recall that even the institutionalization of so-called workers' representations (*Arbeitsvertretungen*) within the business firms was considered an illegal encroachment on the absolute authority of the factory owner, proposals along these lines were considered epoch-making if not revolutionary episodes in the history of the labor movement. The first direct proposal from the large group of social thinkers of the "pre-March" period of the revolution of 1848–1849 to set up workers' representations in the firm was made in 1835 by Robert von Mohl, a professor of political science and economics at the University of Tübingen.[6] Von Mohl, as wel as his fellow teachers Wilhelm Roscher and Bruno Hildebrand at the same university, is to be ranked among the first critics of classical liberalism, which in his opinion failed to solve the social problems of its time. Classical liberalism has to be transcended, which meant for von Mohl that it has to be transformed into a so-called ethical liberalism. The conflicting interests of capitalists, entrepreneurs, and workers could be reconciled if the entrepreneurs would eventually see their way to introduce certain schemes for workers' profit and capital sharing. There is no textual evidence that he actually demanded factual codetermination of employees in managerial decision making. What he intended to introduce by the establishment of workers' representations was no more than a fiduciary control function and consultative assistance to the management, in the hope that the entrepreneurs would recognize the symptoms of the time and finally decide to introduce the appropriate measures to solve the social question. It is rather typical for the arguing of the social reformers of the pre-March[7] that they confined their social criticism mainly to moral appeals to reason and conscience instead of proposing appropriate changes of the system of property rights restricting the behavior of the profit-seeking firms. It is not too farfetched to assert that the prevailing collectivistic perspective explaining the workings of the complex industrial society, a perspective to which they were accustomed by tradition and education, was bound to prevent them from making a correct diagnosis of the social question in the first place.

The activities of the movement for social and economic reforms culminated when the German Legislative National Assembly (*Deutsche Verfassungsgebende Nationalversammlung*) at Frankfurt in 1848 decided on the appointment of an Economic Committee, which was responsible, among other things, for the drafting of an industrial and commercial code (*Gewerbeordnung*) that was to apply to the whole German Empire. An alternative draft by a political minority of this assembly gave utmost importance to so-called factory committees, which were to have the function of regulating and facilitating the labor-management relations. The socioeconomic climate of that time is well illustrated by the more than 500 petitions that were addressed to the Economic Committee, ranging from proposals simply to restore the feudalistic order of the medieval system of guilds, via revolutionary visions of economic democracy and systems of factory commissars, to utopian concepts of a good society. Two leading authorities of the political labor scene should be singled out.

The first was Karl Georg Winkelblech, in Frankfurt, who invented a system of economic federalism.[8] His ideas influenced the minority draft of the Economic Committee at Frankfurt very strongly. The second political leader was Stephan Born, in Berlin, a former student of Karl Marx and Friedrich Engels.[9] Contrary to the vertical class concept of his famous contemporaries, he tended toward a system of cooperative factory bodies, more in accordance with modern notions of equal codetermination on a horizontal level of authority. Small wonder that his proposals were denounced by Engels as revisionistic heresies. However, the German Legislative National Assembly was doomed to failure because it was a parliament without any executive power. In addition, enthusiasm and optimism to introduce political changes were strongly dampened by the political reactions to restore the pre-March socioeconomic conditions.

The following decades are referred to by social historians as the period of voluntarily restricted entrepreneurial authority. Normative and descriptive presentations of the history of great entrepreneurs attribute these social changes to the farsightedness and sense of responsibility of individual personalities, which remained, though, only exceptions in the whole picture of absolute factory authority. Endeavors to look for a systematic economic analysis of the societal conditions of the prevailing economic situations at that time are fruitless. Even for modern economic historians specialized in the history of nineteenth-century Germany, proper analytic standards, as advanced, for instance, by the advocates of the new economic history, remained unknown or at least never got adopted.

Legal regulation of the employer-employee relationship got new strong impetus in 1891 with the Amendment to the Industrial and Commercial Code for the German Empire.[10] This amendment, known as the law for the protection of workers, brought about compulsory work orders (*Arbeitsordnungen*) for factories employing more than 20 workers (but these orders could be laid down unilaterally by the factory owner), official approval of existing voluntarily introduced committees, and legislative regulation for establishing new committees on a noncompulsory basis. The following years brought more stringent regulations for the mining sector in several German states by the legal requirement to establish workers' representations or workers' committees in the respective firms.

During World War I the central government had to comply with labor demand, and it introduced the Act on the Patrial Auxiliary Service (*Gesetz über den Vaterländischen Hilfsdienst*).[11] This act brought legal recognition of unions and provided the compulsory introduction of employees' committees (separately for wage-earning and salaried employees) for business firms with war service functions, provided that they had at least 50 employees.

In November of 1918 the employers and unions instituted the Central Association of the Industrial and Commercial Employers and Employees of Germany, where the compulsory institution of employees' committees for the whole economy was agreed upon. This agreement soon got legislative support.

The Constitution of Weimar[12] of 1919, the Constitution of the German

Reich, explicitly incorporated the concept of codetermination in article 165: "The wage-earning and salaried employees are called upon to cooperate, with equal rights and in community with the entrepreneurs, on the regulation of wage and working conditions and on the total economic development of the productive forces." To guarantee an adequate participation, the constitution provided for the establishment of a federally organized system of workers' councils. The Constitution of today's Federal Republic of Germany does not contain a similar passage, and radical critics of the contemporary social and economic system of the German Federal Republic often refer to article 165 of the Constitution of Weimar when they charge the German capitalistic system with gradually dismantling the rights of the working class. As previously mentioned, the legislation of 1920 and 1922 concretized the somewhat abstract constitutional ideas on labor codetermination by stipulating the delegation of employees into the supervisory councils of the respective business firms.

During the time before and after the foundation of the Weimar Republic, the notion and concept of a liberal economy or economic democracy (*Wirtschaftsdemokratie*) was a central topic of the several regular and special sessions of both the unions and the Social Democratic Party. The 1925 convention of the General German Federation of Unions (*Allgemeiner Deutscher Gewerkschaftsbund*) in Breslau discussed for the first time in full the problem of economic democracy. In the same year, the German Social Democratic Party published at its annual meeting in Heidelberg a program for economic democracy. The discussion culminated in 1928 at the thirteenth convention of the General German Federation of Unions in Hamburg, where a specific program for economic democracy was formulated in the famous report by Fritz Naphtali. "I also hold the opinion: ultimately, economic democracy and socialism are inseparably connected. The goal of economic democracy, i.e., a really democratic structure of the economy, is not attainable within the capitalistic economy."[13] Economic democracy is still an important goal of the German unionist movement in recent times, which is illustrated by the fact that Naphtali's book on economic democracy was republished in 1966 with a unionist introduction and a foreword by the former president of the German Federation of Trade Unions (*Deutscher Gewerkschaftsbund*), Ludwig Rosenberg.[14] This shows quite well that according to the goals of the unions the demand for economic democracy in one version or the other is still an important item on the programmatic agenda for changing social and political conditions in West Germany.

The authoritarian interregnum of the Third Reich (1933-1945) interrupted the development of codetermination in Germany. Works councils and unions were dissolved, the legal right (regulated in the act of 1922) to delegate labor's representatives into the supervisory councils was repealed. The Act to Order National Labor of 1934 deprived the labor representatives in the business firms of their original functions and made them mere functionaries and political agents of the central government.

The Broader Ideological Background

Already during the late fifties, the discussion about economic codetermination in Germany had mushroomed in such a way that even specialists in this field had difficulties in organizing such heterogeneous material in a systematic way. This state of affairs caused the Foundation on Codetermination (*Stiftung Mitbestimmung*) in 1957 to request the Economic Institute of the Unions (*Wirtschaftswissenschaftliches Institut der Gewerkschaften*) to perform a major research program for answering the following question: "Which motives and aspects are asserted in Germany and abroad for and against the introduction and eventual expansion of economic codetermination."[15] The final report was published in 1964. Disregarding the strong unionist bias in the document, this work is still a worthwhile reference book for the German controversy over economic codetermination.[16]

In the postwar discussion one might distinguish five different ideological groupings, whereby the demarcation criteria are taken from an ideal-type concept of the economic-political order, a view popular in the German literature. These different groupings are: neoliberalism, the Catholic social doctrine and the Protestant social doctrine, liberal socialism, and neo-Marxism. Recently, the adjective embroidery of socialism has moved toward "democratic," indicating not so much a purely verbal preference but an ideological move back to the former Marxist basis, which makes it difficult to separate this position from the more direct neo-Marxist orientation. During the last two or three decades both socialism and neo-Marxism have become much more intellectual, but this does not necessarily imply a better theoretical or analytical foundation.

In 1937, under the Nazi regime, Franz Böhm, Walter Eucken, and Hans Grossmann-Doerth started a series of publications under the general title "The Order of the Economy," which programmatically formulated the concept of ordo- or neoliberalism: A social, political, and economic program of a liberal (understood in the traditional European meaning) societal organization, but emphasizing at the same time some institutional corrections that were codifying the strong social feelings of its founding fathers. This social element is, according to its advocates, the curbing ingredient to an otherwise unrestricted liberalism as observed during the eighteenth and nineteenth centuries. This more abstract stock of ideas was then solidified into the concept of the social market economy by Alfred Müller-Armack, Alexander Rüstow, and Wilhelm Röpke, and later politically practiced by Ludwig Erhard. Neoliberal ideas on economic codetermination are expressed in a very influential paper by Franz Böhm, to which I refer summarily in the next section.[17]

The neoliberal position strongly opposes managerial codetermination if the labor representatives in the decision-making bodies of the firm are direct union representatives. This practice would destroy the equilibrium of the bargaining process between employers and employees by challenging the principle of the autonomy of collective agreement. It is denied that union efforts are guided by an economic order concept, union influences on the decision process of the business firm being a mere instrument of political power to organize an all-embracing economic monopoly position unendangered by any possible rivalry or competition. This total monopoly encompasses both economic and political power, with obvious consequences for the survival of the political system of democracy. It is stressed that union representatives are outsiders tending to patronize the insiders and often advocating positions contrary to the employees' interests, whereby their original function is perverted into an independent third interest group. The danger is that market contracts are politicized, that latent and manifest conflicts will become class conflicts, and that the market economy will degenerate to a centrally planned economy. According to the neoliberal concept, the popular notion that economic and political democracy are either necessary supplements or even expressions of the same state of affairs is highly misleading and erroneous. Access to the first kind of "democracy" is open only to an arbitrarily defined group without broad democratic legitimation. Important for the special party association is only the merely accidental position in the labor contract. A kind of institutionalized class struggle cannot solve the familiar democratic exchange of political pros and cons. The strong union influence in this political exchange and the resulting power accumulation will lead to a power polarization of the whole society, with a possible destruction of the democratic political system.

According to the neoliberal position, private ownership of the means of production is a constitutional element of the social market economy. Ownership is not understood in a purely formal way, but implies direct power of disposition and control. The bearing of both positive and negative wealth consequences of the owners' decisions are inseparable characteristics of private ownership. Codetermination introduces bearers of functions without any economic responsibility. This is indirect socialization.

The modern enterprise cannot be understood as a socially isolated entity. The decisions to be taken are related to the wants of the consumer; decisions ignoring the wants will lead to losses. Managerial codetermination could result in a situation in which the wants of the consumers could be ignored for a longer period, which means that economic codetermination will be a disruptive element in a rationally designed concept of competitive order. In any case, the consumer will be placed at a disadvantage. This remaining social party is generally excluded from the codetermination arrangement. The undermining of the entrepreneurial function and the lack of rapid market adjustment will hamper the dynamics of the economic process and slow down the rate of technical progress. The business firms will undertake fewer adjustment and readjustment investments and fewer so-called pioneer investments. In addition, the effects of codetermination resemble standstill agreements between the formerly competing firms of an industry.

Important ingredients for an understanding of the concept of liberal or democratic socialism go back to Eduard Bernstein's revisionist reinterpretation of orthodox Marxism.[18] Certain empirically observed anomalies in the development of the capitalistic system, especially the delay of its alleged breakdown, required the formulation of a political strategy for the transition phase, aiming at a rigorous utilization of system-immanent reform possibilities. But Bernstein's revisionism is only one intellectual trend toward the development of democratic socialism. Neo-Marxian influences, certain elements of a religious and/or utopian socialism, and even left-liberalistic influences also play an important role. This development had its historical background in the totalitarian degeneration of the Marxian thoughts in some European countries. The various groups get a uniform overall orientation by way of a so-called common and unifying understanding of democracy, which amounts to the belief that a comprehensive and well-developed democracy can only be reached through a comprehensive and total realization of socialism. This conception justifies the embroidery with the adjective *democratic*. With respect to economic policies, this name seems to be much more committal than the somewhat outmoded term *liberal,* which was used in express contrast not only to Eastern European social systems as such but also to their Marxian orientation. In our time, Marxian aims and Marxian analysis of social systems are back in favor with the democratic socialists.

The order concepts of democratic socialism are, and have always been, tied together with the union documentations and the program of the Social Democratic Party (SPD). Elements of an ideological reorientation toward Marxian ideas are programmatically included in the new official Orientation Scheme 85 of the SPD,[19] which in this respect closes the interim phase of the former Godesberg Program of 1959,[20] where the Marxian program was rather emphatically excluded.

The early order concept of liberal socialism referred to competition (market competition) as an instrument to be realized as far as possible but to be supplemented by planning (state planning) as far as necessary.[21] The competitive order is seen to require both a public interest supplementation and regulative state interventions aiming at an active full employment, stabilization, and growth policy and trying to reduce the existing income and wealth differences. In this form, the relevance of a liberal socialism is in principle amenable to empirical assessment and evaluation. But nowadays, because socialism and democracy are set as identical almost by definition, the conception of democratic socialism is more and more discussed in a purely ideological manner, without any reference to an underlying analytical-deductive system.

If we exclude the more extreme form of democratic socialism, which consiers codetermination only as a strategic variable in the practical politics of Bernsteinian revisionism, then even today the fund of arguments about economic codetermination from the standpoint of a liberal or democratic socialism is largely supplied by some important commentaries of the fifties. The main points are as follows: in order to restrict the economic forces, the state is naturally legitimated to intervene in the firms' inner constitution. Almost unanimously, the proponents of democratic socialism hold the opinion that outside union representatives are to be sent into the firms' codetermination bodies. The union representatives are seen as acting in the employees' best interest, and because of their alleged better knowledge and superior qualification and their orientation toward the whole economy, they are able to check enterprise egoism and myopia.[22]

The aim of securing and widening the employees' personal rights and freedom is mentioned as the ultimate goal in almost every argument vindicating economic codetermination. In the absence of codetermination there is no control of authoritarian leadership in the firms, which in turn is caused mainly by the one-sided distribution of ownership of the productive capital. Without codetermination, technical progress and bureaucratization make the work environment less human and lead to a loss of individuality and personality. Most of the proponents of democratic socialism believe that only a suitable employees' participation in the managerial decision processes can, in the long run, overcome the class conflicts and avoid a disastrous class struggle. But codetermination is also mentioned as a first step toward socialization of the private sector of the economy, even though it might bequeath to the future—and this is a somewhat unusual argument of a minority group—problems of coordination in the context of a finally all-embracing economic planning. As to the entrepreneurial function, codetermination is considered to have basically only positive consequences. Without codetermination the modern enterprise is believed to operate on the basis of an uncontrolled, discretionary management behavior caused by a far-reaching separation of ownership and control.

These arguments for justifying codetermination are essentially based on the functionlist societal view of contemporary sociology, be it in the integrationist or in the conflict-theoretic variant. As an example of this approach's empirical emptiness combined with a clever technique of argumentation, reference can be made to Dahrendorf's conflict theory, which had a considerable influence in the German controversy over codetermination.[23] Conflict-theoretical aspects are mentioned in a wide variety of circumstances—to support codetermination as a mechanism for solving conflicts or to reject codetermination because it diverts conflicts in an uncontrollable manner (the conservative view) or because it masks the conflicts (the Marxist version) or because it leads to improper pseudo-solutions.

The term *neo-Marxism* characterizes those groups of Marxists who oppose a direct elaboration of Marx's teachings in the sense of Leninism-Stalinism and who do not, like the orthodix Marxists, consider an imminent breakdown of the capitalist system as a basis for an active reorganization.[24] The cause of practically all urgent social and political problems of modern times stems from the allegedly unrestricted decision-making power derived from the existence of private property, especially in the form of productive capital. In principle, this view should lead to a strict rejection of any sort of codetermination, but co-determination is on the other hand considered in a purely instrumental sense and praised as an important intermediate step in the emancipatory struggle of the working class. The labor unions, in this connection, get a very special task, for only the fact of their existence allows a well-directed groundwork in the firms for the creation of the necessary revolutionary class consciousness. Co-determination therefore becomes a system-immanent technique for achieving the true goal, namely the simultaneous realization of socialism and a centrally planned economy. The discussion over planning the economy, though, has ex-tremely polarized the opinions within the neo-Marxist groups. It led to the con-flict between those who believe in workers' self-management with an orientation toward the base (as in Yugoslavia) and those who prefer a "democratic" central-ism, as practiced for example in the German Democratic Republic.

To evaluate the role that the two large German religious communities—the Catholic and the Protestant churches—play in influencing the thinking and the decisions even in economic, social, and political matters, one might first note that more than 90 percent of the total German population are members of one of these two churches.[25] The special position of the churches is shown by the fact that the membership contributions are collected via the public tax system, the church contributions forming a certain percentage of individual wage and income taxes.

The Catholic social doctrine[26] is essentially based on three sources: on the *jus naturale,* on the ecclesiastical teachings (e.g., the social encyclicals), and on "properly" guided scientific endeavors. The *jus naturale* specifies all those rights that any man has as a human being. All normative stipulations posited by the law should be derived from the *jus naturale.* But because such an orientation cannot bring about instructions for particular situations, e.g., parity or non-parity solutions in the codetermination case, the church's authority is needed in order to posit and explain specific norms. The Catholic church's conception of man sees him simultaneously and inseparably as both an individual and a societal being. In the center of this order we find man as a person whose desti-nation aims on the one hand at individual welfare, on the other hand at social welfare, but without any clearcut priority. Two important social principles regulate the organizations of society, namely the principle of solidarity and the principle of subsidiarity. The Catholic social doctrine does not allow a direct derivation of a concrete social order, but at least since *"Quadragesimo Anno"* of 1931 the concept (or the maxim) of an order according to professional cate-gories (*berufsständische Ordnung*) is central to its sociopolitical program. The precise meaning is not specified; it is implied, though, that the social order should establish a social structure based on the subsidiarity principle, thus realizing the idea of an achieving community, with a profession or a firm as the natural unit comprising the members of formerly different classes. This order is to avoid on the one hand the polarization of class interests, criticized as a typical outcome of the liberal order concept, and on the other hand it is to stay clear of egalitarian socialist ideas. The proponents of the Catholic social doctrine take their sometimes very contradictory recommendations about the appropriate social order in general and codetermination in particular mainly from the following official texts: *"Quadragesimo Anno"* of 1931, *"Mater et Magistra"* of 1961, *"Populorum Progressio"* of 1967, as well as the commentaries of the Second Vaticanum of 1962-1964. There is a certain number of influential voices against managerial codetermination, stressing especially the intrinsic relationship between private property and the optimization of the personal existence; but the Catholic social doctrine's functionalistic approach in the context of an organistic view of the world and of society represents the classical justification for a comprehensive concept of codetermination both in the business firms and in the more comprehensive associations and organizations of society as a whole.

The Protestant social doctrine on the other hand does not offer a conceptually unified body of thoughts. It is based solely and exclusively on the interpretation of the Holy Scriptures. The absence of concrete models of societal order restricted each Protestant, responsible only to his own conscience, for a long time to active brotherly love. The Lutherian distinction between the order of the world and the order of God therefore suggests, depending on the ideological starting point of the particular interpreter, a passive-conservative or an open-individualistic relationship toward economic and sociopolitical problems. But the basic attitude has changed fundamentally during the past few years: The Christian's individual uncoordinated activities have been brought into alignment by means of a more and more political or critical theology (somewhat surprisingly not necessarily with theistic notions). Concrete occasions, like rearmament, emergency laws, and so on were first test cases for a collectivistic reorientation of a formerly individualistic attitude toward the state and the economy. A study on the question of codetermination, published by the Chamber for Social Order of the Council of the Protestant Church of Germany in 1968, was still based on the idea of partnership and cooperation;[27] but in recent times many protestant thinkers put increasingly the idea of "democratization of the institutions" in the center of their propositions and programs. An emancipatory Christian faith can bloom only within the framework of a socialist economic order.

The Present Legal Framework

It may appear rather perplexing for an outside observer of the West German labor relations scene that the post-World War II political struggle over labor codetermination has resulted in the enactment of three different pieces of legal regulations, with differing coverage and varying degrees of labor participation in the management of business firms.

The Montan Act of 1951

After the war, the German unions, congenial with declared intentions of the British occupation forces, endorsed proposals to nationalize the "montan" industry (mining and iron and steel producing industry) in the British occupied zone. The changing socioeconomic climate during the ensuing years showed, however, that such a solution was politically unattainable, and a compromise was found in a somewhat different direction. The preliminary organization of the montan industry under British control brought about a full parity solution that amounted to an equal share of seats for the stockholders and the employees in the supervisory council (*Aufsichtsrat*) of the decartelized business firms in the montan industry.[28] Furthermore, the unions obtained the right to nominate the candidate for the newly established position of the so-called labor director, an equal-ranking member of the corporations' executive board (*Vorstand*).

The first postwar German parliament of 1949 saw an unexpected majority for the conservative bloc (Christian Democratic Union, Christian Social Union, Free Democratic Party, and German Party, as well as several other parties), viz. 256 seats as opposed to 146 seats for the left bloc, which was comprised of the Social Democratic Party (131) and the German Communist Party (15). The preliminary parity solution for the montan industry, introduced under the auspices of the British occupation forces, was endangered. Under the massive threat of nationwide strikes, and after heated discussion in and out of parliament, the German government was forced to single out the montan complex for separate legislative treatment. The postwar controversy over codetermination in the montan industry cumulated in the Act on the Codetermination of Employees in the Supervisory Councils and Executive Boards of the Business Firms in the Mining and Iron and Steel Producing Industries of 1951, the Montan Act (*Gestiz über die Mitbestimmung der Arbeitnehmer in den Aufsichtsräten und Vorständen der Unternehmen des Bergbaus und der Eisen und Stahl erzeugenden Industrie*).[29]

Figure 4-1 provides a simple graphical illustration of the characteristic features of this act; it will help to guide our short introductory description.

The Montan Act applies to all firms in the mining and the iron and steel industries if they are operated under the charter of a corporation (*Aktiengesellschaft, AG*), a limited liability company (*Gesellschaft mit beschränkter Haftung, GmbH*), or a joint company of mine owners (*bergrechtliche Gewerkschaft*), and if they have in general more than 1000 employees.

If—unlike in the case of all corporations—the firm's charter doesn't require the institution of a supervisory council, such a council has now to be organized. The council consists of 11 elected members, whereby both the stockholders and the employees respectively appoint four members and an additional external member. The law stipulates that the additional member may be neither a representative of a union nor of an employer organization nor employed by that firm or otherwise connected with it in some economic way.

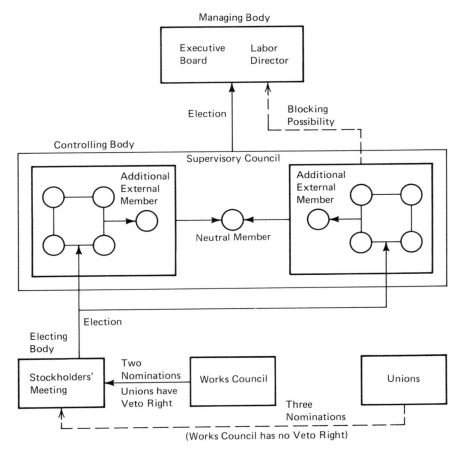

Figure 4-1. Montan Model

The electing body for all members of the supervisory council is the stock-holders' meeting (*Hauptversammlung*).[30] This meeting nominates and elects the owners' representatives and confirms the employees' representatives. Two of the employees' five representatives are nominated by the works council (*Betriebs-rat*),[31] whereby one representative must come from the group of salaried employees and the other from the group of the wage-earning employees. It is interesting to note that the unions concerned can veto that nomination. The remaining three council members, i.e., the two further employee representatives and the additional external member for the labor bloc, are nominated by the unions, with no veto power for the works council. Altogether, only two of the employees' five representatives on the council must come from the firm under consideration; and in addition, labor's direct preference is restricted by the veto right of the unions.

The Montan Act also stipulates the nomination of a so-called neutral member, chosen by the directly elected members of the supervisory council. This eleventh member—the fifteenth or the twenty-first member for extended councils, a case we consider in a moment—deserves our special attention. The neutral member will be elected by majority vote of the council members, whereby at least three of the employees' and three of the shareholders' representatives have to support his election. The notion behind the concept of the neutral member is to prevent possible stalemate situations and to endorse the "public" interest in the decision process of the modern capitalistic enterprise.

In accordance with the German corporate laws, the supervisory council appoints the executive board. The supervisory council elects the so-called labor director, a full and equal member of the executive board but depending in a special way on the trust of labor's representatives. The labor director cannot be elected against the votes of the majority of the employees' members in the supervisory council. But the law does not specify in a concrete and clearcut way the particular tasks and responsibilities of the labor director. Only by assigning distinct areas to the different members of the executive board is the scope of activities for the labor director implicitly demarcated. In practice, the labor director is responsible for personnel and social matters.

In previous discussion we proceeded on the assumption that the supervisory council had 11 members. If the firm's nominal capital exceeds 20 million DM, the maximum number of board members is 15. If the nominal capital is higher than 50 million DM, the electing bodies may appoint 21 members. The change in the number of board members involves a change in the composition of the employees' representatives. In the case of 15 members, the works council nominates three, viz. one salaried employee and two wage-earning employees, and the unions nominate four members, including the additional external member. In the case of 21 members, the works council nominates a further wage-earning employee, and the unions have the option for six candidates. The general rules for the election of the neutral member apply without change.

Managerial Codetermination According to the Works Constitution Act of 1952

As already mentioned, special historical circumstances combined with massive political pressures forced the first German postwar government to single out the montan complex for special legislative treatment. The social constitution for all firms of the private economic sector, the Works Constitution Act (*Betriebsverfassungsgesetz*) was enacted in 1952, one year after the introduction of the Montan Act, which remains *lex specialis* on the issue of managerial codetermination for the montan industry.[32] The legal regulation of labor participation in management fell short of the original union aspirations and their far-reaching realization in the Montan Act. Small wonder that the unions considered this legislative frame only as an uneasy compromise or an intermediate step in a goal-directed process of what they call "democratization" of the economy, a conceptual analogy to the political system.

The Works Constitution Act provides general regulations for three different levels of employees' participation and codetermination. The first complex concerns the independent rights of the single employee on the personal level, e.g., rights to information, hearing, and discussion on issues concerning workshop place, fields of activity, remuneration, and so forth. On the plant level, the act prescribes the institution of a works council, an independent representative body of all employees, which is required if the firm has more than five permanent employees. In addition to this, if the company is employing more than five adolescents (i.e., people below 18), a youth council has to be established.

On the decision level of the whole firm, finally, participation in management found a general regulation. Under the Works Constitution Act, one third of the members of the supervisory council must be labor representatives who are elected by the firm's employees. The structure of managerial codetermination under the Works Constitution Act is illustrated in Figure 4-2.

Before the enactment of the Codetermination Act of 1976, which sets apart large firms for special regulation without invalidating the *lex specialis* of the Montan Act, the Works Constitution Act provided the general legislative frame for the managerial codetermination issue in Germany. In this context, the main provision on managerial codetermination is the one-third share of employees in the supervisory councils of the business firms. In its version of 1952 and the amendment of 1972, the act stipulates one-third codetermination for corporations and partnerships limited by shares (*Kommanditgesellschaften auf Aktien, KGaA*), as well as for limited liability companies, joint companies of mine owners and business cooperatives (*Erwerbs- und Wirtschaftsgenossenschaften*) with more than 500 employees. If the business charter does not already require the institution of a supervisory council, such a council has to be established. The main exceptions from the one-third codetermination are made for family corporations with less than 500 employees, for so-called tendency firms (i.e., business firms with political, unionist, denominational, charitable, educational, scientific, or artistic aims or serving purposes of reporting or expression of opinion) and for religious groups and their charitable and educational institutions.

If the firm's charter prescribes six council members, which requires two labor representatives, only employees of the firm under consideration are eligible for the supervisory council. In the cases of more employee representatives, at least two must be members of the respective firm. Additional members may come from outside, e.g., from unions. It is interesting to note that under the

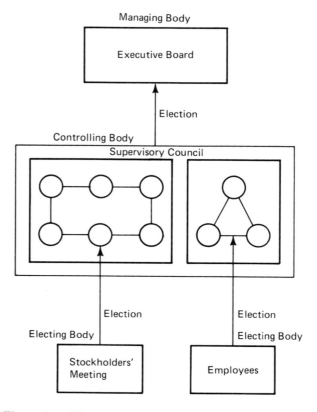

Figure 4-2. The Model of the "Works Constitution Act"

1952 Works Constitution Act the unions have neither a right to nominate the internal employee candidates nor a right to advise the employees on that matter. Even the rights of the works council are rather restricted in this context. Having only the same rights as other employee groupings, the works council may simply propose a list of candiates. The candidates for the supervisory council are elected by all employees according to the rules of direct proportional voting. The voting procedure does not provide a different treatment of salaried and of wage-earning employees. The only structural qualification concerning the list of candidates stems from the fact that the legislators felt the interests of female employees better safeguarded by female representatives on the board. If the firm has more than 50 percent female employees, at least one of the employees' representatives on the supervisory council is to be female.

The Codetermination Protection Acts

In the years after the introduction of the Montan Act, the structure of the West German economy changed quite considerably, so that certain business firms that were subject to the Montan Act underwent so many structural changes that they no longer fitted under that act's criteria. To prevent the firms from escaping the original legal requirements of the Montan Act and thereby becoming subject only to the one-third parity requirement of the Works Constitution Act, the legislators issued several legal amendments, which are referred to as the codetermination protection acts.

The first of these legal amendments was the Supplement Act on Codetermination of 1956 (Act to Supplement the Acts on Codetermination of Employees in the Supervisory Councils and Executive Boards of the Business Firms in Mining and Iron and Steel Producing Industries).[33] This act is more popularly known as the Amendment on Holding Companies. For corporations, limited-liability companies, or joint companies of mine owners dominating a business firm that falls under the Montan Act of 1951, this Supplement Act of 1956 applies as follows. If the production activities of the dominating firm fall themselves under the criteria for the application of the Montan Act, this act remains of course directly applicable. If this is not the case, but the output structure of the business combine is significantly determined by the output of firms falling under the provisions of the act of 1951, the holding amendment of 1956 prescribes that the Montan Act applies to the dominating firm, too.[34]

This act brings about some important legislative changes from the original version of the Montan Act. Remember that in the Montan Model the works council nominates two candidates for election to the supervisory council, with a veto right for the unions concerned. The supplementary act of 1956 introduces a primary election, whereby the electors are directly chosen by the firm's employees. The position of the unions is significantly weakened, because with, in general, 15 members in the supervisory council the unions retain the nomination right for only three members (as compared to four according to the Montan Act). In addition to this, the union veto power concerning the candidates of the firm's employees is abolished. Elected candidates of the union camp become more independent of the unions because their removal from office is rendered more difficult. A court order, pending on the submittal of an important reason for the planned removal, must first be brought about. However, the position of the stockholders is somewhat strengthened, because under the new provisions the labor director may be elected against the votes of the labor representatives in the supervisory council.

The second amendment to the Montan Act was the Modification Act to the Codetermination Act of 1967,[35] which got popular propagation as the *Lex Rheinstahl.* If the sales revenue from montan activities of a business combine falls below 50 percent of the total revenue during two consecutive years, the dominant firm would under the Holding Amendment of 1956 drop out of the montan regulation and would therefore be subjected only to the less stringent regulation of the Works Constitution Act, with the one-third partity requirements. To prevent this consequence, the legislators enacted a modifying law that says that the dominating firm will be taken out of the montan restrictions only if the montan sales revenue of the total business combine falls below the 50 percent limit during an extended time period of five consecutive years. The actual cause for this modifying legislation was the *Rheinstahl AG,* which had brought the *Henschel AG* with the consequence that the orignal Montan Act applied under the Supplement Act for only two more years.

The actual reason for the introduction, in 1971, of the Act on the Limited Further Duration of Codetermination in Business Firms Subject Until Now to the Codetermination Acts was once more the *Rheinstahl AG.*[36] To secure the status quo, the legislators enacted a further prolongation, valid until December 31, 1975. To supplement the prolongation, the scope of application as defined in the original Montan Act was extended. Not only firms in the mining and iron and steel producing industries should be subjected to the act, but also firms engaged in specific forms of iron and steel processing, e.g., rolling mills.

The Codetermination Act of 1976

The controversy over managerial codetermination of employees in West Germany found its preliminary end in the Act on the Codetermination of Employees (*Gesetz über die Mitbestimmung der Arbeitnehmer*), which was passed in 1976.[37] This act, a somewhat moderated version of the Montan Act, applies for large firms in the rest of the economy. Two observations should be stated at the beginning. First, the Montan Act is not annulled by the legislation of 1976, for this legislation explicitly excludes those business firms for which managerial codetermination is settled by the Codetermination Act of 1951 (the Montan Act) and the Codetermination Protection Acts of 1956 and 1967. Second, the one-third parity provisions under the Works Constitution Act of 1952 still apply for smaller-sized business firms not covered by the Codetermination Act of 1976. As in the case of the act of 1952, so-called tendency enterprises remain exempted. These are here defined as enterprises serving, political, coalition-political, denominational, charitable, educational, scientific, or artistic designations or purposes that are conducive to information or to expression of opinion as covered by article 5.1.2 of the German Constitution. In addition, the Codetermination Act also excludes religious communities and their associated charitable and educational institutions. With these exemptions, the act applies to all large business firms—i.e., firms employing in general more than 2000 employees—that are operated under the legal charter of a corporation, a partnership limited by shares, a limited-liability company, a joint company of mine owners, or a business cooperative. To clarify the structure, Figure 4-3 provides an illustration of the characteristic features of the act under discussion.

Indirect voting via an electoral committee will be the rule if the number of employees exceeds 8000. As known, indirect voting could favor organized interest groups, e.g., the unions. The employees may, however, pass a resolution for direct voting. Analogously, the employees of a firm with an employment figure below 8000 may decide on the technically more efficient device of an electoral committee. Voting for the salaried and the wage-earning employees will take place separately if no other resolution is passed by the employees. The number of electors for these two social groups is proportional to the respective number of employees in the business firm. As a specific, much-debated provision under the new Codetermination Act, the group of the salaried employees must include a proportional share of representatives of the so-called managerial salaried employees (*leitende Ange stellte*), i.e., the employees with management functions. The number of electoral representatives in the two groups, whereby one includes the subgroup of the managerial salaried employees, is qualified by a provision protecting minority interests. The electoral group of the salaried employees must include at least one managerial salaried employee.

The electors of the two committees elect the members of the supervisory council in separate pollings according to the rules of proportionate voting, but common voting may be decided upon. Once more, a rule protecting minority interests applies, and guarantees in the actual circumstances that at least one member of the group of the managerial salaried employees will be in the council.

As under the Works Constitution Act, the unions have neither a nomination right nor a veto right with respect to the employees' representatives, all of which must be employed at the firm under consideration. Finally, to benefit the unions' interests, the supervisory council will be completed by two members who are nominated by the unions and elected by the employees' electoral committee. In contrast to the election of the representatives of the two different social groups within the firm, the union members are elected jointly by secret voting of all members of the electoral committee.

A supervisory council with a total number of 12 members is composed of 6 representatives for the stockholders, 4 for the employees, and 2 for the unions of the respective industry, whereby the election of the employees' candidates is qualified by the provision that at least one member of the group of the managerial salaried employees must be represented in the council.

The members of the supervisory council elect both the chairman and the deputy chairman by a two-thirds majority vote. If the majority is not achieved, the shareholders' members of the council elect the chairman and the employees' members the deputy. In general, the members of the managing body will be elected by a majority of at least two-thirds of the council members. If such a

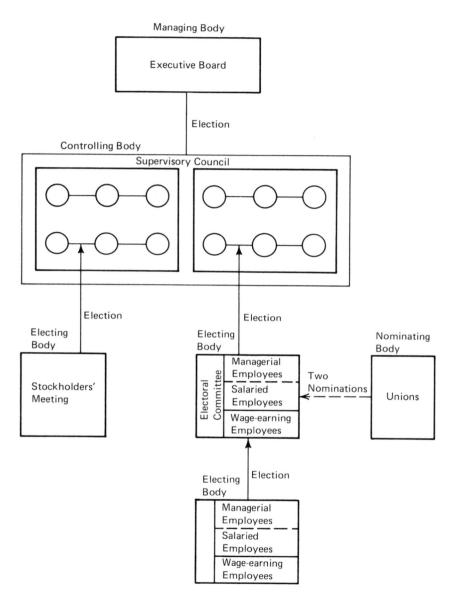

Figure 4-3. The Model of the Codetermination Act of 1976

majority cannot be obtained, a simple majority of the council members is sufficient. In the case of stalemate situations, the chairman of the supervisory council will have two votes. It is interesting to note that the new law does not specify any legal provision for the election of the labor director.

This description applies to business firms with in general no more than 10,000 employees. Between 10,000 and no more than 20,000 employees, the number of council members amounts to 16, including 8 labor candidates, of which only two are nominated by the unions. An additional candidate from the unions will be nominated if the council has a total number of 20 members. This will be the case if the total employment figure exceeds 20,000 employees.

As usual, the members of the executive board are appointed by the supervisory council, and the concept of the labor director is retained from the Montan Act.

Experiences with the Montan Act

"For the evaluation of the previous experiences with codetermination as a basis for further reflections in this area," an independent scientific commission was covened on government assignment in 1968. Two years later, this commission presented its report to the then *Bundeskanzler* Willy Brandt.[38] This report is the most extensive empirical investigation of the codetermination problem so far. It covers the experiences both with the Montan Act and with the one-third parity solution of the Works Constitution Act, but the far-reaching montan regulation attracts the particular interest. Because "the amount of scientifically usable facts of experience that could be gained from the literature"[39] did not seem sufficient, the empirical base was widened through hearings with holders of more or less important positions in the area of economic codetermination and through written interviews with these people. A systematic quantitative assessment of the economic consequences of codetermination was not attempted. Subjective criteria, a priori guesses, and idiosyncracies replaced theoretical analysis, and a narrow documentation had to serve as a substitute for an appropriate empirical implementation guided by the methodological standards of a developed social science. Such an approach is symptomatic for the "empirical" studies in the area of the codetermination problem. Before describing some of the more important results of the commission report, I shall briefly mention the most important earlier studies, not so much for a clarification of the empirical issues but rather with the aim of illustrating how that research proceeded.

Shortly after the Montan Act was passed, Pirkner et al. presented a study, commissioned by the Economic Institute of the Unions, dealing with the first consequences of the new codetermination law.[40] This study and quite a few similar ones published later argued completely under the functionalistic perspective—in those days accepted without reservation—of methodological collectivism, which was a special feature of the then very popular industrial sociology.

Even if we leave out the question of the empirical validity and relevance of this approach, this study does not help in the empirical clarification of the codetermination question, if only because of the fact that the framework of the functionalist sociology does not lend itself to the inclusion of the relevant economic categories, such as capital costs, capital structure, capital intensity, productivity, etc.

Four influential studies published during the years 1953-1968 deal mainly with the problem of how much information the employees had about codetermination institutions and about what was actually happening in those firms that was subject to codetermination.[41] The only research technique used is the interview. These polls were conducted without systematic reference to an underlying theoretical perspective, so that the relevance and meaning of the results presented, e.g., the fact of a low level of familiarity with the codetermination regulations, has to remain open.

The two most important publications before the report of the codetermination commission are the studies by Otto Blume[42] and Fritz Voigt.[43] Both studies, which on the one hand deal with the work of the codetermination representatives and on the other hand with the relationship between the codetermination representatives and the capital owners, come to results similar to the commission report, which we now briefly discuss.

The commission dealt in particular with the following points:[44]

1. The functioning and the consequences of different compositions of the supervisory council
2. The operations of the executive board, especially the cooperation with the works council and the role of the labor director
3. Effects of employee codetermination under the Works Constitution Act
4. Information and cooperation processes
5. The effects of codetermination on the objectives of the firms
6. The influence of codetermination of the position of the firm in the overall economic system.

The following remarks focus on the Montan Act. To the extent that certain differences from the experience with the Works Constitution Act are not caused by the particular legal regulations, the results will be described separately. The majority of the position holders believed that if the employees are to have representative participation in the managerial decision process, then this participation should take place only in the supervisory council. A direct inclusion of employee representatives on the executive board might endanger the functioning of the firm. In practice, though, the supervisory council has more and more acquired the function of a genuine decision body, a development that has blurred the sharp separation of competences as specified in the corporation law.

The Montan Act aimed at a legal institutionalization of the cooperation between labor and capital in the supervisory council of the firm. The nomination of the shareholders' representatives is considerably influenced by the executive board, and this influence is positively related to the dispersion of share ownership. Contrary to common conjectures, the banks' influence, which might be expected to emanate from the deposit voting rights,[45] is not all that important, if influence is identified with presence on the supervisory council. The commission was unable to find much influence beyond that resulting from normal business relationships. As to the recruitment of the employees' representatives in the supervisory councils, those coming from the firms themselves are as a normal rule also members of the works councils. Representatives from outside the firms, i.e., union representatives, are found to an especially high degree in the montan sector, which is due to the legal stipulations. In more than 85 percent of the firms with codetermination under the Works Constitution Act, there are no external union delegates, which shows that the employees strongly prefer their representatives in the supervisory council to come from the firm itself. Whereas the internal members are expected to be strongly oriented toward the firm under consideration, the external members are supposed to look beyond the narrow range of the firm and care more for the wider problem of the economy. The commission holds the opinion, though, that central guidance and control of the union representatives cannot be demonstrated. The majority of all position holders believe that a general participation of employee representatives in the supervisory council cannot be dispensed with any more.

Decisions of the supervisory council are now rarely achieved by discussion in the council meetings, which is due to the fact that the pending problems have already been discussed and decided upon within the constituent groups. Mention is made of an intensive preconsultation between the executive board and the employees' representatives in the supervisory council, with the labor director playing an important role. The unions influence these discussions in a variety of formal and informal ways. Preparatory discussion and formation of separate groups have made the work of the supervisory council almost devoid of real content. The *en bloc* voting of the employee representatives is seen as an important drawback to the parity solution, because in many cases it makes decisions unnecessarily difficult and protracted. However, the employee representatives stressed the possibility of various formal and informal nets of communication and information as a decisive advantage of the Montan Act vis-à-vis the Works Constitution Act.

Concerning the neutral member in the context of the Montan Act, the commission has the impression that the expectations of the lawmakers have not been fulfilled. This member often lacks the necessary knowledge for a sound judgment in the case of controversial decisions, a fact that can be gathered from the high number of voting abstentions. Nor does the work of the supervisory council seem to be enriched by the legally required cooptation of further members. A serious objection against the institutionalization of parity codetermination is the fact that many decisions can only be reached through logrolling processes.

In its study the commission works on the presumption that the managerial decisions are guided by the principle of profitability. The interviews showed that neither internal nor external employee representatives wanted to give up this maxim. But there is a general feeling that because of codetermination the managerial decision process is to a larger extent oriented toward social goals and aspects. The commission notes, though, that this social correction works asymmetrically in the course of the business cycle, the social component being considerably stronger during contractions.

Within the framework of the Montan Act the employee representatives in the supervisory council can influence the firm's investment policy. But the commission did not find any consequences for the business policy as long as the investment decisions do not endanger jobs inside the firm. Nor did the introduction of codetermination in the montan sector hinder the process of concentration in that sector. Of greater relevance were the problems of safeguarding existing jobs and protecting the codetermination rights that had previously been obtained (see the previous discussion of the codetermination protection acts). In the question of dividend policy, too, the commission did not find any systematic influence of codetermination, though the employee representatives seem to be a bit more willing to push up the degree of self-financing.

The employee representatives unanimously believe that collective bargaining matters do not fall within their purview. Also, the institution of the labor director did not bring about any disadvantage for the employer side in collective bargaining with the unions. Social improvements were in most cases attributed to improvements in the labor market situation and not to codetermination per se.

Some chairmen and other members of supervisory councils expressed the fear that the parity regulation might have negative consequences for the composition of the future management, its members being recruited with heavier emphasis on having good relationships with employees. The open market for managers was also seen as being threatened. Concerning the labor director, the loyalty conflicts did not materialize to as large an extent as expected, even though the unions have a strong influence in the nomination of this position.

Executive board and works council often cooperate in an increasingly institutionalized way, and this is true not only for the montan sector. This is a desirable development in terms of making the decision process more rational and reducing information gaps, but it leads to some loss in the functions of the legal codetermination bodies.

The expectation, commonly held when the Montan Act was introduced, that codetermination would be able to control economic power has not been fulfilled. However, one does not see any clear signs that codetermination undermines the functioning of the capital market.

The briefly described results of this elaborate governmental study do not require much commentary. But they show rather clearly the nature of a codetermined research project. The continual concomitance of inadequate logic, unstated assumptions, and unspecified implications; the lack of a clear theoretical framework; and the shortage of systematic factual evidence lead to the conclusion that the commission report did not fulfill the stated objectives.

On the basis of the collected "experiences," the commission members tried to derive their own codetermination model. But this model, as well as more than 30 other models with a similar methodological foundation,[46] was quickly made obsolete by the enactment of the Codetermination Act of 1976.

Notes

1. *Bundeskanzler Willy* Brandt, *Regierungserklärung* of January 18, 1973.

2. The clue to a possible solution of this apparent paradox could lie in the substitution of the term *citizen* for *man,* whereby the first one is interpreted not as an individual actor but as an appropriately conceived role bearer.

3. For an extension and elaboration, see Gèrard Gäfgen and Hans G. Monissen, "Notes on Sociology's Models of Man: An Outside View," paper presented at the Third Interlaken Seminar in Analysis and Ideology, June 1976. Perhaps I should restrict my statement by arguing that methodological individualism in economics is only the accepted methodological principle. In practice, however, I very often find a rash and inconsistent use of an array of holistic or collectivistic terms such as "the" *state, society, common weal,* and so on.

4. Of February 15, 1922 (*Reichsgesetzblatt* (RGB1), p. 209). A short description of the functions of the supervisory council is given in 1 on p. 24.

5. Of February 4, 1920 (RGB1, p. 147).

6. Robert von Mohl, *"Ober die Nachtheile, welche sowohl den Arbeitern selbst als dem Wohlstande und der Sicherheit der gesamten bürgerlichen Gesellschaft von dem fabrikmassigen Betriebe der Industrie zugehen, und über die Nothwendigkeit der gründlichen Vorbeugungsmittel,"* Archiv der politischen Ökonomie und Polizeiwissenschaft Bd, 2, Heidelberg, 1835.

7. For a detailed discussion of the ideas of the social reformers of the pre-March, see Hans Jürgen Teuteberg, *Geschichte der industriellen Mitbestimmung in Deutschland,* Tübingen: 1961, pp. 1ff.

8. Winkelblech wrote under the pen name of Karl Marlo; see *Untersuchungen über die Organisation der Arbeit oder das System der Weltökonomie,* 2d ed., Tübingen: 1884–86.

9. Stephan Born, *Erinnerungen eines Achtundvierzigers,* 3rd ed., Leipzig:

1898. For a detailed elucidation of the ideas of Winkelblech and Born, see Teuteberg, *Geschichte der industriellen,* pp. 59ff. and the references cited there.

10. Of June 1, 1891 (RGB1, p. 261).

11. Of december 12, 1916 (RGB1, p. 1333).

12. Of August 11, 1919 (RGB1, p. 1383).

13. Fritz Naphtali, *"Die Verwirklichung der Wirtschafts-demokratie,"* *Referat auf dem Hamburger Kongress des Allgemeinen Deutschen Gewerkschaftsbundes,* 1928, *Protokoll,* pp. 172ff.

14. Fritz Naphtali, *Wirtschaftsdemokratie–Ihr Wesen, Weg und Ziel,* Frankfurt: 1966.

15. See Otto Kunze and Alfred Christmann, *Wirtschaftliche Mitbestimmung im Meinungsstreit,* Vol. 1, Colone: 1964, p. 19.

16. A recent extension of this earlier work is offered by Bernhard Muszynski, *Wirtschaftliche Mitbestimmung, Konflikt- und Harmoniekonzeptionen,* Meisenheim: 1975. This independently written book takes an even stronger pro-union and anticapitalistic position, a change somewhat symptomatic for the development of the intellectual climate during recent years in Germany.

17. Franz Böhm, *"Das wirtschaftliche Mitbestimmungsrecht der Arbeiter im Betrieb,"* *Ordo* 4 (1951), pp. 21–250.

18. Eduard Bernstein, *Voraussetzungen des Sozialismus,* Berlin: 1921.

19. *Ökonomisch-politischer Orientierungsrahmen für die Jahre 1975–1985 in der vom Mannheimer Parteitag der SPD am 14. November 1975 beschlossenen Fassung, mit einem Geleitwort von Willy Brandt.*

20. *Grundsatzprogramm der SPD, Bad Godesberg* 1959.

21. See, for example, Eduard Heimann, *Soziale Theorie der Wirtschaftssysteme,* Tübingen: 1963; Carl Landauer, *Theory of National Economic Planning,* 2d ed., Los Angeles: 1947; Karl Schiller, *"Sozialismus und Wettbewerb,"* in Erich Potthoff, Karl Schiller, and Carlo Schmid (Hrsq.), *Der Ökonom und die Gesellschaft,* Stuttgart: 1964; Gerhard Weisser, *"Freiheitlicher Sozialismus,"* in *Handwörterbuch der Sozialwissenschaften* 9, pp. 509–523.

22. See Otto Kunze and Alfred Christmann, *Wirtschaftliche Mitbestimmung,* pp. 249–333 for a more detailed discussion and elaboration.

23. Ralf Dahrendorf, "Toward a Theory of Social Conflict," *Journal of Conflict Resolution,* Vol. 2, 1958, pp. 170–183. Cf. in this context the critique by Gèrard Gäfgen und Hans G. Monissen, op. cit.

24. See Gèrard Gäfgen and Hans G. Monissen, "Notes on Sociology's Models of Man," for a further substantiation of this point.

25. About 47 percent are professed Protestants; about 45 percent are professed Catholics.

26. This social doctrine is specifically Catholic only insofar as it represents a certain religious understanding that is in a special way connected with the Catholic ministry. The essential propositions and instructions could easily be formulated without direct theistic references.

27. See Bernhard Muszynkski, *Wirtschaftliche Mitbestimmung, Konflikt- und Harmonie konzeptionen,* p. 261.

28. The German corporation law (reformed in 1965) does not know the American-type "board of directors" with its mixture of management and non-management members. Instead, there is a separation into a top management body (*Vorstand*) and a controlling body (*Aufsichtsrat*), though certain kinds of decisions can be made conditional on the supervisory council's approval. The members of the executive board are appointed—and removed—and have their salaries determined by the supervisory council. The supervisory council's remuneration is determined by the stockholders' meeting or by the firm's bylaws.

29. Of May 21, 1951 (*Bundesgesetzblatt* (BGB1) I, p. 347; as amended by the acts of August 7, 1956, BGB1. Im, p. 707; of July 15, 1957, BGB1. I, p. 714; and of September 6, 1965, BGB1. I, p. 1185).

30. Individual stockholders who have their stocks and shares on deposit with a bank can and often do transfer their voting rights to the bank. The stockholders' meeting decides upon the discharge from responsibility of the members of the executive board and of the supervisory council. It also decides upon the distribution of profits and upon such matters as alterations of the firm's charter, changes of share capital, etc.

31. The rights and duties of the works council are regulated by the Works Constitution Act. The works council is elected by the employees and has the task of representing—on an honorary basis—the employees' interests in the firm's decision-making process. A variety of decisions in personnel, social, and economic matters require by law the works council's cooperation and consent.

32. Of October 11, 1952 (BGB1. I, p. 681). This law was reformulated in the act of January 15, 1972 (BGB1. I, p. 13), considerably strengthening the position of the employees and the unions in personal affairs but without changing the original provisions for labor management via representation in the supervisory councils.

33. Of August 7, 1956 (BGB1, I, p. 707; as amended by the acts of July 15, 1957, BGB1. I, p. 714; of September 6, 1965, BGB1. I, p. 1185; and of April 27, 1967, BGB1. I, p. 505).

34. If the business combine's sales revenue from montan activities exceeds 50 percent of the total revenue, this act applies.

35. Act to Modify the Act to Supplement the Act on Codetermination of Employees in the Supervisory Councils and Executive Boards of the Business Firms in the Mining and Iron and Steel Producing Industries. This act amends § 16 of the Supplement Act on Codetermination of 1956.

36. Of November 29, 1971 (BGB1. I, p. 1857).

37. Of May 4, 1976 (BGB1. I, p. 1153).

38. *Mitbestimmung im Unternehmen, Bericht der Sachverständigenkommission zur Auswertung der bisherigen Erfahrungen bei der Mitbestimmung (Mitbestimmungskommission), Bundesdrucksache* VI/334, Bonn: 1970.

39. Ibid., Part. II, section b. These "facts of experience" are opinions and

guesses, not systematically performed empirical studies on the basis of a theoretical concept. The main arguments comprising this stock of "experience" were summarized in the second section of this chapter.

40. Theo Pirkner, Siegfried Braun, Burkhard Lutz, and Fro Hammelroth, *Arbeiter, Management, Mitbestimmung*, Stuttgart: 1955.

41. *Institut für Sozialforschung Frankfurt* (ed.), *Betriebsklima, Eine industrie-soziologische Untersuchung aus dem Ruhrgebiet*, Frankfurt: 1955; Heinrich Popitz et al., *Das Gesellschaftsbild des Arbeiters, Soziologische Untersuchungen in der Hüttenindustrie*, Tübingen: 1957; Viggo Graf Blücher, *Integration und Mitbestimmung, Hauptergebnisse, Tabellenauswahl und Modellnachweis einer Untersuchung des Emnid-Instituts für Sozialforschung*, Sennestadt: 1966; and *Umfrag Mitbestimmung des Instituts für Demoskopie*, Allensbach: 1968.

42. Otto Blume, *"Zehn Jahre Mitbestimmung,"* in Erich Potthoff, Otto Blume, and Helmut Duvernell, *Zwischenbilanz der Mitbestimmung*, Tübingen: 1960.

43. Fritz Voigt, *"Die Mitbestimmung der Arbeitnehmer in den Unternehmungen,"* in Walter Weddingen and Fritz Voigt (eds.), *Zur Theorie und Praxis der Mitbestimmung*, Vol. 1, Berlin: 1967.

44. *Mitbestimmung im Unternehmen*, Part III, pp. 29-55.

45. See note 30.

46. See Siegfried Hergt (ed.), 35 *Modelle und Meinungen zu einem gesellschaftlichen Problem*, Opladen: 1974.

5

Labor Participation in the Management of Business Firms in Sweden

Rune Ryden

The Historical Development of Labor Participation (Codetermination) in Sweden

Organizations on the Swedish Labor Market

The Swedish labor market is dominated by a small number of organizations representing the greater number of employers and employees. The terms of employment of the overwhelming majority of employees are governed by national collective agreements concluded between national unions and employers' associations representing particular industries.

The dominant employers' association is SAF (*Svenska arbetsgivareforeningen*, The Swedish Employers' Confederation), with over 25,000 member companies employing some 1,250,000 people. SAF has 38 member federations. State-owned industry has its own organization, SFA (*Statsforetagens fohandlingsorganisation*, the Bargaining Organization of Swedish State-Owned Enterprises), comprising 70 firms with some 50,000 employees. A third organization of employers is that for the cooperative enterprises, KFO (*Kooperationens forhandlingsorganisation*, The Cooperative Labor Negotiation Organization). Today KFO represents 400 enterprises employing a total of about 90,000 people.

The leading organization for manual workers is LO (*Landsorganisationen i Sverige*, the Swedish Confederation of Trade Unions), which has a membership of 1.8 million covering some 90 percent of the organizable blue-collar workers in Sweden. LO has 25 affiliated national unions varying in size from the Swedish Metal Workers' Union, with 412,000 members, to the Swedish Chimney Sweepers' Union, with about 1350 members. Most of the national unions of workers are structured by industry rather than by trade. The most important top organization for white-collar workers is TCO (*Tjanstemannens centralorganisation*, the Swedish Central Organization of Salaried Employees). Affiliated with TCO are 22 unions with a combined membership of 840,000. The third main organization is SACO (*Sveriges akademikers centralorganisation*, the Swedish Confederation of Professional Associations) with upwards of

85

150,000 members, mainly graduates. About 75 percent of organizable white-collar workers in Sweden are union members. In bargaining matters of a general nature, including matters connected with board representation, TCO and some SACO unions cooperate via PTK (*Privattjanstemannakartellen,* the Private Salaried Staff Cartel).

The rise of trade unions can be traced back to the middle of the nineteenth century. At that time, individual local trade unions began to be formed, mostly of craftsmen, their main task being to work for good relations with employers and for the improvement of their members' general and vocational education, their sobriety, etc. Toward the 1880s, when industrialization became increasingly intensive, the trade unions changed character and the organization of the workers was undertaken on a larger scale. Under the influence of the experience of the British trade unions and influenced by the growing Swedish social democracy, the trade unions readjusted their outlook in favor of less liberal, less friendly attitudes toward employers and in favor of unions more dedicated to the notion of struggle. The local character of the trade union was modified with relation to the formation of national unions. In 1898 the unions combined to form a national organization, initially with the limited tasks of providing strike pay to unions involved in disputes affecting unions, to draw up common statistics, and to agitate for the formation of new unions.

Common characteristics in the further development of the Swedish trade union movement were work for the principles of industrial unions rather than for unions of craftsmen, as well as assertion of the sovereignty of the individual trade union.

From 1898 onward we can distinguish three periods in the development of the Swedish trade union movement. The first lasted until the Great Strike in 1909. During this period an attempt was made successively to develop the strength of the trade union movement and the position of the Confederation of Swedish Trade Unions (*Landsorganisationen*–LO) with regard to the trade unions' pay and wage questions. Further, during this period, various unions endeavored to strengthen their position in relation to the local unions. The number of trade union members increased from about 60,000 in 1898 to about 230,000 in 1907. The Great Strike of 1909 and the bad economical situation of the same period showed, however, that the trade union cohesion was very loose. During the four years between 1907 and 1911 the number of trade union members declined to scarcely 50 percent.

The second period of development of the trade union movement lasted from the unsuccessful Great Strike of 1909 until the mid-thirties. This period was characterized by reformation and consolidation, and it became increasingly evident that it was the trade unions and not LO that formed the nucleus of the trade union movement. The total number of members did not attain the 1907 figure until 1917. This rise in the union membership is evidence of its firm cohesiveness. Labor disputes and mass unemployment of the 1920s and 1930s provided, according to Swedish and contemporary international experience, an unusually unfavorable environment for stability and growth of the trade union movement. For about 25 years the actual powers and activities of the central LO were very limited—it is typical that on no occasion between 1909 and 1936 did negotiations take place between LO and the Swedish Employers' Confederation (*Svenska Arbetsgivarforeningen*—SAF).

When LO entered into negotiations with SAF at Saltsjobaden in 1936, the Swedish trades union movement had embarked upon a new phase in its history, with improved contacts between the principal organizations on the labor market —documented, among other things, in a series of *"Saltsjobaden* agreements" and occasional collective bargaining.

For employees other than workers, the efforts of the trade union organizations were more sluggish, among other things, because of the greater difficulties experienced by the administrative personnel of various branches of business and commerce in having their rights to organize themselves and negotiate on salaries and so on acknowledged. However, in shipping and banking, as well as in some branches of education, professional associations were founded as early as the nineteenth century, and in the early 1900s other groups also began to organize. A national organization for salaried employees in industry and commerce was founded in 1931, and a corresponding top organization for the salaried employees in state and local government bodies was established in 1937. In 1944 these two principal organizations were united in the "new" TCO (*Tjanstemannens Centralorganisation,* the Swedish Central Organization of Salaried Employees.

On the side of the employers, the end of the nineteenth century saw the founding of scattered employers' organizations. These combined in 1902 to form the Swedish Employers' Confederation (SAF—*Svenska Arbetsgivareforeningen*). During the first years of the twentieth century the Swedish Mechanical Engineering Association, also founded in 1902 and incorporated in SAF in 1917, was the strongest employers' organization, and it fought, with the aid of numerous lockouts, the most extensive disputes with the trade union movement. In 1903 the Central Employers' Association (*Centrala Arbetsgivareforbundet*—CEA) was established, recruited mainly from small firms in the building industry. In 1919 this association was absorbed by SAF. These and other federations on the part of the employers were originally founded with the idea of defence, and their character of "defensive organizations" is still their most obvious feature.

The development of organizations on the Swedish labor market took place, in contrast to the conditions prevailing in many other countries, without any conflict with regard to obtaining legal status. When comparing the development in other countries we also note that the organizational efforts of the workers and employers were not split by any political or religious motives—the organizations are neutral in matters of religion—and apart from some attempts at the end of the nineteenth century to form liberal workers' associations, the various political parties have not attempted to split the trade unions along political lines in accordance with the pattern prevailing in Southern Europe. Today the labor market organizations are stronger in Sweden than in any other country, and therefore they exert greater influence on their sector of social development than is the case in any other country. Contributory to this development toward strength and influence is not only the fact that the state has permitted the organizations great scope to build up their activities but also that the parties on each side of "the front line" have respected each other and have indirectly stimulated each other's activities. Without LO it is unlikely that there would ever have been SAF; without SAF's occasionally tough policy it is unlikely that LO andits unions, as well as other salaried employees' organizations, would have been able to advance their positions in various sectors, as has in fact been the case.

In Sweden there is a labor market with well-developed, strongly consolidated, and relatively "mature" organizations that respect each other and work with each other in a mainly relaxed and constructive manner.

The Present Constitution and Activities of LO, TCO, and SAF

Common to the structure of the principal organizations on the Swedish labor market is their character of federations of societies. For every national organization the problem has always been, and still is, how much power and how much influence the head organization should have over the activities of its member organizations.

The head organization with the greatest influence on its member organizations, and thereby the greatest concentration of power and centralization, is formally and in reality SAF. This is expressed in the fact that the statutes for the member organizations of SAF are laid down by the board of SAF, that a member organization may not enter into a collective agreement without first gaining the approval of the board of SAF, and that the economic power in the form of funds and so on is centered in SAF instead of its member organizations. In LO and TCO, on the other hand, the case is the reverse, both with regard to finance and other matters. There it is the member organizations that draw up their statutes, reach wage agreements for the employees of their individual trades, and dispose of the greater part of their strike and other funds. In reality LO now has greater influence in wage policy and other matters than TCO has on its members. Among other things, since 1951 LO has been empowered to try to coordinate the wage policies of the various unions, and since the mid-1950s LO has conducted coordinated wage policies, the unions having given LO the right to negotiate on their behalf.

Another difference between the organizations of the wage earners and the employers is that whereas each of the wage earners' unions has a network of local sections (trade unions, professional associations, etc.), the individual employers are members of their organization without local federations as an intermediate link. LO has thus about 7300 local branches, and TCO about 2500. It is in these local branches that the individual wage earner mainly carries on his activities, requests and receives help in negotiation, criticizes the agreements on wages reached and puts forward demands for future agreements, participates in conferences and studies, receives information on wage policy and so on, and possibly also assists in determining the collective backing of his or her branch for a particular political party, etc. The local branches have intensive mutual contact with their respective union or professional association, usually located in Stockholm, and appoint representatives to the committees of their unions, representations, congresses, delegations, etc. The local branch of a union in a particular place is often obliged to collaborate with the local branches of other unions in the same place through union central organizations or TCO committees. These committees are supported by LO and TCO respectively and are in lively and direct contact with their main organizations—in fact they constitute on-the-spot miniature LO's and TCO's. If LO and TCO wish to have contact with their individual members, there are thus two channels, one indirectly through the unions and the other directly through thelocal committees. And if the individual wage earner wishes to contact LO or TCO, the same two channels are available in the opposite direction.

The system with local branches leads inevitably to relatively considerable activity of the members in the wage earners' organizations, a relatively "living democracy." In the LO sector it is estimated that the approximately 7300 local branches have a total of about 50,000 to 60,000 committee members. If we add to these the committee members of shop stewards, sections, study committees, joint councils, women's committees, etc. existing within the framework of at least the larger local branches, the number of LO members on committees amounts to more than 100,000. At least every fifteenth LO member thus plays an active part in the movement.

The objective of the labor market organizations in accordance with their statutes are per se self-evident. For the activities of LO, as well as for those of the majority of the trade unions, it is laid down that the organization shall "safeguard the interests of the employees on the labor market and in business and industry as well with respect to this and in general actively participate in developing the community on the basis of political, social and economic democracy." In the statutes of some LO unions it is also stipulated that "these tasks include working for increased right of codetermination in enterprises and in supporting the demand for the socialization of production."

For TCO and its member associations the political elements in the aims are strikingly absent and the main purpose of the organizations is stated in the statutes as being "the safeguarding of the economic and social interests of the salaried employees." In the statutes of SAF the aim is stated as being, among other things, "to further the common interests of employers" and "to work for good relations between employers and employees."

It should be observed, in this context, that the labor market organizations are, in accordance with their statutes, politically uncommitted, although particularly LO and SAF have on a number of occasions declared party-political viewpoints. Within LO, there is a special circumstance that individual local unions (that is to say neither the regional unions nor LO itself) have often collectively made their members into members of the local Social Democratic party organization. At present, about 500,000 LO members (about one-third of the membership) are connected to the Social Democratic party, corresponding to a little more than half the total membership of the party. It may be added that both LO and the unions made contributions to the party's election funds, that they also give economic support to the so-called labor press, and that the leadership of LO has been represented since the beginning in the Social Democratic Party Council and take part in regular talks with the members of the Social Democratic government. Corresponding cooperation is most frequently the case on the local political level also.

And now for a brief description of the administrative bodies of the labor market organizations. The activities of the local unions are handled by a committee of five to nine members, whose term of office is usually two years and who are appointed by the members at union meetings. Many unions are divided in turn into shop steward organizations active within an enterprise and whose matters are managed by special committees. The unions covering the regional level, like the decision-making and administrative bodies of the salaried employees organizations, consist normally of three bodies. The first is the congress, the highest decision-making body, which meets every third to fifth year. It consists of elected representatives from the local branches in addition to members of the council and board of the trade unions' regional level. The second body is the trade union council, which is responsible for activities between the congresses and which meets two to three times annually. It consists of representatives of various groups of employees and geographical areas covered by the regional union in addition to committee members at regional union level. The third body is the committee of the union at regional level, which is responsible for day-to-day leadership of the regional union and which, in the case of the larger unions, meets once every week. The number of members is usually seven, of whom three or four are functionaries employed on a full-time basis (ombudsmen) in the union of regional level. The council of the regional union conducts the affairs of the regional union office, where functionaries are responsible for publishing the regional union bulletin, reports, and central negotiations, as well as for assisting in local negotiations on wages and other matters of employment; for expressing their views on proposed legislation to the head organization or government authorities on various matters; for contact with the main organization or other unions; etc.

LO and TCO are, in principle, of similar structure. The highest body of each is the congress, which in LO meets every fifth year with about 300 delegates and in TCO every third year with about 200 delegates. Between the congresses the local and regional delegates are the governing body. Normally, they meet twice annually; in LO they have about 140 members, in TCO about 100. The day-to-day business of the head organization is managed in LO by the national secretariat, with 13 members; in TCO by its board, with 10 members. The chairman of the national secretariat is at one and the same time the chairman of LO and acts in addition as "the managing director." The board of TCO is managed by the chairman of TCO, who is now also the manager of the TCO head office. In the LO and TCO head offices a number of ombudsmen and functionaries are employed with salary and organization matters as their principal tasks. In addition, there are experts on economic, statistical, and legal matters, among other things. LO and TCO also run schools, publish newspapers and pamphlets, run lecturing and information activities at local committee meetings, represent their movements on national reporting committees and authorities, and express their views on miscellaneous proposals.

Within the employers' organization, the administrative bodies are to some extent of a similar structure. The pattern is reminiscent of the wage earners' organizations. There is an annual meeting, the executive council meets somewhat more often, and a board with working committees functions as the governing body. The SAF annual meeting has about 330 members, the executive council about 75 members, the board about 25 members, and its working committee 4 members. SAF is managed by a managing director who has authority over a number of sections and departments for negotiations, contact with the community, and reports. Under the auspices of SAF there is the Institute of Foremen, for the training of factory engineers, foremen, etc. SAF also runs courses for managers, issues bulletins, and conducts ergonomical research at the Council for Personnel Administration. SAF is also represented on various government committees and bodies, and like LO and TCO, it is frequently used as a body for expressing specific points of view on given legislative proposals.

The most important task of the labor market organizations has, however, always been and still is wage policy. Here we have the wage earners' wage-dispute associations whose task is to demand and endeavor to bring about increases in wages and other improvements in working conditions, while the employers' associations are "defensive" organizations. Thus so that wage policy may be carried out effectively and powerfully, the organizations have developed special rules for the structuring of wages. As already mentioned, SAF has special rules for its members such that firms or branches of industries and commerce may not reach collective agreements without obtaining the approval of the board of SAF.

Nor may lockout be introduced for a member company or a branch organization without the approval of the board of congress of SAF. However, lockout authorized by these organs is binding on all member enterprises. If a member enterprise breaks SAF's statutes, it may be compelled to pay damages and/or be expelled from SAF. But SAF pays compensation to member enterprises from its funds and assets for economic losses resulting from disputes, provided that measures taken by the enterprise in question were not the cause of the dispute and provided that the enterprise follows SAF's instructions and statutes. Within LO it is laid down that the union committees shall be sovereign with reference to agreement and dispute questions, which among other things means that new votes in such matters among the union members may only be of a consultative nature. Without a statute of this kind, the ability of the union to conduct an effective and (with other unions) co-ordinated wage policy would be considered too restricted. It is further prescribed that before dispute measures are undertaken by a union within LO, when the dispute concerns more than 3 percent of the members of the union, the national secretariat of LO shall approve the measure. If the union goes on strike against the veto of LO, the only consequence will be that LO's economic support for the dispute will be withheld. In addition, the unions are obliged to keep LO informed on agreement negotiations and disputes and to allow LO representatives to take part in negotiations.

Within TCO there is no automatic obligation to provide support in the case of disputes, but the board of TCO is empowered to take part in its member organizations' negotiations in matters of general nature or where principles are involved. The registered capital assets of LO and TCO in 1961 were about 550 million and 170 million Swedish crowns respectively, of which the largest part was disposed of by the individual unions.

The wage agreements, reached peacefully or after disputes between the parties on the Swedish labor market, are regulated for wage earners normally by means of collective agreements. As a rule, these national agreements—that is to say, applicable to all the enterprises of a particular branch of industry or commerce within the country—are valid for one or two years. For a large number of government and local government employees, unilateral wage agreements made up by the employers are in force and the employees have no right to strike. These agreements, however, are now always drawn up following negotiations with the employees' organizations. In the case of TCO associations that have members in the private sector, wages are regulated for some branches— banks, insurance companies, chemists, journalists, merchant navy, etc.—by means of collective agreements, whereas for most of the salaried employees the salaries are not determined collectively but individually on the local level. Snce 1952, however, in the case of industrial salaried employees, wage negotiations have acquired a collective nature, since the central parties have reached agreement about general salary increases, vacation pay, etc.

Under the wage political system worked out by the labor market parties in Sweden also come rules of negotiation of a relatively detailed type. Among tese, the so-called *Saltsjobaden*-agreements between LO and SAF, accepted by a majority of the associations affiliated to the head organizations, occupy a leading place. The first *Saltsjobaden*-agreement—the main agreement—was reached in 1938 to prevent government intervention in the freedom of the labor market. The main agreement contains negotiation procedure for solving disputes during an agreement period in force and provide rules for the dismissal and laying off of workers by employers in the event that employers are compelled for economic reasons to limit the operation of their enterprises. Further, the main agreement contains standards for the settlement of disputes that can affect functions of vital importance to a community. Disputes of the type dealt with in the main agreement shall ultimately be heard or sometimes decided by a labor market committee, with three members from LO and SAF, respectively. A main agreement of a similar nature now applies to a couple of TCO associations. Further agreements between LO and SAF have been subsequently reached for labor safety activities (1942), the training of apprentices (1944), joint councils (1946), the worktime studies (1948). The agreement on joint councils has also been recognized by TCO.

Industrial Democracy in Sweden

It is now more than 50 years since the discussion of industrial democracy began in Sweden. In 1920, the first Social Democratic government appointed a commission on industrial democracy. The parallel was drawn to the contemporary triumph of political democracy that took place in Sweden during the years 1918 till 1921. The ideas of the commission in 1923 were surprisingly up-to-date by our standards. Two principal motives—job satisfaction and productivity—were emphasized. Proposals were put forward for a consultative factory committee for enterprises with at least 25 employees in which management and labor would together discuss company problems. These committees were to comprise elected workers' representatives and management representatives, and the aim would be "to afford the workers a deeper insight into production and a better capacity for active participation in the promotion of the same," and also to bring about "closer cooperation between workers and management." The joint committees thus proposed were to be consultative bodies only.

For various reasons it became apparent that both the employers and the trade union movement adopted a negative attitude toward the proposals of the commission. The employers considered that they went too far. LO took the view that the proposals took no account of the necessary class struggle. Via the labor market disputes of the 1920s and early 1930s, during the remainder of the 1930s a gradual relaxation occurred on the labor market.

The main agreement of 1938 was the first fruit of the Saltsjö spirit of

1936. It was followed by a number of other main agreements regulating various sectors. Some had industrial democratic features in the specific sense that they granted increased rights to the employee organizations within an enterprise. This was the case with the following agreements: the agreement on obligation to give notice and enter into consultation in laying-off and dismissing workers already in the first main agreement 1938, the agreement on local labor safety activities in 1942, the agreement on vocational training in 1944, and the agreement on worktime studies in 1948. The climax of these industrial democratic features was the main agreement on joint councils in 1946, which closely resembles the proposals put forward in 1923. This agreement was reviewed for the first time in 1958, when, among other things, the limit for the compulsory establishment of joint councils was moved from enterprises with 25 employees to those with 50 employees, and it was reviewed for the second time, more extensively, in 1966. The so-called *Saltsjö* spirit and *Saltsjö* methodology gradually went out of fashion during the years after 1966.

Agreement and negotiation methodology was abandoned and largely replaced by legislation. It might be said that if both parties had lived up to the industrial agreement of 1966, many of the questions that had been the subject of government commissions, bills, and parliamentary decisions could have been solved in a smoother manner.

The negotiating competence of the parties on the labor market need not have become such a delicate matter if the joint council agreement of 1966 had provided for the delegation of the right of determination to joint councils. With regard to labor safety, vocational training, worktime studies—which themselves opened the door to technology—and job security, there were also rules on the labor market that could have formed a basis for further development. However, such a development of the joint councils did not appear attractive to the trade union movement at the time of the revision. The very aim—the transition from inside and joint consultation to the right of codetermination—still seemed too remote and doubtful. When, two or three years later, this aim became attractive, a development of joint councils and indeed very soon the path of negotiation itself no longer seemed suitable. There were various reasons for this attitude. Joint councils and negotiation appeared much too slow and uncertain. The new climate evidenced changes and often stricter attitudes in the wage earner organizations, both with regard to discrepancies in the interpretation of the new rules and questions of tactics and methods. This change was met by increased interest in the political parties in involving themselves in industrial democratic questions.

In 1966 LO adopted an attitude toward the industrial question as a result of a 1956 committee that studied "the trade union movement and industrial democracy." Three main points were stressed: job security, participation in enterprise policy, and the question of the encouragement and leading of local activities. The third point applied mainly to the position of the labor market committees and the establishment of a special council for matters affecting joint councils.

With regard to job security, item one, it was determined that the conceptions in the so-called Ahmann laws should be revived. The employers' free right of dismissal should be entirely excluded from agreements in force and be replaced by a protection against dismissal and the right to a place of employment.

With regard to participation in enterprise policy, item two, the commission first dealt with the question of whether the consultative activities of the joint councils should be given up in favor of powers of decision making. A wish was expressed, however, to separate the question of the right of codetermination for employees in enterprise management from the question of the activities of the joint councils. One condition for the right of codetermination was stated to be that the employees' representatives should become members of the boards of the enterprises. Experience gained from union participation in the task of enterprise management was, however, regarded as being much too negative. Double loyalty to the company or enterprise and to the employees could arise.

However, it was claimed that there could be good reason to take part in the work of bodies not directly concerned with enterprise management but in which general policies were formulated and before which enterprise management reported measures taken. But still it was considered that the organizational structure of enterprises did not give scope for such action, over and above that attainable by intensified joint council activities.

The debate on industrial democracy has acquired strength in recent years, and demands for greater democratization of working life have become progressively more insistent. The concept of industrial democracy has come to include the degree of joint influence exerted by employees, the collective decisions taken at various levels of an enterprise, and also the degree of self-determination enjoyed by employees in the course of their daily work.

In the fall of 1969 LO's national secretariat appointed a committee, "the LO committee on increased industrial democracy." The committee's proposals were expressed in the report "Democracy and Enterprises," which was submitted to the LO congress in 1971. The report contains, among other things, the demand for workers' representation on the boards of enterprises as a stage in an extensive program for increased industrial democracy.

In 1969 TCO also appointed a group whose task was to study matters of cooperation at places of employment. The committee submitted an interim report, entitled "The Democratization of Employment," to the TCO congress in 1970. This report also recommended, among other things, experimental activities involving representation on the boards for employees.

Both congresses adopted the proposals-for-action programs that had been drawn up. Both reports contained relatively detailed wishes as to how representation on the boards should be worked out technically. The employees should have the right to appoint a minority of the members of the board. This right should be exercised by the local union organizations. The employees representatives should have the same powers as the other members. After the congress LO requested negotiations with SAF, with the aim of securing by means of agreement the representation of the employees on the boards of joint stock companies. Similarly, negotiations were subsequently commenced between TCO and SAF. These negotiations, however, were discontinued during the winter of 1972 when SAF had declared that it lacked the power to make agreements binding on the individual enterprises.

In a report to the Director General of the Department of Industry, LO and TCO then demanded that the rights of the employees to representation on the boards should be secured by means of legislation. A working group was appointed with representatives of the Departments of Industry, Justice, and Internal Affairs. The group drafted a proposal for a bill on representation for employees on the boards of certain joint stock companies that subsequently formed the basis of the bill presented by the government in 1972. In the departmental memorandum it was pointed out that the debate on industrial democracy had been carried on with increasing intensity and that demands for increased democratization at places of employment were growing stronger and stronger. Views on industrial democracy had also been extended and deepened. More and more attention has been focused on the need to extend the possibilities of influence by the individual on his own duties and the conditions of his own working place. At the same time there remains for wage earners the need to acquire influence on matters of great importance to them as a collective group.

The way to acquire influence on questions of this kind must, it is stated in the memorandum, proceed via representative systems, where representatives of employees obtain the possibility to exercise influence on and participate in the formulation of decisions together with management and specialists of the enterprise.

The two lines of development within industrial democracy—increased individual influence and broadened collective influence—must be regarded as interdependent. In such a context representation on the board for employees appears to be an important element in development toward increased industrial democracy. Representation should thus be regarded as one element and one stage in the development toward increased influence by wage earners. This basis is decisive both for the justification of such reform and the more detailed formulation of representation, states the departmental memorandum.

According to the current Association Law of 1944, the annual general meeting is the decision-making body with regard to the business of an enterprise. The board is the governing body and responsible for administration, but it is obliged to comply with special regulations laid down by the annual general meeting. If the board appoints a managing director, day-to-day administration shall be dealt with by him. The status of the board and its manner of work can in practice vary considerably between different companies, according to the memorandum. In large companies the ownership of shares is often widely spread, and only a minority of the shareholders exercises the right to vote. This may be assumed to strengthen the position of the board. However, this has led to an accentuation of the position of managing director. Thus in many companies today management lies in fact in the hands of the managing director, while the board has a more supervisory, long-term planning function. In small companies the board is assumed to have a very strong position, which is probably due to the fact that board members own either all or a great deal of the share capital in such enterprises.

According to the memorandum, effective management requires that the board have the power and capacity to reach decisions. This implies some basic common interest on the part of board members. The legislator assumes that the owners and the board representatives appointed by them are deeply committed to the survival and development of the enterprise. The memorandum states that the employees, both individually and collectively, share this interest. The employees are dependent on a favorable development in order to earn their living. In general they are relatively closely bound to their place of employment, and change of work and relocation can be both painful and lead to economic loss. If the employees are granted representation on the boards of enterprises, this does not therefore mean a weakening of the basic, common interest of the members, a necessary condition in order for them to act as an effective decision-making body.

According to the departmental memorandum, representation on boards should be regarded principally as a further development of the representative system of safeguarding the wage earners' interests already incorporated in enterprises in the form of joint councils and their subordinate bodies, such as departmental committees, consultation committees, etc., as well as labor safety and proposal committees. Certainly the work of a board can vary widely with respect to both intensity and content. Nevertheless, representation on the board in most cases would be likely to give employees added insight into the problems of central importance both to the enterprise and to the employees, especially with regard to future possibilities and plans for development. This increased insight into the problems of the enterprise, in turn, ought to create conditions that allow the changes that must continually take place in a dynamic enterprise to be implemented in satisfactory ways.

The reform, however, not only grants insight but also implies the possibility of employee influence on company policy. An individual member of a board can take the initiative and request information from management. The insight of the employee representatives in the company from points of view other than those of the other members of a board can raise demands for supplementary reports on the problems of the enterprise. This can raise demands for more detailed information and wider discussions on the board and thereby result in a better basis for decision making. Representation on boards can give employees direct contact with the groups of major owners, and thus the employees can share the owners' views on the future of the enterprise. But representation on boards must also be regarded in some degree as an instrument for making shareholders representatives share the experiences, points of view, problems, and evaluations of employees. As a result of employee representatives entering the decision process at earlier stages, it should be possible in many cases to find solutions that reduce the risks of conflict and friction within enterprises at later stages.

In the long run, employee representation should contribute to the creation of greater understanding between the two principal interests in enterprises with respect to problems that are to a great extent mutual. Increased participation on the part of the employees should have a directly positive effect on productivity. Thus board representation for employees ought to be of value not only to the collective group of employees but also to the enterprise as such and thereby to the owners, states the memorandum.

In the bill submitted to the *Riksdag*, the Director General of the Department of Industry states that no consulting body has taken a negative view of the aim of the reform. During the fall of 1972 the *Riksdag* enacted the bill for employee representation on the boards of joint stock companies and economic associations (1972:829 App I). This was a matter for a three-year experimental period and the law came into force on June 30, 1976.

In April 1974, the National Industrial Board (NIB) was instructed by the Department of Industry to evaluate the current experimental activities and thereby report on the implementation of the reform and the problems that have arisen. The NIB submitted its report "Board Representation for Employees" (SIND 1975:4). The following paragraphs present some of the comments and evaluations of this study.

The study carried out by the survey group to gauge the extent to which employees have exercised their right of board representation covers 2056 enterprises, i.e., all joint stock companies and cooperative associations having at least 100 employees, according to the most recent figures available from the Central Bureau of Statistics (data supplied by the enterprises for 1972).

The exempting clauses in the act refer, among other things, to enterprises with less than three board members. The study revealed that about 5 percent of the 2000 or so enterprises were affected by this provision. Another 5 percent are exempt because trade union membership is below 50 percent (more than half the personnel of an enterprise must be trade union members in order for the act to entitle the employees—or rather, the local trade union—to appoint board representatives). Rather less than 15 percent of the enterprises have undergone such changes since 1972 that they no longer fulfill the basic requirement of at least 100 employees (resulting from closures, mergers, sleeping companies, etc.).

Employees have exercised their right of board representation in 82 percent of the remaining 1556 enterprises—enterprises actually coming under the experimental legislation. The trade union clubs in 3 percent of the enterprises stated at the time of the interview that representatives were going to be appointed, while the employees of 6 percent of the firms are indirectly represented on the boards of parent companies (the board of the individual firm in cases of this kind being for the most part a pure formality). This leaves a "residue" of firms, equaling 9 percent of all those affected by the legislation, in which employees have abstained from the exercise of their right of representation.

An examination of the reasons given by the trade union organizations for the nonexercise of the right of board representation reveals three principal motives. In a relatively large group of enterprises, employees are awaiting the end of the experimental period and/or have not suitable candidates at present. In a second group of enterprises, the trade union clubs saw no point in the reform because, in their opinion, it did not give the employees a strong enough position on the board. A third reason for the nonexercise of the right of representation is that cooperation between employees and management has been organized on other lines and is working well.

When the data are grouped according to size of enterprise, a positive relation emerges between size and the exercise of representation rights: 3 percent of firms with 500 or more employees have no employee representatives on their boards of directors, while the corresponding figure for enterprises employing between 100 and 199 people is 15 percent. The smaller enterprises often lack suitable employee candidates for board appointments, and consequently these enterprises tend more often than the larger ones to postpone the exercise of their right of representation. A sectoral grouping has shown that in most sectors the extent to which the right of representation is exercised is in the region of 80 to 90 percent.

Working Forms of the Company Board

The board representation reform has raised the membership of the average board of directors from 5.8 to 7.7 people. Enterprises quoted on the Stockholm Stock Exchange average 8.7 board members, the corresponding figure for family businesses being 6.7. Big firms tend to have larger boards than small firms, but figures vary a great deal.

The intervals between board meetings also vary a great deal, namely from 1 to 13 meetings a year. The boards of the enterprises quoted on the Stockholm Stock Exchange average 5.1 meetings a year as opposed to 3.8 for family businesses. Subsidiaries of foreign companies have the lowest average, at 3.5 meetings a year. A small number of boards are said to meet only once a year, and 10 percent of the enterprises concerned have two board meetings a year.

Most board meetings last between one and three hours, which means that the boards of many enterprises probably meet for a total of between 5 and 15 hours per annum. But it is also quite common for meetings to last between three hours and a whole day, the latter being the case with many of the enterprises registered on the Stockholm Stock Exchange. Meetings tend to last longer in large firms than in small ones.

In 11 percent of the enterprises, board work involves the use of another language besides Swedish. Usually the second language is English, but it may sometimes be French or German. It is unusual, however, for all working material to be in the foreign language and/or for all board proceedings to be conducted in that language. In the majority of cases, the use of the foreign language is confined to a more limited use of foreign terms and technical expressions, and this is said to present no difficulties to the employee representative.

Of the enterprises concerned, 18 percent have a working committee within the board, and in 70 percent of such cases the working committee does not include an employee representative. Most working committees were set up before the reform came into effect, but the replies to the questionnaires show that about 20 percent of them were set up at the time the act was introduced.

The ability of board members to influence board decisions depends to a very great extent on their access to prior information before the actual board meeting. Employee representatives who have not had any previous experience in board work and who often lack a general economic perspective are likely to have greater difficulty than shareholder nominees in rapidly penetrating complex items on a board's agenda. This, coupled with the fact that the reform is aimed at securing greater influence for employees as a whole not merely for their representatives, points to a need for extensive and well-timed advance information.

The replies to the questionnaires indicate serious deficiencies in this respect. Fist of all it should be recorded that as a rule the employee representatives receive the same prior information as their shareholder-nominated colleagues, but that in many cases this information is distributed very late (often it is not distributed until the actual meeting). Almost half the employee representatives find the decision-making material incomplete. This is bound to inhibit their prospects of penetrating the problems concerned.

The Content of Board Work

It is observed in the terms of reference for the study that "the functioning of board representation, generally speaking, is probably connected with the functioning of the board itself." If board representation is to help improve the insight and influence available to employees, the board meeting must be the occasion on which important decisions concerning company development are actually taken. Only a limited amount of empirical data is available concerning the role of the board of directors in business enterprises, but the predominant view seems to be that the substance of power is vested in management and not in the board of directors.

This assumption is borne out to a certain extent by the material from the survey. Both the questionnaire studies and special studies made of groups of companies and family businesses suggest that in many cases the board of directors is a passive institution, an institution "in the hands of" the managing director and his assistants. For instance, the questionnaire surveys have shown that only about half the employee representatives interviewed believe that "the important decisons in the company are taken by the board of directors." This picture becomes clearer if we group the replies according to the forms of ownership of the different enterprises. It then becomes apparent that the highest proportion of enterprises with active boards of directors is to be found among consumer and producer cooperatives and among enterprises whose shares are traded on the Stock Exchange, while, on the other hand, active boards are fewer particularly among the subsidiaries of foreign-owned companies, subsidiaries of privately owned Swedish companies, and family businesses.

The data contain examples of enterprises that have made alterations to their group structure or product range or have closed down production facilities and the like without any previous discussion of the matter by their boards of directors. During the experimental period, there have also been cases of changes being made in the ownership of enterprises without any prior consultation of the boards of directors. Instead the matter has been dealt with exclusively by the managing directors and their assistants or—in subsidiaries— by the group management together with the heads of the subsidiary enterprises. However, in the overwhelming majority of enterprises where important changes were made during the experimental period, decisions were preceded by discussions in the boards of directors.

Almost one-fifth of the employee representatives replying to the survey group's questionnaire believe that the reform has involved changes in the work of boards of directors. In the majority of cases, the changes are considered to be for the better: "discussions have become more penetrating," "the board seems to be working more seriously and efficiently," "more consideration of personnel questions, otherwise hard to say." Those respondents taking a negative view of the changes that have occurred generally believe that decisions are made informally outside the boardrooms. By way of comparison, it is worth noting that the proportion of board chairmen and managing directors believing that board work has changed is almost as large as the proportion of employee representatives. Here again the majority believes that a change has taken place for the better: "board work has become more orderly," "there are more meetings now," "more active now, previously a formality," etc. Those who take the negative view maintain that meetings have become more formal and last longer.

The employers' questionnaire included a question concerning matters usually discussed at board meetings. Their replies indicate that matters of finance, investment, and production are discussed "often" in more than half the boards of directors, while it is less common for the agenda to include marketing, personnel questions, and questions concerning the working environment. Personnel matters are discussed "seldom" in 21 percent of the boards of directors, and work environment "seldom" in 23 percent.

Data Concerning Employee Representatives

In almost 20 percent of the boards concerned, both the employee representatives appointed are LO members; and in 5 percent of them, both employee representatives are PTK members. In 75 percent of the enterprises, the two employee representatives belong to separate main organizations.

The act says that "an employee representatives should be elected among the employees within the enterprise." This paragraph has given rise to a great deal of discussion, and the employers want the word *should* replaced by *shall*. The material from the survey shows that 98 percent of the employee representatives appointed are employees of the firm where they become board members. Some of the "external" employee representatives are previous employees of the firm, while in other cases they are employed with a subsidiary. In a very few cases the representatives of a central trade union organization serve as employee board representatives. The reason for this in two such cases is that the activities of the enterprise are scattered over a wide area so it would be a full-time job for an "internal" employee representative to go to the rounds of different units. In one other case, the "external" appointment is a temporary arrangement pending the reorganization of the enterprise.

Most of the employee representatives (94 percent) are men, and on average they are considerably younger than the director appointed by the shareholders. Most of them have had previous experience in committee work in their trade union clubs, and many of them have been club chairmen. In addition, several have received a certain amount of training in trade union affairs.

In the majority of enterprises, the employee representatives have the support of some form of liaison or reference group, i.e., a group of three or four people primarily responsible for communications between the employee representative and the groups they represent.

The Activity of Employee Representatives on Company Boards

In the majority of company boards, the employee representatives get in touch with one another before board meetings, but scarcely half of them get in touch with their managing directors or are approached by them. The employee representatives can also get in touch with senior officers within the firm prior to board meetings. Contacts outside the firm are limited, usually being confined to the representative's own central trade union organization.

Most employee representatives report back to their liaison or reference groups after board meetings, but the proportion of representatives stating that they do not consult these bodies is surprisingly large (some 40 percent). Only a very limited number of employee representatives report back to the joint councils in their firms.

A problem is presented by the frequently deficient contacts occurring between employee representatives and other employees. Most employee representatives complain of a lack of interest and inactivity on the part of other employees. Probably one reason for these deficiencies is the difficulty of communicating information to all employees concerning board work and matters discussed at board meetings. This is primarily a task for management, but local trade union organizations also have an important part to play. A particular problem in this connection is posed by regulations, expressed or implied, concerning secrecy.

Current company and cooperative legislation does not make any express provision concerning the duty of board members to observe secrecy, but there is a paragraph saying that a board member (as well as a managing director, an auditor, and others) can become liable for damages to the enterprise if they intentionally or negligently injure that enterprise. The provision is taken to include a duty of silence concerning matters whose disclosure might injure the firm. The trade unions have emphasized the importance of the employee representative being enabled to inform employees of board decisions and the state of the firm, but employee representatives must also be enabled to consult their trade union organizations.

Nearly one-fifth of the firms replying to the employers' questionnaire observe general secrecy concerning all business discussed by the board of directors, both before and after board meetings. Half the firms report that during the experimental period the entire board consented to the observation of secrecy concerning certain issues on their agendas. However, problems connected with secrecy appear to be diminishing, and the material from the survey indicates that employees are tending to take more interest in the reform and in the opportunities of insight and influence that it can imply. This suggests that employee representatives can look forward to a gradual improvement in the backing they receive from their colleagues.

The opportunities available to employee representatives for influencing boards and their decisions are among other things a function of such factors as formal position, knowledge, and information. The material from the survey shows that most representatives have had previous experience in trade union work and that nearly all of them undergo the board training provided by their union organizations. These training activities should result in a gradual improvement of the employee representative's knowledge of financial and economic matters, parallel to their growing experience in board work. This in turn should lead to more active participation by the employee representatives and, presumably, enable them to exert greater influence.

Bearing in mind the short time the experimental activities had been in progress at the time of the survey, it is remarkable that no less than 40 percent of the employee representatives reported that they had "pushed one or more questions particularly hard in the board of directors." In some cases this resulted in decisions in line with the representative's views, while in others it led to the appointment of a committee of investigation. It is uncommon for a board of directors to adopt a decision on matters of this kind running clean contrary to the wishes of the employee representatives. This could imply that even if the activity of employee representatives in board discussions has otherwise been low—"getting the lie of the land"—many employee representatives have tried, with the aid of boards of directors, to find solutions to the problems they have encountered.

Moreover, only 8 percent of the employee representatives have on occasion dissented to board decisions. Most such dissents have concerned decisions on closures, layoffs, and donations to political parties.

Attitudes of Employers and Employees toward the Reform

An overwhelming proportion of the board chairmen and managing directors replying to the questionnaire were favorably disposed toward the reform (or perhaps it would be more accurate to say "not unfavorably disposed"). The problems they report, such as educational problems, will presumably diminish with the passing of time. It is true that one-third of the employers replying to the survey questionnaires did not believe that the reform had enhanced their employees' influence as yet, but more than half of them stated that it had done so "to some extent." Otherwise the majority of employers regard the reform as being "to a great extent" or "to some extent" a suitable means of increasing the influence wielded by employees.

Only 10 percent of the employers replying to the questionnaire report negative consequences of the board representation of their employees. These 10 percent refer to "lack of competence" and maintain, for instance, that ignorance makes the employee representatives uninterested and prevents them from making any significant contributions to board work. For this reason, many of them also feel that board work proceeds more slowly and sometimes takes on the character of "lessons." ("It must be painful for the employee representatives to participate in discussions without understanding what is being said.")

Another relatively common reply is that boards have become "more prudent," that the presence of the employee representatives inhibits discussions. Other respondents maintain that the contribution of employee representatives to board proceedings are biased and that the employee representatives "have difficulty in living up to their electors' expectations." However, this problem of divided loyalty is only mentioned by representatives of five firms. Finally, there are three firms that feel that problems have arisen concerning secrecy.

At the same time, however, employers are somewhat skeptical concerning the contributions made by employee representatives to board work. In fact, 74 percent of them feel that the employee representatives have made little or no contribution to discussions of personnel questions, and still lower levels of activity are reported on the subjects of production, investments, and finance. One-third of the employers feel that employee representatives have "quite often" taken the initiative or contributed when work environment questions have come up for discussion. It is also worth noting that a quarter of the board chairmen or managing directors feel that the contributions made by employee representatives have gradually improved during the experimental period, while hardly any of them feel that it has deteriorated.

The favorable attitudes professed by most employers toward the reform as such are shared by spokesmen for the employees. The data reveal that problems have been encountered in certain areas (lack of prior information, the use of foreign languages in the course of the board work, working committees without employee representatives, etc.), but the reform is interpreted as a step toward greater democratization of working life.

Only 3 percent of the employee representatives state that they have had no opportunity during the experimental period to influence "matters closely concerning the employees and discussed at board meetings" (25 percent feel that their opportunities to influence such matters have been great or very great). The corresponding figure for "matters concerning investment plans or finance" is higher—18 percent (while 15 percent of the respondents feel that they have great or very great opportunities to influence matters of this kind).

In some other cases those reporting that they have had good opportunities to influence matters that closely concern employees have given examples: "On my advice, a personnel manager was appointed to organize a sounder personnel policy"; "When the question arose of changing to a new printing method, we were able to influence the purchase of machinery and the design of the premises"; "At my suggestion, project groups are now working for improvements in these matters"; and so on. Other respondents observe in more general terms that boards are interested in hearing the opinions of the employee representatives.

The most negative representatives maintain that decisions by boards of directors are foregone conclusions and that employee representatives are seldom able to influence the decision-making process. Other negative replies suggest that boards as a whole (and with them the rest of the enterprise) have worked badly, thus precluding any employee influence. The PTK replies make a rather more negative impression on this point than the replies from the LO representatives.

The most common remark made by the PTK representatives concerning their ability to influence investment plans or finance is that they themselves lack the requisite knowledge of general economics and, more particularly, of the economics of their firms. The LO replies do not emphasize this problem to the same extent. Members from both organizations tend in some cases to regard the possession of specialists' knowledge as an advantage where the exertion of influence is concerned.

It is even more common with matters concerning investment plans or finance than with matters closely concerning the employees for boards to make merely formal decisions. In most cases these questions have formerly been settled without the employees being consulted. Another relatively common explanation given for the slight influence exerted by employees is that matters concerning investment plans and/or finance are not raised at all, as a result, for example, of lack of planning.

Both the preceding questions have elicited such remarks as: "Question premature, we are still new in the job." Another interesting viewpoint is: "This question presupposes differences of opinion; there have been none."

Another indicator of the fundamentally positive attitude of the employee representatives can be seen in the fact that 60 percent of them believe their fellow employees to be "pleased" or "very pleased" with the reform. Only 1 percent believe their fellow employees to be dissatisfied.

Group Study and Family Firm Study

The Group Study. Some of the employee representatives interviewed in the group study regard the group board of directors as "purely a matter of form— the group president always gets his own way." One representative remarks, "It is all laid down in advance, so that there is nothing much to be said." However, there are exceptions to this rule, i.e., combines in which the group board of directors is said to play a very active part in the decision-making process.

Most employee representatives on the boards of groups of companies regard the act as "a step in the right direction." In the majority of cases the skeptical view taken by most of the representatives when they were elected has given way to a more favorable attitude. Most representatives agree that the reform has not yet conferred any direct influence, but they regard the group board of directors as a valuable source of information. Board representation has also served to enhance the status of trade union work and made it easier to establish "upward" contacts within organizations.

Most of the group presidents interviewed also profess themselves in favor of the reform, though the majority observes that this evaluation is premature and that the employee representatives have not yet had time to "get the feel of things." Emphasis is placed on the need for competent board members, and many of the respondents feel that the employee representatives do not have much to offer at group level. The majority also underlines that the employee representatives are not to be regarded as representatives of one "side" against the other where board work is concerned. "All board members—employee representatives included—must work for the best interests of the company." Most group presidents advocate employee representation at the local level instead. "They ought to be represented at the organizational level where they will be most useful."

The Family Firm Study. The family firm study is too limited to provide the foundation for any real conclusions, but most of the employee representatives interviewed are relatively indifferent to board representation because of the existence of other forms of industrial democracy (mainly joint councils and informal channels) and also because of the frequently short-term and formal nature of board business.

With one exception, the managing directors interviewed in the study of family firms are favorably disposed toward the employee representation reform. Some of them feel that the employee representatives bring additional knowledge to the board, e.g., concerning "shop floor problems." Others point out that one advantage of the reform is that it gives employees a closer view of activities. One managing director remarks that "it gives us a spokesman among the employees," while another appreciates the fact that "information is now distributed in the right way, so that false rumors can be avoided." The negative views advanced by the managing directors concerning employee representation have usually concerned the part played by the representatives themselves in board proceedings: "They just sit there listening and never say anything themselves"; "They don't understand the terminology—it's all Greek to them. But they are fairly well up to the mark when it comes to reading a balance sheet."

Labor Participation in Sweden Today

In effect since July 1, 1976, the new law covers board representation of employees in joint stock companies or cooperative associations that during the fiscal year now ended in Sweden employed an average of at least 25 wage earners. The preamble to the bill states that the limit of 25 wage earners should not be regarded as final. Whether or not it can be lowered further will be decided on the basis of experience. The government intends to consider the matter once more in three years' time. The local union organizations have the right —though they are not obliged—to bring about representation on boards. The parties within an enterprise are free to solve the problem of the employees' interest with respect to insight and influence in other ways than by means of representation on the board. The law does not apply to individual private firms, trading companies, or limited partnerships. The question of employee representation on the boards of trading companies is currently under review by the Companies' Committee of 1974. Special legislation is applicable to banking institutes and insurance companies. Certain economic societies are exempt. In enterprises affected by the law the employees normally enjoy the right to appoint two members and two deputy members. This right remains unchanged from the previous law. Unlike the provisions of the former law, this rule applies even if the board consists only of two shareholder-nominated members. If the company board consists of only one shareholder-nominated member, the employees are entitled to appoint a wage earner member and a deputy member. Thus the employees in certain cases can have as many members on the board as the shareholders. When there is an equal division, the chairman has a casting vote. It is assumed that the chairman is appointed by the shareholders at the annual general meeting. The right to make decisions with regard to employee representation is exercised by the union organization or organizations committed by the collective agreement involving the enterprise and representing more than half the employees. At least 50 percent of the employees must be union members before the law becomes applicable. The union organizations must reach mutual agreement as to the distribution of membership of the board. If they are unable to do so, the following applies: if more than four-fifths of the wage earners bound by the collective agreement belong to the same head organization, the latter shall appoint both members. If an organization represents more than 5 percent of the organized wage earners, it is entitled to appoint deputy members. In other cases the local wage earner organizations representing the largest number of wage earners each nominate a member and a deputy member. Local organizations belonging to the same head organization count as a single organization. Once the employee representatives have been appointed they may still remain in office, even if the number of employees falls below 25. Employee representatives should be appointed from the employees of the enterprise or in the case of a parent company from among the employees of the concern. In practice, only employees of the individual enterprises have been appointed hitherto. The period of office is determined by those who appoint the employee representatives, but should not exceed four financial years and should terminate at the annual general meeting. After a decision has been reached as to employee representation, the board of the company should be informed in writing. Unlike previous practice, deputy members are granted the right to attend and to speak at meetings of the board, even if members are also present. In such cases, however, deputy members are not entitled to vote. The preamble to the bill also provides that deputy members, like members, should have access to background material and should otherwise also be granted full possibilities of participating in the work of the board. If a board has a special working committee to prepare matters for later decision by the board, an employee representative is entitled to participate in the work of such a committee.

Normally the employee representatives are nominated by the largest head union organization represented in the enterprise. The employee representatives are for almost all practical purposes on a par with the other members of the board. Thus, with respect to company statutes on qualification, employee representatives on the board enjoy the same status as members appointed by the annual general meeting. The bill for employee representation lays down, however, that employee representatives may not participate when certain matters are dealt with by the board or working committees, namely negotiations with employee organizations, the cancellation of collective agreements, and lockouts. The new bill on representation on boards contains no provisions with respect to the form of work to be carried out on the boards. However, a summary regulation of the forms of work is provided by a minor amendment to the Company Act of 1975. This amendment means that the board may not make a decision on a matter unless, whenever possible, all members of the board are able to participate in dealing with the matter and have access to adequate material to reach a decision on the matter. It is stated in the preamble that this amendment means that not only shall the employee representatives have access to the background material within a reasonable time but also that it must be furnished in a manner suitable to the circumstances in question. Thus if written or oral material is presented in a foreign language of which not all the members of a board have a command, these members have a right to be furnished with at least a summary in translated form. The employee representatives' obligation to observe secrecy is not touched upon in the bill. The employee representatives are, however, bound to the same extent as other members of a board to observe secrecy concerning matters which, if made known, could do damage to the company. In the preamble reference is made only to what the Director General of the Department observed on the matter of secrecy in connection with the law of 1972: ". . . the weighing up that must, in my opinion, lead to the question being taken up for discussion by the board in each individual case. In this way it should be possible to evolve a praxis whereby both the interests of the enterprise and those of the employees are provided for." The obligation to observe secrecy is a difficult matter. On the one hand, the employee representatives may feel it necessary to discuss matters with other employee representatives in the enterprise. On the other hand, it is obvious that certain matters cannot, having regard to the interests of the enterprise, be discussed outside the board. Information on what is dealt with by the board must remain within the enterprise. If information is to be spread outside the enterprise, a decision to that effect is required by the entire board of the managing director.

In Sweden the question of employee representation on company boards is regarded as less important. The question of codetermination or industrial democracy is considered more important.

A major labor law reform was adopted by the *Riksdag* at the beginning of June 1976. The new law on codetermination at work replaces, among other things, the laws currently regulating relations between the parties on the labor market—above all the Law on Collective Agreements of 1928 and the Association and Negotiation Law of 1936 (App II).

The most important feature of the new bill is the rules making it possible for employees to gain influence on management matters by means of negotiations and agreements. The rule that has for many years left its mark on relations between the parties on the labor market—that the employer alone is entitled to manage and distribute the work as well as freely to employ and dismiss workers—is replaced by a codification of the desirability of collective agreements being reached as to the right of codetermination for employees. Another important new feature is that the union organizations that sign the collective agreements have the right of interpretation of the new provisions in the case of disputes on obligation of job performance and the application of agreements on the right of codetermination. Further, a reduction of the employers' right of interpretation in wage disputes is effected. In addition, the position of the union organizations is strengthened in matters not regulated in collective agreements by means of rules on increased rights of negotiation and improved information.

The increased right of negotiation consists primarily of rules on the so-called primary negotiation obligation for the employer. According to the bill, the employer must negotiate with the union organizations on his own initiative before making decisions on important changes at the place of work, for example, relocation of production, organizational changes, change of ownership of the enterprise, etc. Also important changes of significance to individual employees, such as relocations, are covered by the primary negotiation obligation. In other matters the employer may be obliged to negotiate if the union organizations request negotiations. The proposed negotiation obligation exists only with respect to the local employee organizations that have signed the agreement concerned. If agreement is not reached on a decision the employer intends to take, the matter can be taken up at the central level with the trade union concerned. According to the bill, it is the duty of the employer to put off making a decision or implementing a proposed measure until negotiations have been concluded. In emergencies and comparable situations, the employer is exempted from his duty to delay procedures, but the obligation to negotiate as such remains.

In the bill the primary right of negotiation is combined with rules on the right to obtain information. It is proposed that the employer should be obliged to inform the local organizations that have signed the collective agreement of the economic and productive development of the company's activities and on guidelines for personnel policy. It is also proposed that the organizations be entitled to access to balance sheets and other documents to the extent necessary to safeguard the common interests of the employees in relation to the employer. According to the bill, the employer is also obliged to a reasonable extent to assist such survey work required for these purposes. Protection for the interests of the employer and private persons is provided by means of rules on the obligation to observe secrecy. The obligation to observe secrecy is determined in the first place by negotiations between the parties at the place of employment.

The principal aim of the bill is, however, to encourage collective agreements on the right of codetermination for employees. According to the bill, the influence of employees shall be brought to bear on all matters affecting relations between employers and employees, i.e., also matters of management, etc. It is also proposed that the employee organizations should be entitled to use active union measures to the extent collective agreements on the right of codetermination are not reached. However, one condition is that the claim for the right of codetermination be made in connection with negotiations for collective agreements on wages.

An important question in the relationship between the parties at the place of employment is whose opinion shall apply when disputes arise on the interpretation of rules determining the internal relationships. This so-called right of interpretation, which is currently considered to lie with the employer by virtue of his right to manage and distribute work, is proposed in the future to be transferred to the trade union responsible for signing the collective agreement. The right of interpretation of the employee party does not apply if it should involve breaking the law or other extraordinary cases. In wage disputes it is proposed that the employer's right of interpretation be limited in such a manner that the employees views of the correct meaning of the wage agreement shall apply if the employer does not immediately take the initiative to start negotiations or bring the matter to court.

Codifications are proposed to give the union organizations responsible for signing the collective agreements a right of veto against contracts that may be assumed to imply disregarding of laws or collective agreements or in any other way conflicting with what is generally accepted in the branch of industry in question.

With regard to the Association Law, i.e., the right to form and belong to organizations on the labor market and play an active part in such organizations, no important changes in the present law are proposed.

In addition, rules are proposed on the obligation of employers and the local trade unions concerned to commence negotiations as soon as an unlawful dispute has broken out and to work together for a settlement. When determining the consequences of participation in unlawful conflicts, special consideration should be paid to the circumstances resulting from the negotiations and their effects. There are no changes in the legislation with respect to political strikes and union measures of sympathy in connection with events abroad.

Finally the bill contains some provisions of a merely technical nature, such as rules for negotiating disputes and law suits. In addition, a summary is given of intermediation activities in labor disputes. Many of the codifications are not compulsory so that the parties on the labor market can adopt the new legislation by means of collective agreements to the special conditions prevailing in different branches of industry. The basic association and negotiation laws, however, are obligatory.

These rules for negotiation must be subjected to practical application before it will be possible to reach any definitive concept of how far the development of industrial democracy in Sweden can proceed.

References

Brantgärder, Elvander, and Viktorin Schmidt. *"Konfliktlösning på arbetsmarknaden.*" Lund: 1974.

Holmberg, P. *"Arbete och löner i Sverige."* Solna: 1963.

Öhman, B. *"Svensk arbetsmarknadspolitik."* Halmstad: 1970.

Samuelsson, K. *"Medbestämmande och medinflytande."* Uddevalla: 1974.

SIND 1975, Stockholm: 1975.

Part II
Economic Analysis of
Codetermination

6 Governments, Voluntary Organizations, and Economic Life: The Preindustrial Development of Western Europe

Douglass C. North

Introduction

Exclusive property rights in factor and product markets have been the exception and not the rule throughout history. The emergence of such markets in the Western world in the past millennium prepared the way for the unique economic expansion of the past two centuries. Moreover, the movements toward better specified and enforced property rights is neither unilinear nor irreversible throughout historical experience. The challenge to economic historians is to provide an explanation for this changing institutional structure (and consequent performance) of economies over time.

In this chapter I attempt to briefly summarize the major forces that shaped the preindustrial development of Western Europe. In the course of the explanation I shall have occasion to explore in more depth the interrelationships between economic and political policies, the various kinds of institutional arrangements that ensued, and the contrasting kinds of property rights that produced stagnation and relative decline on the one hand and induced sustained economic growth on the other. The mix between voluntary organizations, government, and the market changed during the period. Economic historians have traditionally viewed the market as replacing other institutional arrangements (i.e., the "self-sufficient" manor) and government as absorbing some of the functions of both the market and voluntary organizations with the rise of the nation state. No such simple unilateral movement occurs with this analysis. Rather at various moments in time over this eight-century span we find various combinations between voluntary organizations, the market, and government.

At the beginning of our period the self-sufficient manor and the ruling of the local lord predominated and the sector devoted to market activity was small indeed. In the twelfth and thirteenth centuries the market grew at the expense of the manor, and gradually larger political units grew at the expense of the power of the manorial lord. In the next two centuries there was probably some relative decline in market activity and a relative growth of organizational forms that used the market less (such as guilds and a relative expansion of self-sufficient agriculture). Government also grew at the expense of the market. In the final

115

two centuries under review the pattern diverges; in England and the Netherlands there is probably an expansion in both the market and voluntary organizations at the expense of government, while in seventeenth century Spain the reverse is occurring.

The primary change that took place was population growth. This led to:

1. A change in relative factor scarcities and factor prices. The result is to induce the modification of the structure of property rights.
2. An increase in trade as population growth induces extensive expansion and increasing differentiation in the factor endowments (both physical and human) occurring in areas with diffferent degrees of population intensity and resource endowments.
3. Changes both in the gains and costs of forming different institutional arrangements to realize economies of scale in all those activities with some attributes of "public" goods.
4. An alteration in the scale of warfare induced by both the development of an exchange economy as a consequence of the growth of trade and technological changes. The consequence was to radically alter the efficient size for survival of a political unit.

Classical Feudal Organization

The characteristics of tenth-century Western Europe gave rise to the following initial conditions: order generally existed only within settled areas, a condition that severely limited trade and commerce: goods were generally less mobile than labor because they were subject to higher transaction costs; land was abundant but only valuable when combined with labor and the semipublic goods of protection and justice; labor exhibited constant costs when combined with land to produce goods because of the abundance of land; because of the indivisibility of the castle there were economies of scale in protection. However, as the numbers of inhabitants increased and the distance of farmed lands from the castle so increased, eventually protection cost more. In short, protection exhibited a U-shaped cost curve and the "efficient" size of the manor would be limited to the point at which the marginal cost of providing protection equaled the value of the lord's share of the marginal product of labor (i.e., the tax). Later I shall discuss the changing character of warfare, but it is sufficient here to point out that a local castle and knights were the key to protection. However, there was a hierarchy that reached all the way up to the greatest lord—the king.

Feudalism (and in particular *manorialism*) may be best described as a contractual arrangement in which villains and free labor provided labor services for the lord in return for the provision of the semipublic goods of protection and justice. In turn, local lords provided knight service and other payments in kind for superior lords extending up the hierarchy to the king in return for the same public goods. In the context of the initial conditions previously described, these institutional arrangements represented an efficient solution. The extremely high transactions costs of forming organized markets precluded specialization and exchange, and the desired consumption bundle could be achieved at a lower cost by allocating labor services to produce the desired mix of goods and services in kind despite the obviously high shirking costs entailed in such arrangements. (Shirking costs were reduced by the customs of the manor that specified the amount of labor time for various tasks).

In this world, property rights were ill-defined and the protection was usually done by local voluntary associations. Land, while abundant, had location value; accordingly, while the manor had some common property uses of land from its very beginnings, various customs of the manor evolved to limit the number of users of land (as well as the intensity of use). Thus rents did accrue to those who had the rights to use land, but the transferability of these rights was limited. Subinfeudation (the granting of land to a lesser lord in return for knight services and some other payments in kind) was a controversial issue because higher lords frequently found it more costly to exact labor services from a longer chain of the hierarchy. Where trade did exist, its protection was typically in the hands of the traders themselves. Caravans and ships had their own armaments. Perhaps the most striking feature of transactions costs was in the transfer of goods and services. There was frequently no impartial third party to enforce the bargain. The bargains were enforced by interested parties—the manorial court in which the lord of the manor resided was the judge enforcing the customs of the manor—the unwritten law. Yet the lord of the manor was frequently an interested party in dealing with his serfs. It was the opportunity costs of the serf that enforced the contract. Labor was scarce and lords were frequently in competition for serfs (and accordingly unlikely to return a runaway serf). As towns developed, they too frequently provided a haven for the serf. Therefore the lord did have an incentive to abide by the contractual arrangements imbedded in the custom of the manor and to interpret them with "restraint."

While the classic manor was largely self-sufficient, trade did persist throughout the Middle Ages. Witthout any central coercive authority, the protection of property rights was frequently localized; and the division between voluntary groups (providing their own policing) and a sanctioned public coercive authority was difficult to distinguish. The *Cambridge Economic History* provides a graphic description of tenth-century traveling merchants:

In order to protect themselves against high risks, they formed bands and "fraternities" which, in northern Europe, were called merchant guilds. Such a guild existed apparently in the tenth century among the merchants of Tiel, a town near the mouth of the Rhine, at that time presumably a Frisiain settlement. The monk, Alpert, who reports on their activities, considers them as wicked and lawless men, and relates, what is more significant for us, that they pooled their resources, shared their profits and spent part of their gains in licentious feasts. Unfortunately, he does not go into more detail about the operation of this profit-sharing scheme. From the statues of another guild, the frairie or brotherhood of Valenciennes, portions of which probably date back to the tenth century, we also learn that the members did not stay at home but were constantly exposed to perils "on sea, water, and land." They probably traveled together in armed caravans, since an article of the statutes fines the member who appears in the ranks without armour and bow. Once a caravan has left town, the statutes provide, no one is allowed to leave but all are to stay together and to give each other aid and assistance in case of emergency. If anyone dies on a journey, his companions are under obligation to carry the corpse for at least three nights and to bury it, if possible, according to the wishes of the deceased.[1]

Towns developed their own bodies of law and gradually their own commercial courts. While early enforcement may have been by ostracism, they subsequently had the police power of the local political unit. As these merchant codes became elaborated they were recognized over a wider area—the Chart D'Oleron (near La Rochelle, France) containing judgements from the twelfth century was widely recognized in Flanders, Holland, and England.

The property rights surrounding the production of nonagricultural goods was inextricably tied to the guild, which in its early form defies description as either a voluntary association or a part of the state. They did provide an early set of rules for the protection of the property of their members (private policing), but already by the end of the twelfth century they had become a part of the political administration in the Italian cities.

Colonization

The revival of population growth as a result of the relative improvement in order led to local crowding and diminishing returns in local areas. The logical outcome—given the conditions described in the previous section—was colonization, the creation of new manors carved out of the wilderness frequently in order to provide incentive to peasants, conveying more liberal labor obligations and better specified property rights in land than the earlier manor. Settlements filled out Northwest Europe and in consequence encouraged trade (1) by reducing the unsettled areas between manors that harbored brigands, (2) by encouraging the growth of towns in thickly settled areas where specialized skills were developed to produce manufactured goods, and in particular (3) by resulting in areas with very differentiated factor endowments, which increased the gains from trade. The wine of Burgundy, Bordeaux, and the Moselle; the wool of England; the metal products of Germany; wool cloth from Flanders; fish and timber from the Baltic all betoken different factor endowments (both in terms of resources and human capital investment). In short, the frontier settlement movement was a sufficient reason to reduce the transaction costs of trade and increase the gains.

The growth of trade and exchange economy basically altered feudal institutional arrangements, since the existence of an organized market negated the advantages of labor services as compared to a market system of landlord, tenant, and wage labor.

In the twelfth century, general diminishing returns appear to have set in, leading to changing relative factor scarcities. The rising value of land led to increasing efforts to provide for exclusive ownership and transferability. Thirteenth century England witnessed the development of an extensive body of land law, the beginnings of enclosure, and finally the ability to alienate land. Similar developments took place in Burgandy, Champagne, and France.

The twelfth and thirteenth centuries were a period of the flowering of international commerce. There is not sufficient space in this chapter to trace out the institutional arrangements that were innovated in the development of organized product and factor markets to replace local self-sufficiency and barter. The Champagne fairs; the burgeoning Mediterranean trade of Venice, Genoa, and other Italian cities; the urbanization of metal and cloth trades of Flanders were only a few of the major manifestations of commercial expansion of the era. From the viewpoint of this chapter, the most interesting aspect was the shift in the protection of property rights from private policing by voluntary groups to the state. Everywhere kings and princes were guaranteeing safe conduct to traveling merchants, protecting alien merchants (and providing them with exclusive trading privileges), enforcing the enactment of commercial courts, and granting or delegating property rights to the burgeoning towns.

There can be little doubt that there was a substantial productivity increase in the nonagricultural sector as a result of reducing transaction costs, but this was still a tiny fraction of economic activity. Equally, there is no doubt that population growth was resulting in rising prices of agricultural goods and falling real wages. The famines that enveloped much of Western Europe in the early fourteenth century were a harbinger of things to come. The plague followed in 1347 and became endemic to the population, raging again and again so that population probably fell for over a century. Trade and commerce declined in volume. The most striking feature in the nonagricultural sector was the emerging strength of guilds to protect the share of local artisans in declining markets. The strength of the guilds in preserving local monopolies against encroachments from outside competition were frequently reinforced by the coercive power of kings and princes. On a large scale, the Hanseatic League represented such a defensive alliance of cities to protect their shrinking markets from the competition of other rival cities.

In the agricultural sector there was a return to an era of abundant land and scarce labor. Everywhere poorer land went out of production, there was a shift from crops to livestock production and real wages rose (and rents fell). Despite repeated efforts to regulate maximum wages, competition among landlords led to increasingly liberal terms for tenants as well as rising wages gradually; the master-servant aspects of serfdom gave way to recognition of copyhold rights and an end to servile obligations (although it was not till 1666 in England that they were legally swept away). Freemen had already escaped the jurisdiction of the Manorial Court in England in the thirteenth century and had come under the aegis of the King's court. Gradually villains also came under the King's justice and the manorial court slowly lost jurisdiction.

These changes existed throughout Western Europe. There were regional variations in population pressure and incidences of famine and the plague, but to one degree or another all of Western Europe felt the changing relative factor scarcities. However, the response in terms of evolving institutional arrangements and property rights differed throughout Western Europe. In order to understand the diverging pattern of adjustment to these changes we must turn to another consequence of the growth of a money economy—the change in the scale of warfare.

Change in the Scale of Warfare

The lack of order that followed the decline of the Roman Empire resulted in literal chaos. Despite temporary large-scale military-political units, such as the Carolingian Empire, the basic unit of protection was the individual castle protected by the lord's vassals and knights. A distant king and army was little protection against the marauding bands of Vikings, Moslems, and Magyars. Typically lesser lords provided knight service to greater lords, which entailed the military services of a given number of knights for 40 days a year. While it is true that under conditions of invasion or similar major military perils a superior lord could call up knights to protect the "realm," labor services in kind tended to impose severe restrictions on major military operations.

The first change in the feudal system after the growth of a money economy was the payment of scutage—a money payment to the superior lord in lieu of knight service. It enabled the superior lord to pay a standing army and hire mercenaries. It also decreased the de facto power of his vassals, who had always posed the potential threat of becoming militarily more powerful than the king.

Between the thirteenth and fifteenth centuries there was also a series of major technological changes in military warfare, of which the longbow, the pike, gunpowder, and in consequence the cannon and the musket were the most important. Whether the development of an exchange economy was a sufficient condition for expanding the optimum scale of warfare or it was augmented by the aforementioned innovations is not clear. However, the overall consequence was that the conditions for political survival were drastically altered and entailed not only larger numbers for an effective army but also much more training and discipline (particularly important for effective pikemen) and much more costly equipment in the form of cannons and muskets. The age of the armored knight with lance, and the era of chivalry, was passed. Instead it was the age of the Genoese crossbowman, the English (or Welsh) longbowmen, and the Swiss pikemen, all for hire to the highest bidder.

At this point I can usefully pause in my historical narrative to offer an analogy from economic theory. Take the case of a competitive industry with a large number of small firms. Introduce an innovation that leads to economies of scale over a substantial range of output so that the efficient firm size must be larger. The path from the old competitive equilibrium to a new (and probably unstable) oligopoly solution will be as follows. The original small firms must either increase in size, combine, or be forced into bankruptcy. The result is a small number of large firms of optimum size, but even then the results are unstable. There are endless efforts toward collusion and price fixing, but equally ubiquitous is the advantages that will accrue to an individual firm to cheat on these arrangements. The result is periods of truce interrupted by eras of cutthroat competition.

When we translate the preceding description to the political world of this era, we have an exact analogy. Between 1200 and 1500 the many political units of Western Europe went through endless expansions, alliances, and combinations in a world of continual intrigue and warfare. Even as the major nation states emerged, the periods of peace were continually interrupted. In short it was an era of expanding war, diplomacy, and intrigue. The magnitude of the increasing costs was staggering. A year of warfare represented at least a fourfold increase in costs of government—and most years were characterized by war not peace. Monarchs were continuously beset by immense indebtedness and forced to desperate expedients, the spectre of bankruptcy was a reoccurring threat and for many states a reality. The fact of the matter was that princes were not free— they were slaves to an unending runaway fiscal crisis.

As late as 1157 the Count of Flanders received a significant share of his revenues in kind, and such revenues show up in French crown receipts well into the thirteenth century. Indeed in the feudal world it was customary for the king's court to move from one part of the country to another to consume the goods (and services) in kind that had comprised his revenues. With the growth of a money economy, there was a change over time to money payments and the incidents of Feudalism were increasingly monetized. However, the feudal incidents were continually declining, as the basic structure of feudal society was being altered.

In the face of declining revenues and growing financial needs, the princes of Europe faced an ever-growing dilemma. Custom and tradition set limits to the exactions they could obtain from lesser lords; and as the Magna Carta amply attests, a king who stepped over the boundary of accepted custom faced the ever-present possibility of revolt. Many of the king's vassals were almost as powerful as he (in fact the dukes of Burgundy were much more powerful than the kings of France), and certainly in concert they were more powerful. There was frequently more than one active contender for the throne; but even in the absence of an active contender powerful vassals posed a continuous imminent threat to the king either from within or from without through collaboration with outside invastion threats (as the Burgundians did with England against the French).[2] There was the possibility of borrowing the money—and indeed as a long succession of first Italian and then German bankers can attest, this was a major source of meeting the short-term crisis of a war. However, a prince could not be sued, and accordingly the lender exacted a high interest rate (usually disguised to avoid usury laws) for the high risk or collateral (early it was crown lands, then crown jewels, or farming the customs or monopoly concessions). Still default was common. Edward III ruined the Peruzzi and Bardi, and at a later date Charles V and Phillip II ruined the Genoese and Fuggers. The capital market was not only one of the most thriving activities of this period but a major force in the development of the major capital centers of Florence, Antwerp, and Amsterdam.

Yet loans, if they were to be repaid, required fiscal revenues. Loans could tide a king through a war, but then he faced the awesome task of repayment. If loaning to princes was a major influence in the development of capital markets, the development of a regular source of revenue to repay the loans was the guiding influence in the relationships between the state and the private sector.

The degrees of freedom of a prince varied widely. He could confiscate wealth, but if dissipated, it was by necessity a once and for all source of revenue. He could exact a forced loan when he could convince his subjects that they were threatened by attack or invasion. He could trade the granting of privileges for revenue. These privileges essentially consisted of the granting of property rights or a guarantee of the protection of property rights for revenue. Clearly there were economies of scale in state take-over from voluntary associations of the protection of property rights. As trade and commerce grew beyond the boundaries of the manor and the town, the farmers, merchants, and shippers found that the private costs of protection could be reduced by a larger coercive authority. The basis for a mutually advantageous exchange existed, but no two monarchs were confronted with identical economies. Since individuals in the private sector always had the "free rider" incentive to evade a tax, the monarch must of necessity discover an income stream that was measurable and easy to collect. In contrast to present-day tax structures, there was no institutional structure available to undertake such activities; and as a result, in most cases, the information costs were so high that they precluded modern alternatives. Two polar extremes illustrate the dilemma and possibilities open to a prince. First, where foreign trade was a significant part of the economy, the costs of measurement and collection were typically low—even lower in the case of water-borne trade, since the number of ports were limited. Second, where trade was primarily local within a town or small geographical area or primarily internal to the economy, the cost of measurement and collection were typically much higher.

In the space of this chapter I can do no more than list some of the multi-tudinous (and ingenuous) ways by which princes traded property rights for revenue. The right to alienate land was granted in England by the Statute of Quia Emptores in 1290 (1327 for Nobles) because the king would otherwise lose revenue by subinfeudation; still later the Statute of Wills (1540) was en-acted to permit inheritance because he was losing revenue through the exten-sive devise of "uses." Similar developments in France, Champagne, and Anjou occurred not only to prevent loss of revenue but to tax land transfers in the thirteenth century. Towns were granted trading and monopoly privileges in return for revenue; alien merchants were granted legal rights and exemption from guild restrictions in return for revenue; guilds were granted exclusive monopoly privileges in return for payment to the crown; customs duties were established on exports and imports in return for monopoly privileges; and in some cases the crown was forced to grant "representative" bodies control over tax rates in return for the revenue.

This last point requires special emphasis and further elaboration since it is the key to the differential patterns of development that we observe. What did the prince have to give up in order to get the essential tax revenues for survival, i.e., what determined his bargaining strength vis-à-vis his "constituents"? The preceding argument suggests three basic considerations (1) the incremental gains to constituents of the state taking over protection of property rights from the voluntary associations; (2) the closeness of competitors to providing the same service; (3) and the structure of the economy that determined the benefits and costs of alternative forms of taxation.

The Late Medieval World

While the late medieval world may not be strictly characterized as a stationary state, it was a society in which the revival of population growth resulted in Mal-thusian cycles of extensive expansion (900–1300), followed by famine, pesti-lence, and economic contraction (1300 or perhaps 1350–1475), and then a second cycle of expansion and contraction. But by the end of the second con-traction in the seventeenth century it was clear that England and the Nether-lands had escaped the Malthusian cycle and output was growing faster than population; France, while perhaps not stagnating, was clearly falling relatively behind England; and Spain, once the most powerful nation in Europe, was in a state of absolute decline.

The effects of the differential fiscal policies upon the growth of these four countries was not only in terms of the "deadweight" effect of the taxes but specifically upon the private rate of return in engaging in productive pur-suits. Obviously these are overlapping categories but nevertheless worth separat-ing in terms of their effects. In the case of the first two countries, property rights had evolved that directed by incentive economic effort toward productivity-raising types of activity. These property rights had raised the private rate of return toward the social rate, thereby providing incentives to use factors of production more efficiently and to direct resources into inventive and innovating activity. In the case of the last two, the absolute level of taxation and the specific forms of taxation resulted in these incentives being partly or completely lacking. In the space of this chapter I can only suggest the promise of the explanation advanced in previous sections to account for the difference.

The story in England begins with the development of land law. However, it is in the famous struggle over taxation of the wool trade by the three Edwards that we see the evolving structure of the English fiscal system and property rights coming most clearly into focus. As an early export trade, wool ideally fitted the requirements as a source of tax revenue. Thus the tripartite struggle between the wool exporters, Parliament, and the Crown over the taxation of wool was a major turning point in English parliamentary history. The development of Parliament as a body convened in order to obtain tax revenues is clear, but the powers that Parliament obtained in return are central to our history. Eileen Powers documents the story in a classic account of the wool trade.[3] The wool exporters; Parliament, representing, as its most powerful interest, the wool growers; and the Crown gradually evolved an arrangement in wich the wool exporters as the merchants of the Staple got a monopoly of the export trade and a foreign depot in Calais; Parliament gradually got the power to set the tax; and the Crown got the revenue. The monopoly served the king well, the duty providing collateral for land. The series of steps in the evolution of the structure of the wool trade and its implications for property rights are detailed in Eileen Powers' study, and throughout the study the Crown's guiding interest was fiscal necessity. In her final chapter on the emergency of a middle class, Powers ties the growth of a broadly based group of merchants to the outcome of this struggle. The most noteworthy contrast between English fiscal policy (and that of the Netherlands as well) as compared to France was that the export trade faced competition from other sources of supply and limited the degrees of freedom of the Crown (of the duke of Burgundy in the case of the Netherlands). Too heavy taxation could kill the trade and the revenue.

The development of the English customs on exports and imports and the farming of the customs are a frequently told story. But the main thread of the story surely must follow the outlines developed in Stubbs' *Constitutional History of England*[4] on the growth of parliamentary powers. The development of Parliament was bound up with the development of royal finance. Taxation was a major reason for calling Parliament into session, and over time Parliament, representing the major economic interests, traded revenues for increasing control over the property rights evolving in English common law. While the issues did not finally get settled until 1689, the major steps along the way, including Gresham's policies, the controversy between Coke and James I, the Statute of Monopolies which attempted to prevent Crown monopolies and created a patent law, the development of the joint stock companies, and Charles I desperate expedients to raise money in the face of a hostile Parliament, all are well known history.

In terms of the three criteria that determine the structure of property rights, the English case was one in which the bargaining strength of the voluntary groups was always great relative to the Crown. The net gains from royal protection (as compared to protection by the voluntary association) were quite limited. The degrees of freedom of the Crown were circumscribed by the persistent power of the lords and gradually other groups (i.e., there was always potentially close substitution for the services provided by the Crown). The structure of the economy, which made for a very "visible" export and import trade, had at least two important consequences. The costs of measurement and collection were relatively low and did not lead to a vast bureaucracy directly dependent on the Crown, and the tax yield on exports was (as in the case of the Low Countries) directly dependent on the health of a trade that faced international competition.

The critical period in French fiscal policy is also during the One Hundred Years War. Earlier French fiscal history had also involved representative bodies —*Estates-General* in various parts of France voting special levies to the Crown in cases of emergency. Unlike England, there was no great export trade to serve as a ready source of taxation (Gascony and the Bordeaux wine trade were in the hands of the English) so taxes had to be direct and at the local level (reflecting the pattern of trade and commerce of the private sector). Moreover, the monarch was beset by powerful and quarreling vassals, by English invasion, and by the widespread plundering of both the quarreling lords and English troops by bands of roving unemployed (or unpaid) mercenaries. The complete lack of protection of property rights in this chaotic era led to the *Estates-General* granting special levies (the taille) and other taxes to the Crown. Charles VII gradually consolidated his position vis-à-vis competition, but the English occupation and plundering mercenaries provided leverage for him not only to exact further special levies but to make them de facto—a permanent feature of French fiscal policy without the consent of the *Estates-General.* After the meeting of the *Estates-General* in 1439, Charles VII not only assumed power to make the taille regular but also to change the rate at will. In fact the levy increased fourfold between the middle and end of the fifteenth century—yet the important feature of this account is not the deadweight effect of the taille (from which nobles and clergy were exempt) but the consequences for Charles VII, his less than loving son, Louis XI, and subsequent monarchs. They had a degree of monopoly power for themselves and their wholly dependent bureaucracy that made the dispensing of property rights the whim of the monarch and of his subordinates who farmed tax revenues that were for sale by the Crown. The long-run consequence was to bolster those economic activities which could immediately produce revenue for the Crown at the local level.

With the decline of economic activity in the fourteenth and fifteenth centuries, the guild became a growing power in the towns to protect the shrinking markets from outside competition, and the Crown found in the guilds an already developed infrastructure for fiscal revenue. The Crown strengthened the guilds by guaranteeing a local monopoly in return for revenue and as a result prevented mobility of capital and labor between towns and equally prevented innovation by minute regulations of every detail of the production process. With Colbert the fiscal system was sytematically organized. In addition, Colbert's policy of subsidizng inefficient industry and trading companies, the selling of offices to court favorites, and forced loans were all contributors to the Crown's arbitrary doling out of specific property rights in return for revenue.

In contrast, therefore, to the English case, the gains to voluntary groups of protection of property rights were so great that they gave up control over taxation; the Crown steadily increased its degree of monopoly power and ensured against the hostility of potential competitors by exempting the nobles and clergy from major taxation; and finally, the structure of the economy led to high initial measurement and collection costs that required a large bureaucracy whose loyalty and largesse depended on the Crown. Moreover, once the bureaucracy existed, the marginal costs of raising the rate were very small.

Spain is in sharp contrast to the other two countries. While land was still abundant, the wool industry developed and sheepherding between the highlands in summer and the lowlands in winter became the pattern. Local sheepherders guilds called *mestas* were consolidated into a single guild by Alfonso X in 1273 called the Honorable Assembly of the Mesta of the Shepherds of Castile.

. . . The motive was merely one of the king's financial embarrassments; he realized that it was much easier to assess taxes on livestock than on men, and formed the mestas into an organization that would provide considerable sums to the monarchy. In exchange for these taxes the herders wrested a series of privileges from Alfonso X, the most important of which was the extension of supervision over all migratory flocks, including stray animals, in the whole kingdom of Castile. This supervisory function was gradually extended, in time, even to "permanent" sheep pastured in local mestas and to the "riberiegas", animals which were pastured along the river banks within the district of a particular town. . . .[5]

In return for being the principal source of the Crown's revenue to finance the war with the Moors, the privileges of the *Mesta* to move back and forth across Spain expanded and for centuries thwarted the development of effective property rights in land.

The Council of the Mesta by the sixteenth century had become a privileged institution, with protected routes across the kingdom, with its own itinerant legal staff and armed guards accompanying the annual flocks, with authority to override conflicting interests, to prevent the enclosure of fields in their path, empowered to engage in collective bargaining with the most powerful land-owners, exempt from the payment of the *alcabala* and from municipal sales taxes. It had judicial powers and economic perogatives which placed it outside the reach of other institutions.[6]

It was under Ferdinand and Isabella that a nation-state emerged from the centuries old strife with the Moors and the ceaseless internal warfare of feudal lords. Over the years 1470 to 1540 tax revenues grew 22 fold; and as in the case of France, the representative body, the *Castille Cortes,* lost control over the revenues, as a populace weary of endless plunder and internal strife turned the power over to the Crown in return for internal order. As in the case of France, the centralization of the granting of property rights in the hands of the Crown made property rights the object of royal whim and immediate necessity.

The *Mesta* was the major explanation for the failure to develop property rights in land right through the seventeenth century. But other arbitrary fiscal policies of the Crown also contributed to Spain's decline. It is ironic that the inflow of revenue from the Netherlands that gave the Spanish Crown vastly increased income for a time was ultimately responsible for forcing the Crown to desperate expedients. The growing revenues made possible the Empire of Charles V, but when the net revenues began to fall off, with revolt in the low countries, the military commitments continued. The result was a series of ex-pedient policies that determined property rights in other factor and product markets. The granting by the Hapsburgs of monopoly privileges to town guilds in return for revenue led to a failure to permit factor mobility, to widen mar-kets, and to provide incentives for innovation in industry. Consequently, industry and commerce stagnated. The successive confiscations of property and bank-ruptcies of the Crown (in 1557, 1575, 1596, 1607, 1627, 1647) as a result of the bankruptcy of its creditors drove merchants and entrepreneurs out of productive activity. In fact, the widely held explanation for Spain's decline on the grounds of the aversion of the hidalgo for trade and commerce and his pref-erence for church, army, and court activities is perfectly consistent with the explanation of this chapter. The structure of property rights that evolved in response to fiscal policies drove individuals out of economically productive pursuits into those which were sheltered and protected and clearly offered a higher rate of return than economic pursuits.

The similarity between France and Spain with respect to the first two cri-teria that determined property rights is striking. In both cases the gains to voluntary groups from government protection of property rights were so great that the "representative" bodies were willing to give up control over taxing power; in both the monarchy gradually acquired a substantial degree of monop-oly power. It was the difference in the structure of the economy that produced widely divergent results. The *Mesta* and then the revenue from the Netherlands both provided a ready and growing source of income to the Crown. The consequences of the former on the efficient utilization of land have been made clear; the consequences of the latter were to permit Charles V to have the greatest army and to dominate Europe as no other monarch had succeeded in doing since Roman times. But the Empire he had created required the maintenance and expansion of fiscal revenues, and here the contrast with France is critical. Spain was basically dependent on revenue from abroad, whether from the Netherlands, the Kingdom of Naples, or the New World. As these sources disappeared or declined (as in the case of New World treasure), the costs of army and empire were still growing. The result was a resort to such desperate measures as confiscation, default, and short-run considerations that granted monopoly privileges. The consequence was a structure of property rights that produced economic stagnation.

Postscript

By 1700 England and the Netherlands had evolved a structure of property rights that produced sustained economic development. An integral part of this institutional change was the development of a body of impersonal law in which private property rights were imbedded. They provided for the right to own, derive income from, and alienate land; they gradually evolved a similar body of law dealing with the rights of joint stock companies. The master-servant doctrine of early modern times, as embodied in Elizabethan England's Statute of Apprentices (1524), gradually evolved into a contractual relation between employer and employee.

But there is a long gap between the end of this chapter and the modern problems of labor participation in management that are the subject of this book. It was not part of my assigned task to fill this gap, nor indeed do I know anybody of literature in economic history that would fill this gap. There is very little serious historical study of the evolution of property rights, and here I wish only to suggest some major threads that would have to be followed.

There seems to me to be two such threads—one tracing the reduction in restrictions to ownership rights that occurred between the Statute of Monopolies (designed to curb Crown monopolies) in 1624 and general incorporation laws in the nineteenth century. Thereafter the direction of change is reversed as we move into the twentieth century, with increasing attenuation of ownership rights.

The other thread would trace the evolution of labor's status from the master-servant doctrine spelled out in the Statute of Apprentices through nineteenth-century law, which declared that trade unions per se were not illegal (*Commonwealth v. Hunt,* 1842 in the U.S.), to the Clayton Act, which exempted trade unions from the Sherman Antitrust Act in the United States.

I expect that one would want to distinguish the threads between Europe and America. In the former, labor participated through the political process, sometimes actually forming political parties. In the latter, labor has practiced the policy of "rewarding their friends and punishing their enemies" but has shown little interest in direct political parties. A partial explanation may be that in the United States, as a consequence of its exemption from the Sherman Antitrust Act and the National Labor Relations Act (1935), trade unions' bargaining positions with management have been superior to their European counterparts, and the latter in consequence have opted to pursue political policies to achieve similar results. Whatever the explanation for this divergent development, it does seem to be a part of the reason that labor in Europe has, by political fiat, achieved ownership rights that have not so far occurred in America and at least at this point—does not appear to me to be an imminent development. If it occurs in the United States, it appears more likely that it will occur within the existing property rights structure in the ownership claims of union pension funds. In that case, the implications with respect to decision making and resource allocation may be quite different from those in Europe.

Notes

1. *Cambridge Economic History,* Volume III (London: Cambridge Univ. Press, 1965), p. 47.

2. It is beyond the scope of this chapter to give adequate treatment to the role of the church. However, the church may best be regarded as a competitor in providing the same range of services as other "states." There was not only a Papal State, but the church was also an actual competitor in the intrigues, alliances, and warfare of this entire period. It may be argued that the church not only sold protection and justice but salvations as well.

3. Eileen Powers, *The Wool Trade* (London: Oxford Univ. Press, 1941).

4. 3 volumes (London: Oxford Univ. Press, 1876).

5. Vincent Vives, *An Economic History of Spain* (Princeton, N.J.: Princeton Univ. Press, 1969), p. 25.

6. Maurice Schwarzman, "Background Factors in Spanish Economic Decline," *Explorations in Entrepreneurial History* (April 1951): 237.

7

The Economic Consequences of Codetermination on the Rate and Sources of Private Investment

Eirik G. Furubotn

Introduction: The Significance of Codetermination for the Operation of a Capitalist Economy

In recent years various European countries have initiated legislation providing for worker participation in the management of private business enterprises. Thus in the period 1973-1974 the Netherlands, Norway, Sweden, Austria, Denmark, and Luxembourg joined Germany and France as states actively promoting "industrial democracy" through the use of codetermination schemes. Since Great Britain is now considering comparable legal changes and preliminary debate on the issue is taking place in the United States, there can be little doubt that the topic of labor participation is important. What is more uncertain, however, is the significance these new programs will have for capitalism and the future development of Western economies.

The granting of effective decision-making power to the firm's employees implies some attenuation of private property rights in capital and, indeed, can be expected to touch off a general reorganization of the structure of property rights. In particular, it appears that company law will require progressive modification if the conflicting interests of the different parties involved in production are to be resolved satisfactorily. European experience to date does not give any clear indication of how far this restructuring process will proceed; but there is at least some suggestion that major change in society is desired so that, as it is sometimes expressed, "the arbitrary pursuit of private interest" will no longer be dominant. Of course, insofar as different content is given to private ownership rights, the pattern of incentives in the system will change and economic behavior will be conditioned accordingly. One crucial question that arises in connection with labor participation, then, is whether the incentives generated by the new institution are likely to be efficient. In other words, we should like to know whether the incentives created are consistent with a Pareto optimal allocation of resources and equilibrium growth or whether they are counterproductive and lead to economic stagnation. Given the interventionist political climate, and initial failure of codetermination could be disastrous, since it would probably mean that further regulation and control of the system would be undertaken by the state. Then a cumulative movement away from traditional organization might well be started, and capitalist economies could be transformed into something quite different from the relatively free systems currently known in Western Europe and the United States.

Codetermination represents more than a mild experiment in labor relations. By giving sanction to fundamental changes in private property rights, the policy must inevitably have the potential for altering the normal operation of a market economy. Implicitly, at least, the exclusive right of the entrepreneur to claim and dispose of profits is called into question. This must be so because the firm's workers have the legally acknowledged power, under codetermination, to participate in decisions on the nature and conditions of production as well as to bargain for remuneration. The breach of convention carries profound consequences for the conduct of the firm. Even in the traditional capitalist economy, the role of profits in directing resources is frequently misunderstood; but the institutional arrangements of codetermination tend to reinforce the view that profits emerge from the exploitation of labor and are the legitimate object of redistribution. In short, there are good reasons to believe that participatory legislation will encourage labor to behave in ways that conduce to the misallocation of resources and to the reduction of the volume of voluntary private investment.

It might be objected at this point that whatever the theoretical grounds for concern with codetermination programs, the empirical record does not bear out the view that their existence causes capitalism to face imminent ruin. Although relatively brief, European experience seems to indicate that the effects of codetermination are quite modest and that, in general, labor participation in corporate decision making has not forced governing boards to adopt policies different from those which they would have chosen in the absence of worker representation on the board. As a practical matter, labor influence has not been much greater than it would be in a purely consultative situation where management's goal is merely to secure information and opinion from employees on topics of mutual interest.

There are, of course, various explanations for the meager results achieved so far by the new institutions designed to promote "industrial democracy." Thus it is asserted that when labor representatives have nothing more than a minority position on the firm's governing board, as may legally be the case, they can always be outvoted by the capital owners. Given such circumstances, workers can never win on crucial issues and labor's input may well be largely ignored. Parity representation might help to redress the voting imbalance but, as has also been pointed out, further problems tend to arise because the worker-directors are often ill equipped by education and experience to serve effectively on the board. And even if they should be capable decision makers, the labor representatives often do not have strong links to and support from the total constituency whose interests they are supposed to promote. At any given period, the employees of the firm are likely to hold somewhat divergent opinions about the nature of optimal policy, and there is, presumably, an ongoing political process within the firm that can affect the attitudes of the worker representatives. Thus the latter must have other considerations in mind than the pure interests of the laboring class.

Moreover, the relation of the firm's worker representatives to external labor unions, and the role such unions play in the firm's decision making activities, can vary considerably. In theory, a labor-participation scheme represents a potential substitute for the union because either institution can serve as the means for advancing the interests of the firm's employees. It follows, therefore, that unions may be ambivalent about supporting codetermination; unless they are assured of controlling the worker representatives, unions may wish to oppose the new arrangement or see that it functions inefficiently. Certainly, if unions show little real enthusiasm for codetermination and workers become apathetic about the plan, it may well become inconsequential. Business opposition to reduced decision-making power can always be expected, and this force must be countered strongly by labor to make participation effective. That is, unless labor is able and willing to bring pressure to bear on the firm's owners and managers, the latter will probably attempt to evade the full impact of codetermination by reducing the possibilities for meaningful discussion at board meetings. Various devices can be employed to subvert the intended objectives of participation; for example, special committees that exclude worker representatives can be formed to carry out the serious business of the board, detailed agendas of the topics to be considered need not be made available to workers in advance of meetings, limitations can be placed on the dissemination of sensitive or confidential data relating to the operation of the firm, etc. In these and other ways, then, capital owners are able to place obstacles in the way of true codeterminationist solutions; whether such obstacles can be maintained as permanent impediments, however, would seem to depend on what happens in the world outside the firm.

It is not difficult to account for the limited effectiveness of codetermination as the policy has been developed in Europe over the past decade or so. But the present lack of success in reducing private property rights in capital does not imply that the participatory approach is fundamentally incapable of effecting profound changes in traditional capitalist organization or of altering dramatically the way in which a market system functions. The important element in the program is public acceptance of the idea that it is legitimate and proper for the state to limit the decision-making power of those who supply capital funds to the firm and assume the risks of production. Once this principle is established, the extent of reorganization depends largely on the political process and on the determination of those who are the prospective gainers to bring about effective implementation of the new scheme. In other words, codetermination can become a real force in the economy provided an appropriate legal and institutional structure is created—a structure that will support the extended claims of labor and, at the practical level, confer greater bargaining power on the firm's employees. That a critical role is played by the politicoeconomic background conditions of the system is, no doubt, obvious; but, in any event, if labor participation does not have a potential for radically changing ownership rights and behavior, the whole issue of codetermination would possess little interest.

To assert that serious long-term consequences are likely to emerge from the implementation of codetermination is not to suggest that all, or even most, supporters of the program are intent upon destroying the capitalist system. Indeed, the question of why demands have been made for labor to participate in the management of private business firms is very complicated and one to which no simple answer can be given. There has, of course, been a long-standing tendency to view the modern corporation as a type of political entity and to insist upon democratic participation of all stockholders in the governance process. If this "political" conception of the firm is held, it is an easy step to the further belief that workers as well as stockholders should take part in decision making. On this interpretation, both workers and stockholders are affected by the policies of the firm, and both must have effective political means for registering their preferences so that minority stockholders or managers do not impose arbitrary policies on a disenfranchised majority. Of special interest here is the implied partiality to the use of the *political* mechanism over the market mechanism.

A general predisposition to political solutions may be one force impelling a move to codetermination, but additional support for "industrial democracy" comes from the writings of the growing school of neo-Marxist economists whose members are found both in Europe and the United States. Although the critique of capitalism is general, the capitalist organization of production is the target of special denunciation. As this line of argument goes, the very structure of the industrial system forces workers to lead fragmented, unfulfilling lives. Inevitably, labor or work activities will be uninteresting drudgery that must be undertaken to secure income. Moreover, the nature of capitalism ensures that the quality of the work process will always be sacrificed in the interest of capitalist dominance and greater profits. Workers are, therefore, *alienated;* and indeed, the problem of alienation is inescapable because workers do not own or control the means of production, do not participate in the choice of production technology, do not determine what commodities are to be produced, etc. Workers must be frustrated in any attempts to achieve a more humane and meaningful work environment. The capitalist system, in short, has no way of responding to labor's desire for creative, self-developmental work activities, and workers can find no interest in their jobs as such.

According to the neo-Marxists, what is required to eliminate or reduce the problem of alienation is nothing less than the restructuring of institutions. In particular, things have to be arranged so that workers are able to control production and determine both the technological and social organization of the work process. There is fairly general agreement that the ideal productive organization would be something akin to the *socialist labor-managed firm*. That is, to ensure a democratic atmosphere and a fulfilling work environment, the new structure should be based on social ownership and permit workers to have virtually unlimited powers in management and decision making. Also implicit is the understanding that labor will be guaranteed a definite share of the firm's profits. Obviously, codetermination schemes do not go quite this far since private ownership rights in capital are recognized as legitimate. It is true, nevertheless, that codetermination represents the type of industrial reorganization that is generally consistent with the objectives of neo-Marxist reform.

The implicit link of codetermination to the alienation critique is especially significant because insofar as the Marxist ideas about alienation are accepted, they provide intellectual justification for very sweeping reduction in the powers traditionally left in the hands of the capital owners. Labor unions, of course, have always had some interest in the working conditions maintained by the employers of union members, but the chief concerns of unions have been the wage contract and immediate fringe benefits. Given the basic philosophy of labor-participation schemes, however, priorities are quite different. Thus, under a true codetermination program, the emphasis is shifted from wages to the total reward (pecuniary and nonpecuniary) going to the worker. In the limit, anything in the firm that affects the welfare of labor is a legitimate subject for worker control. Effectively, the firm's working environment becomes a "variable" that must be adjusted appropriately for labor. But since the internal productive organization of the firm depends on many factors, the consequences of labor's intervention in decision making are profound. Owners lose unequivocal authority to determine such matters as the type and quality of output, the scheduling of production, the supervisory structure within the firm, etc. This means that the general efficiency of production may decline and, thus, that consumers and the public at large, as well as the firm's owners, may suffer a significant reduction in welfare. The labor-participation argument tends to play up the gains the approach implies for labor while ignoring the probable losses generated for the economy as a whole. As with many policy questions in economics, however, there is danger that the full implications of labor participation will not be understood by all those who will be affected by it and who will, ultimately, be required to bear the costs of the program.

A Model of the Capitalist Firm under Codetermination

From the preceding discussion of labor participation, it is apparent that under the proposed reorganization, decision-making power in the enterprise will no longer reside exclusively with those who supply equity capital (or with those who are the agents of the capital suppliers). This attenuation of private property rights can be expected to have an important influence on the firm's actions in both the short run and long run. Thus the objective of the present section is to develop a simple theoretical model of the capitalist enterprise subject to co-determination, and to deduce from the model the behavior that such a firm is likely to display over time. Underlying the analytic construction will be three fundamental assumptions concerning the economic environment in which the firm operates.

1. The legal and institutional structure characterizing the politicoeconomic system gives the employees of the firm substantial, if not overwhelming, bargaining power on the firm's governing board. While the workers cannot always expect to have their views prevail, they are in a position to demand reasonable compromise solutions from the firm's owners.

2. Individual workers will show significant differences in objectives, planning horizons, and reward preferences, but all workers are concerned with the working environment maintained within the firm. In short, the alienation argument is accepted in the limited sense that the welfare level of the worker is taken to depend in a systematic way on the character of the firm's production environment.

3. Labor unions play no role in the process by which labor representatives are elected to the firm's governing board, and unions exert no influence on the decisions made by the members of the board.

In addition, the following assumptions will be made relative to the organization of the firm itself:

4. The governing authority of the firm is single-tiered and consists of a board of directors representing shareholders, managers, and workers.

5. The worker-directors who sit on the governing board are elected directly by the employees of the firm on the basis of a majority voting procedure.

6. The workers, as distinct from the shareholders and management, have parity representation and control 50 percent of the seats on the board.

7. Workers hold no stock in the company and are free to leave the firm at any time they wish.

The institutional arrangements outlined are by no means the only ones conceivable for a participatory economy, but they are sufficiently representative to provide some basic insight into how codetermination is likely to function. Of course, to predict how the actions of the participatory firm will differ from those of the standard capitalist firm, it is necessary to possess relatively detailed knowledge of the decision-making system under codetermination and to determine the way in which this system affects economic incentives. Consequently, as the analysis proceeds, the crucial questions to keep in mind are: Who are the individuals actually making decisions for the firm? What are the objectives (and planning horizons) of the decision makers? How do the latter acquire information on which to act? How are the activities of the decision makers monitored by other interested parties? What is the penalty-reward structure (or opportunity set) facing the decision makers? By having the answers to these questions, it becomes possible to understand the effective rewards associated with different behaviors and, hence, to understand the probable policy line the firm will take with respect to such matters as employment, wages, output, investment, etc.

To begin systematic analysis of the effects of codetermination, it will be useful to set up a simple formal model of the participatory firm. Thus, assume that the following economic situation holds. Substantial investment opportunities exist in a particular industry[1] and a private entrepreneur is considering the establishment of a new productive organization. Competition rules in the economy so that the prospective firm's actions will have no influence on the product price in any period (p_t) or on the price of capital equipment (Z_t) or the interest rate (i_t). Since the entrepreneur's planning horizon is assumed to be fixed at T, the firm is concerned not only with existing prices but also with the prices that are expected to exist in each time period to T. Definite expectations are held relative to future market developments, and the entrepreneur is able to make single-valued estimates of the respective price parameters for each period over the planning interval.

The firm's effective production function at any period t is given by the stock-flow relation:

$$q_t = {}_t f(L_t, K_0, E_t) \qquad t = 1, 2, \ldots, T \qquad (7.1)$$

Only one type of capital good is considered in the model and the input in question is assumed to have a durability of T periods. At the end of the Tth period, the equipment is completely worn out but progressive physical depreciation does not affect its productive powers during the effective lifespan over periods 1, 2, $\ldots$, T. For simplicity, the analysis involving the stock-flow function (7.1) will confine attention to the case in which investment is of the point-input-multipoint-output type. That is, units of the capital good are put in place (and paid for) at the end of period 0, and thereafter, no further investment is made.[2] Problems of capital replacement are not considered; the planning horizon is coextensive with the lifespan of the capital good.

Under normal circumstances, quantities of the variable input (i.e., flows of labor service L_t) are employed each period to work with the capital stock; and output emerges at the end of each period to form the stream $q_1, q_2, \ldots, q_T$. Planned commodity output can, of course, show substantial variation from period to period if the firm has to adjust L_t to meet changing wage (w_t) or price (p_t) conditions. Another reason for output variation, however, can arise because of deliberate alterations in the internal productive organization of the firm over time (E_t). Specifically, the bargaining powers conveyed to workers through codetermination may be used to force the owners to change the working environment of the firm in ways that are regarded as desirable by the workers. If, as the arguments for industrial democracy suggest, labor alienation is a major problem under traditional capitalism, workers will, presumably, take the opportunity afforded by the new system to improve the firm's environment and reduce alienation. In the model, workers are assumed to be concerned with both pecuniary returns (w_t) and nonpecuniary rewards (via E_t).

The magnitude of the environmental variable in any period (E_t) is supposed to indicate the general character of the firm's technological and social organization at that time. It is somewhat artificial, but convenient, to think of each E_t as being continuously variable. Then, at every cross-section of time, a full range of organizational forms exists, and it can be assumed that as E_t grows larger the work environment becomes less alienating. Many things influence a firm's working atmosphere or environment, but *ceteris paribus* worker satisfaction will tend to vary with such factors as the strictness of labor discipline, the pace of work, the nature of production scheduling, the way in which responsibility for productive tasks is assigned, etc.[3] It is not difficult to believe that the "quality" of the work process is important to workers and contributes to their nonpecuniary incomes from the firm. Unfortunately, however, it is also likely to be true that as the work environment becomes less strongly hierarchical and controlled, and as the technological organization is decided by considerations other than narrow concern for output, the productive efficiency of the firm will drop. From a formal standpoint, the marginal products of labor and capital can be assumed to fall as the level of E_t is increased. Variation in E_t generates effects analogous to those which arise from neutral technological change; more concretely, the model treats an increase in the magnitude of E_t as tantamount to neutral technological retrogression.

With the interpretation of the production function established, the next step is to consider how the entrepreneur determines the level of investment in plant and equipment (K_0) when he knows that he must operate subject to codetermination. To limit the complications of the model still further, we assume that the entrepreneur expects the market rate of interest (i_0) and the price of capital input (Z_0) that hold at the end of period 0 to remain unchanged over the T periods to the planning horizon. Then the objective of the firm can be conceived as one of maximizing the yield (or the present value of the cash flow) of investment made in capital goods subject to certain constraints that appear because of the institutional arrangements under codetermination.

Given the various price estimates (P_t, i_0, Z_0) the net present value (Π) of capital goods installed at the end of period 0, and utilized over periods 1, 2, ..., T, can be obtained from the expression:

$$\Pi = \sum_{t=1}^{T} \left\{ [p_t \cdot {}_tf(L_t, K_0, E_t) - w_tL_t] \cdot \frac{1}{(1+i_0)^t} \right\}$$

$$- Z_0K_0 \qquad t = 1, 2, \ldots, T \qquad (7.2)$$

The variables in (7.2) are: (1) the successive employment levels (L_t) for periods $1, 2, \ldots, T$; (2) the corresponding wage rates (w_t); (3) the initial capital stock (K_0); and (4) the environmental levels (E_t). This interpretation of the problem is somewhat unorthodox, for in the standard model of the competitive firm the wage rates pertaining to the different periods are taken as externally established market parameters which the firm must simply accept.[4] Similarly, the environmental level (or technical organization) of the firm tends to be viewed as given.[5] Under codetermination, however, wage rates and environmental levels are likely to be the subjects of negotiation. That is, because of their representation on the governing board, the firm's workers can be expected to press for some local control over these key variables (w_t, E_t). And, depending on their bargaining skill and economic power, the workers may be able to secure particularly favorable wage streams and working conditions from the firm's owners.

Since the firm being considered in the present model is merely contemplating entry into the industry, it does not have an existing labor force and there are no worker representatives to deal with in the board room. Nevertheless, in planning its operations, the firm must take account of the *probable reactions* of those employees who will ultimately be hired if active production is undertaken. Prediction of employee desires over an extended planning interval poses obvious difficulties, but estimates of some sort have to be made. What the firm's owners must do specifically is establish the maximum reward levels that workers can be expected to demand over the planning interval $1, 2, \ldots, T$. Since labor is concerned with both the pecuniary (w_t) and nonpecuniary (E_t) returns the firm provides, projections of the reward maxima can take the following form:

$$U_t^0 - {}_t\phi(w_t, E_t) = 0 \qquad t = 1, 2, \ldots, T \qquad (7.3)$$

From the standpoint of the owners, there is a separate criterion function, or community welfare function $({}_t\phi)$, defining worker policy preferences at each period $1, 2, \ldots, T$. Workers are assumed to reach a definite level of satisfaction (U_t) for any stipulated values of the wage rate and the environmental index. The variables w_t and E_t represent "goods" and, in each time period, tradeoffs between the two "goods" are possible that leave workers at the same level of satisfaction. Indifference curves are assumed to have conventional shapes; more generally, each function ${}_t\phi$ in (7.3) is taken as globally strictly quasiconcave and is presumed to yield ordinal rankings that are meaningful (and consistent) for the particular group of workers considered.[6]

If it is true that workers are interested in the *total satisfaction* employment yields, rather than the wage rate alone, bargaining discussions between the firm's owners and employee representatives on the board will focus on the *welfare level* (U_t) the firm's policies promise. Effectively, labor remuneration in any period will be measured in terms of the index U_t; and, in making investment plans, the owners can guard against overoptimism by estimating the maximum welfare levels U_1^0, U_2^0, . . . , U_T^0 that will be demanded from the firm. Of course, the lower the levels of these maximum demands (U_t^0, $t = 1, 2$, . . . , T), the brighter will be the prospects for capital investment. Each separate equality in (7.3) can be interpreted as a constraint that affects the maximization of net present value (7.2); at worst, however, the values of w_t and E_t need be no larger than those consistent with the attainment of U_t^0. Moreover, in each period, the owners will attempt to generate the required level of welfare (U_t^0) at the lowest possible cost by substituting appropriately between pecuniary (w_t) and nonpecuniary (E_t) benefits in the reward vector.

Whatever labor's preferences may be with respect to the firm's production environment, it remains true that existing technology imposes an effective lower limit (E^*) that the value the environmental index E_t can assume. Thus, in any period, $E_t \geq E^*$ and the following constraints hold for the maximization problem:

$$E_t - E^* \geq 0 \qquad t = 1, 2, \ldots, T \qquad (7.4)$$

These relations have direct significance for the interpretation of the stock-flow production function (7.1) introduced earlier. Maximum output of marketable product (q_t) is obtainable only when the firm's productive organization is characterized by the particular set of technological and social conditions represented by E^*. To the extent that E_t becomes larger than E^*, the working atmosphere improves and worker alienation may diminish, but the physical productivity of inputs declines.[7]

Once the sets of constraints in (7.3) and (7.4) have been established, the way is open to determine whether or not investment in the industry is justified. In formal terms, the problem is to maximize the net present value function (7.2) subject to (7.3) and (7.4).[8] Then, following a standard decision rule,[9] positive investment is indicated if the calculated net present value or yield of the capital project (Π) is greater than or equal to zero. Of course, in addition to deciding investment feasibility, the optimization procedure also yields information on the ideal level of capital stock (K_0).

Given the situation of a firm as described above, two different types of solutions are distinguishable for the system (7.2) through (7.4). In what would seem to be the most likely case, worker preferences, as revealed in (7.3), can be expected to emphasize improvement of the productive environment so that the equilibrium value of E_t will always be greater than E^*; in short, the constraints of (7.4) will not be binding in any period.[10] Under these circumstances, "corner" solutions are avoided, and the relevant Lagrangian expression reduces to:

$$V = \sum_{t=1}^{T} \left\{ [p_t \cdot {}_t f(L_t, K_0, E_t) - w_t L_t] \cdot \Psi_t \right\}$$

$$- Z_0 K_0 + \sum_{t=1}^{T} \lambda_t \left[U_t^0 - {}_t \phi(w_t, E_t) \right] \qquad (7.5)$$

where $\Psi_t = 1/(1 + i_0)^t$. The unknowns in (7.5), whose values are to be determined, are K_0, L_t, w_t, E_t plus the Lagrangian multipliers λ_t ($t = 1, 2, \ldots, T$). By differentiating (7.5) partially with respect to each of these variables, the necessary conditions for the maximum[11] emerge as:

$$\frac{\partial V}{\partial K_0} = \sum_{t=1}^{T} \left(p_t \frac{\partial q_t}{\partial K_0} \Psi_t \right) - Z_0 = 0 \qquad (7.6)$$

$$\frac{\partial V}{\partial L_t} = (p_t \frac{\partial q_t}{\partial L_t} - w_t) \Psi_t = 0 \qquad t = 1, 2, \ldots, T \qquad (7.7)$$

$$\frac{\partial V}{\partial w_t} = -L_t \Psi_t - \lambda_t \frac{\partial U_t}{\partial w_t} = 0 \qquad t = 1, 2, \ldots, T \qquad (7.8)$$

$$\frac{\partial V}{\partial E_t} = p_t \frac{\partial q_t}{\partial E_t} \Psi_t - \lambda_t \frac{\partial U_t}{\partial E_t} = 0 \qquad t = 1, 2, \ldots, T \qquad (7.9)$$

$$\frac{\partial V}{\partial \lambda_t} = U_t^0 - {}_t \phi(w_t, E_t) = 0 \qquad t = 1, 2, \ldots, T \qquad (7.10)$$

The economic interpretations to be given to these first-order conditions become obvious when they are rewritten as:

$$\sum_{t=1}^{T} \left[p_t \frac{\partial {}_t f(L_t, K_0, E_t)}{\partial K_0} \Psi_t \right] = Z_0 \qquad (7.11)$$

$$P_t \frac{\partial_t f(L_t, K_0, E_t)}{\partial L_t} \Psi_t = w_t \Psi_t \qquad t = 1, 2, \ldots, T \qquad (7.12)$$

$$-\frac{\partial w_t}{\partial U_t} L_t \Psi_t = \lambda_t \qquad t = 1, 2, \ldots, T \qquad (7.13)$$

$$p_t \frac{\partial_t f(L_t, K_0, E_t)}{\partial E_t} \cdot \frac{\partial E_t}{\partial U_t} \Psi_t = \lambda_t \qquad t = 1, 2, \ldots, T \qquad (7.14)$$

$$U^0 = {}_t\phi(w_t, E_t) \qquad t = 1, 2, \ldots, T \qquad (7.15)$$

Conditions, (7.11) and (7.12) are quite standard and merely require the "efficient" allocation of resources. Thus, (7.11) states that if the firm is to use capital advantageously in the particular institutional conditions given, the sum of the input's discounted marginal value products over periods 1, 2, . . . , T must equal the initial supply price of capital. Similarly, (7.12) indicates that the discounted value of the marginal product of labor, applied during any period t, must be equated to the discounted wage labor receives at t. Conditions (7.13) and (7.14) show that the Lagrangian multiplier for each period (λ_t) is negative; in other words, an incremental *relaxation* of any reward constraint in (7.15) causes the firm's costs of operation to become greater and leads to an incremental reduction in net present value.[12] The equalities (7.13) and (7.14) also imply that the firm should minimize the cost of providing workers with any given level of welfare (U^0) by manipulating the composition of the reward vector (w_t, E_t). At equilibrium, the cost of generating a marginal increment of worker satisfaction should be the same whether the means used is an increase in the wage rate or an improvement in the productive environment.

This last requirement can be seen from a different perspective if (7.13) and (7.14) are equated and cast in the form:

$$-\frac{\partial w_t}{\partial U_t} \frac{\partial U_t}{\partial E_t} L_t \Psi_t = p_t \frac{\partial q_t}{\partial E_t} \Psi_t \qquad t = 1, 2, \ldots, T \qquad (7.16)$$

By assumption, $\partial q_t / \partial E_t < 0$, and thus the indication given by (7.16) is that at equilibrium the decrement in the discounted wage bill is just equal to the decrement in the discounted value product so that no further change in environment is justified. As the magnitude of E_t is increased, alienating features of the productive organization are reduced and the wage rate (w_t) that will be accepted by the firm's workers will fall. The precise relation between the two variables is, of course, determined by the shape of the indifference curve: $U^0 = {}_t\phi(w_t, E_t)$; and the marginal rate of substitution $dw_t / dE_t = -\partial w_t / \partial U_t \cdot \partial U_t / \partial E_t$ is relevant. Since any reduction in the wage rate applies to all units of labor employed by the firm, it follows that, *ceteris paribus,* the total wage bill must be lowered as E_t is increased. Such lowering of the wage bill is advantageous, but there is, unfortunately, a productivity effect to be considered too. Technical efficiency declines in step with the increase of E_t; thus, with a fixed commodity price p_t, the total revenue of the firm falls, *ceteris paribus*.

Clearly, it is in the interest of the firm to increase E_t as long as the diminution of the wage bill exceeds the diminution of total revenue. The movement toward an improved work environment (higher E_t values) will always come to an end, however, if the relevant total revenue curve falls more rapidly than the corresponding curve representing the total wage bill. This type of outcome is to be expected. The slope of function $_tf$ will tend to become steeper as E_t is made larger and the slope of function $_t\phi$ will tend to become less steep because, from an economic standpoint, there can be little doubt that continuing efforts to modify the work environment will exert an increasingly adverse effect on physical productivity and cause output to fall more and more rapidly; while, as far as worker preferences are concerned, improvements in the environment will be valued less and less highly relative to money wages as substitution proceeds. The implication of this state of affairs is that an alienating work environment will not be banished entirely; rather, conditions will be improved consistent with technology and the willingness of the workers to forgo money income in favor of other nonpecuniary rewards.

Having established the economic interpretations of the necessary conditions for the maximum of V (or II), the next objective is to find the equilibrium values of the variables in the model. In principle, this can be done by solving equations (7.11) through (7.15) simultaneously. Since there are $4T + 1$ variables $(K_0, L_t, w_t, E_t, \lambda_t)$ and $4T + 1$ equations present, the problem is straightforward. By assumption, the system is mathematically well behaved, and it follows that a unique solution for the various unknowns can be expected. In other words, we are able to determine simultaneously the optimal amount of physical capital for the firm $(\hat{K}_0)$, the optimal level of employment in each period during the lifetime of the capital equipment $(\hat{L}_t)$, the ideal magnitude for the wage rate in each of these T periods $(\hat{w}_t)$, and the optimal environmental level in each period $(\hat{E}_t)$. In addition, values are found for the respective Lagrangian multipliers $(\lambda_t^0, t = 1, 2, \ldots, T)$. The solution secured here indicates, of course, that the values of the $4T + 1$ variables are functions of the parameters entering into equations (7.11) through (7.15); thus, the specific magnitudes of $\hat{K}_0, \hat{L}_t, \hat{w}_t, \hat{E}_t$ $(t = 1, 2, \ldots, T)$ depend on the known values or estimates made for p_t, i_0, Z_0, etc. and on the technical characteristics of the functions $_t\phi$ and $_tf$.

The information obtained concerning the optimal input magnitudes and environmental levels permits discovery of the ideal output quantities over periods $1, 2, \ldots, T$. Technically, all that need be done to determine the output program $\hat{q}_t$ is the insert $\hat{L}_t, \hat{K}_t$, and $\hat{E}_t$ $(t = 1, 2, \ldots, T)$ into the general production relation (7.1). Along the same lines, the optimal magnitudes yielded by the solution of (7.11) through (7.15) can be used in equation (7.2) to establish the crucially important measure—net present value (Π). This calculation is central because, from the standpoint of the entrepreneur considering investment in the industry, net present value has to be nonnegative. That is, if $\Pi = 0$, the proposed investment $Z_0\hat{K}_0$ is just acceptable; it is expected to earn an average rate of return over the interval $1, 2, \ldots, T$ that is precisely equal to the market rate of interest i_0. Under these circumstances, the entrepreneur is indifferent as to whether he invests the sum $\hat{Z}_0\hat{K}_0$ in the particular type of capital equipment represented by $\hat{K}_0$ or makes a routine financial investment that has the same period (and risk level) and offers the market rate of interest i_0.

So far, discussion of the optimization model (7.2) through (7.4) has presupposed that the constraints in (7.4) have not been binding. In other words, it has been assumed that worker preferences in each period are so oriented that $\hat{E}_t$ is always greater than E^*. Figure 7-1 illustrates this case. The equilibrium position in period τ is represented by point A where the indifference curve

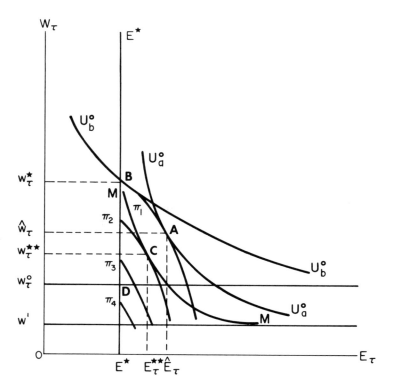

Figure 7-1. The Optimization Model

$U_a^0 U_a^0$ is just tangent to the isoyield curve $\Pi_1 \Pi_1$. As shown, the solution values $\hat{w}_T$ and E_T permit the workers to achieve the level of welfare they demand (U_a^0), but these values also allow the firm to realize a net present value of Π_1 when optimal adjustment of all remaining variables in the system (over all periods) has been accomplished.

Cases analogous to the one just considered, where equilibrium is reached at one *interior point* like A, are important and are likely to be encountered very frequently. Nevertheless, it must be recognized that the preference relation (7.3) can reflect relatively lesser worker interest in a firm's environment than is implied by indifference curve $U_a^0 U_a^0$. In short, a differently shaped curve such as $U_b^0 U_b^0$ can appear as the effective reward constraint in any period. With this preference orientation, of course, the nature of the solution changes. Specifically, if $U_b^0 U_b^0$ holds, no point of tangency is reached with an isoyield curve;[13] the equilibrium conditions (7.13) and (7.14) will not be met as equalities in period τ and a type of *corner solution* will emerge. In the diagram, point B indicates the operating position of the firm. The environmental level is E^* and the wage rate is w_T^*.

From a formal standpoint, both types of constraints, (7.3) and (7.4), are binding in the time period considered here (τ). The situation is such that $U_\tau^0 = {}_\tau\phi(w_T, E_T)$, $E_T = E^*$ and the two curves must intersect at some point. Since the environmental level is specified as E^*, the corresponding wage rate (w_T^*) is determined automatically by the preference constraint (7.3). Thus, for the period in question, w_T^* and E^* can be regarded as data and introduced directly into the net present value equation (7.2). Similar procedure can be followed for corner solutions occurring in other periods than τ. Then, after all independently determined wage rates and environmental levels have been inserted into (7.2) as parameters, the maximization problem reverts to the type examined earlier. That is, (7.2) has to be maximized subject to the remaining constraints of (7.3).

As Figure 7-1 is constructed, the corner solution at B is consistent with a net present value of Π_1—on the assumption that all the variables in the system subject to control have been adjusted optimally. However, if the isoyield curves in the diagram are so ordered that $\Pi_3 > 0$, $\Pi_2 = 0$, and $\Pi_1 < 0$, it is obvious that investment is not feasible in the case shown. The magnitude of net present value or yield depends on various factors, but one critical determinant of Π is the reward policy enforced by the firm's worker-directors. Thus, if the demands made in this area were reduced, capital formation would be encouraged correspondingly. In the diagram, movement from $U_a^0 U_a^0$ or $U_b^0 U_b^0$ to MM would raise the attainable net present value to Π_2 and permit investment to take place. The conditions under which workers will be disposed to compromise on rewards, and the extent of such compromise, are important issues that will be taken up later.

Alternative Institutional Arrangements and the Firm's Level of Investment

Implicit in the discussion of the preceding section is the assumption that the worker-directors elected by the employees of a firm have substantial influence on the board and can, in fact, push forcefully for the adoption of policies that are beneficial to the constituency represented. Thus, in the model, the real rewards demanded (or thought to be demanded) by labor were indicated by a succession of relatively high welfare levels: $U_t^0 = {}_t\phi(w_t, E_t)$, $t = 1, 2, \ldots, T$. It follows, of course, that to the extent the worker-directors are able to secure concessions from the capital owners and gain unusually favorable wages and working conditions, the profitability of capital investment will tend to be reduced. Under plausible assumptions about the technical conditions of production and the elasticity of commodity demand, the net present value of capital goods will be diminished by labor's policies; and even if investment is positive, capital accumulation will be carried less far than it would under circumstances where the wage rates demanded over time were lower and where the productive organization was permitted to take on technically more efficient configurations.

What is of interest at this point, then, is to contrast the investment solution that emerges under conditions of active labor participation in decision making with the solution that might be expected to appear in a traditional capitalist regime. Given competition, and the same general set of assumptions adopted in the earlier codetermination model, the standard capitalist model can be handled in a straightforward fashion. Analytically, two basic cases are conceivable. In the first and simpler case, the firm is said to operate with the best known technology (E^*) and to purchase labor services each period (L_t) from a single competitive market in which a uniform price w_t^0 holds. The situation is such that all workers in the industry have to acquiesce to the given production environment (E^*) whether the particular working conditions implied are regarded as optimal or not. Presumably, information costs and transactions costs generally are so high that workers are unable to bargain with potential employers and secure improved working conditions ($E_t > E^*$) in exchange for accepting lower wages ($w_t < w_t^0$). Thus each firm pays the same wage rate (w_t^0), employs the same technical organization (E^*), and offers the same environment.

If this rather special setting is accepted, the calculation of net present value becomes routine. That is, equation (7.2) reduces to:

$$\pi = \sum_{t=1}^{T} \left\{ [p_t \cdot {}_tf(L_t, K_0, E^*) - w_t^0 L_t \cdot \Psi_t \right\}$$

$$- Z_0 K_0 \qquad t = 1, 2, \ldots, T \qquad (7.17)$$

As usual, the objective is to find the values of the variables that make π a maximum; but, in this application, the only effective variables are K_0 and L_t, $t = 1, 2, \ldots, T$. Since each successive wage rate w_t^0 is determined in the open market, free of any monopoly influence, there is reason to believe that labor costs will be generally lower here than in the case of codetermination. Moreover, the conditions of the new problem require that the technical efficiency of production be as great as possible ($E_t = E^*$, $t = 1, 2, \ldots, T$). Thus the implication is clear. In the traditional capitalist world, conditions are relatively more favorable to investment in capital goods than they are in a system in which codetermination is practiced and, *ceteris paribus*, the absolute volume of capital investment will be larger.

Insight into the investment situation can be gained by considering the first-order conditions for the maximization of (7.17). The latter are:

$$\sum_{t=1}^{T} \left[p_t \, \frac{\partial_t f(L_t, K_0, E^*)}{\partial K_0} \, \Psi_t \right] = Z_0 \qquad (7.18)$$

$$p_t \, \frac{\partial_t f(L_t, K_0, E^*)}{\partial L_t} \, \Psi_t = w_t^0 \Psi_t \qquad t = 1, 2, \ldots, T \qquad (7.19)$$

In the work so far, attention has been confined to a two-factor model (per period), and thus the $T + 1$ equations of (7.18) and (7.19) can be solved for the optimal values of these inputs. It would be a simple matter, however, to extend the analysis to the multifactor case by positing the existence of, for example, other current inputs than labor. Then additional conditions analogous to (7.19) would hold. In the context of this more general model, the various productive inputs can show relations of complementarity or competitiveness.[14] Quite possibly, technical conditions are such that the labor input (L_t) and the capital input (K_0) are complementary—in which case, the quantity of capital demanded must fall as the price of the labor input rises. But regardless of the reaction of the individual firm, it is true that the total volume of investment in the industry can fall in response to rising wage costs if the elasticity of demand for the industry's output is large.

This line of analysis points up the need to define more precisely the basis on which the codeterminationist model is to be compared with the traditional capitalist model. Equilibrium conditions (7.11) and (7.12) of the former are essentially the same as (7.18) and (7.19) of the traditional model, but sensible interpretation of the respective cases requires some assumptions to be made about the general nature of the economy in which the codeterminationist firm is operating. Thus, to begin the discussion, it will be useful to conceive of the existence of a single codeterminationist industry functioning within an otherwise conventional capitalist system. The firm of model (7.2) through (7.4) is in the process of deciding whether or not to join this codeterminationist industry. Because of the special institutional arrangements in the industry, the firm will, presumably, be required to face a higher wage rate each period $(\dot{w}_t)$ than it would if the industry were of the traditional competitive type. In effect, codetermination implies that each firm must deal with a small but potent local union comprised of the firm's employees; and thus it seems reasonable to assume that the equilibrium wage rate $\dot{w}_t$ will always tend to be greater than the general market wage w_t^0.

If this new condition on wages $(\dot{w}_t > w_t^0)$ were the only change brought about by codetermination, the analysis would be straightforward. An industry tied to labor participation would be analogous to a conventionally organized capitalist industry facing abnormally high wage costs because of location or some other special circumstance. The relatively high cost structure in the industry would mean that it was vulnerable to competition from any firms that could produce the same product under more favorable wage conditions—for example, new firms producing the product might spring up in other locations where the wage rate was lower. For the codetermination case, the implication is that labor participation schemes must be extended to *all* firms manufacturing a given commodity or class of commodities. Unless the coverage is complete, codetermination is not viable; partial enforcement of the plan would permit those outside the codetermination program to undersell those within it. Then subnormal profits would be made by firms in the codetermination sector and, ultimately, the latter would disappear.

Of course, even if all the firms producing a common product are committed to codetermination, survival of the industry requires a market price for output that is high enough to cover opportunity costs and yield normal returns to investors. The commodity price in question must be higher than the price that would be charged by a hypothetical competitive industry producing the same product under conditions of lower wage cost $(w_t^0 < \dot{w}_t)$. In other words, codetermination implies a higher cost structure and long-run equilibrium price than traditional capitalism; thus, insofar as the demand for the industry's output is relatively elastic, it follows that industry sales must be significantly smaller than they would be for an industry organized along conventional lines. The possibility of this output effect means, in turn, that the *total volume* of capital investment in the codeterminationist industry may well be limited to rather low levels.

From the standpoint of any firm in the industry, the high wage rate $(\dot{w}_t)$ brought about by codetermination may tend to encourage the substitution of capital for labor, and in consequence, the firm's capital-labor ratio can increase as transition is made from normal capitalist organization to the new arrangement. This development is, of course, quite consistent with an overall reduction in *industry* investment. It should also be recognized, though, that a net increase in the firm's demand for capital need not occur as the wage rate increases. If L_t and K_0 are complementary inputs, so that the partial elasticity of substitution between the two is negative, an increase in the wage from w_t^0 to $\hat{w}_t$ will lead to a diminution in the amount of capital used by the firm. And, along the same lines, the environmental factor $(\hat{E}_t)$ is likely to play a very important role in diminishing the volume of investment undertaken by the co-determinationist firm. The reason is simple. Insofar as negotiation leads to an equilibrium environmental level $(\hat{E}_t)$ that is greater each period than E^*, it follows that the firm's technical organization of production is less well suited to producing marketable output than it would be under traditional capitalism (where E^* holds). But, then, the marginal productivity of capital (and labor) must be lower in the codeterminationist firm and, *ceteris paribus,* the equilibrium volume of capital investment $(Z_0\hat{K}_0)$ must be lower. At equilibrium, the first-order conditions (7.11), (7.12), . . . are satisfied in the codetermination model; the optimal values $\hat{L}_t$, $\hat{K}_0$ are, however, smaller than the corresponding values that emerge in the capitalist model via (7.18), (7.19), ... Since both the wage rate $\hat{w}_t$ and the environmental index $\hat{E}_t$ are likely to be set at higher levels than w_t^0 and E^* when labor has effective representation on the firm's governing board, there is no escaping the general inference that a codetermination system may act to retard voluntary investment in capital goods and reduce employment. Moreover, at the industry level, the effect of codetermination will be observed in the form of higher output price and lesser production.

On this accounting, a capitalist system that operates along traditional lines, and is unemcumbered by labor participation schemes, has both advantages and disadvantages. To its credit, such a system will encourage capital accumulation and growth; but, at the same time, it will be unresponsive to the desires of workers for less-alienating production environments. In other words, if there is truth in the contention that transactions costs under traditional capitalism are so high as to preclude negotiation over the relative mix of the pecuniary (w_t) and nonpecuniary (E_t) elements in a worker's reward vector, the standard capitalist model is open to criticism. Specifically, a case can be made for codetermination on grounds that the changed institutional structure will have the effect of reducing transactions costs, of permitting a finer adjustment of the working environment to the preferences of labor, and thus of increasing welfare within the system.

To the extent that a capitalist economy is inflexible and operates so as to maintain uniform but alienating work conditions within each firm, only a second-best solution can be expected. In effect, a series of special constraints of the type $E_t = E^*$ must then hold and the requirements for Pareto optimality cannot be met. Ultimately, the argument for labor participation in management seems to rest on this general conception of the problem. The basic premise is that high transactions costs rule out the use of markets and freely negotiated contracts as means for achieving an optimal working environment within the firm;[15] thus, alternative institutional arrangements have to be introduced that will ensure the appearance of more desirable conditions of work. But the specific legislation needed to implement a program of "industrial democracy" has its own drawbacks; and, at base, the choice seems to be between a structure that promises to improve the firm's environment $(E_t > E^*)$ and one that conduces to a high rate of capital investment and lower commodity prices.

A serious question can be raised, however, as to whether choice must, in fact, be restricted to these second-best alternatives. In theory, optimal adjustment of the firm's production environment does not require the creation of institutional conditions that diminish the incentives for investment. If markets are competitive and transactions costs are zero, the behavior of profit-maximizing entrepreneurs and utility-maximizing workers will lead automatically to a wage-environment-investment solution that can be considered ideal. In particular, the firm's environment will be optimal in the sense that the "quality" of the work process will be as high as it can be each period, given technological alternatives, the structure of market prices, and the willingness of workers to substitute nonpecuniary for pecuniary rewards.

Insofar as the alienation of labor represents a major problem for traditional capitalism, it follows that workers must be concerned with both pecuniary and nonpecuniary returns. By implication, then, there is not one supply schedule of labor facing an industry at any period t, but many different schedules based on different possible work environments. In other words, each period, for every wage-environment pair (w_t, E_t), there is a corresponding supply of labor potentially forthcoming. Competition is assumed and thus, from the standpoint of any firm in the industry, the conditions of labor supply per period are reflected as a set of horizontal schedules. There is a completely elastic supply of labor available at each of many different wage rates, but, at each wage, a definite type of production environment must be provided by the firm. As the wage rate offer is increased, the environment can become more alienating, and conversely. The firm, of course, is free to secure any volume of labor services it desires from a given type of market by offering the appropriate reward vector (w_t, E_t) to the workers.

When viewed collectively, the various labor markets (based on different environmental guarantees) imply a general tradeoff relation between money wages and the work environment. In effect, then, a tradeoff curve can be drawn that reflects the subjective preferences of workers regarding the balance to be maintained between pecuniary and nonpecuniary income. Curve MM in Figure 7-1 represents such a preference relation. Presumably, labor will insist on comparatively high wages when the quality of the work process approaches some lower limit such as E^* in the diagram and will resist dipping below a minimum money wage w'. Of course, individual workers have different objectives, and thus, in a free system, each worker will tend to move to the particular market that offers him the most desirable reward vector (w_t, E_t). In this way, all workers will sort themselves out into the many different markets that are available.

To simplify the analysis, it will be convenient to assume that the various markets in existence are differentiated very finely. Then, at each period, the general tradeoff curve showing worker attitudes toward rewards can be expressed as a continuous mathematical function:

$$w_t = {}_tG(E_t) \qquad t = 1, 2, \ldots, T \qquad (7.20)$$

In Figure 7-1, MM indicates the tradeoff curve for period τ. It is typical of the family represented by (7.20); but all these curves are subject to change as opinions about the appropriate working environment shift. For example, MM would change shape and the lower limit E^* would be displaced to the right if money income were valued relatively less highly. Similarly, the limit w' would move upward if workers became less willing to trade wages for improved working conditions. In subsequent discussion, however, labor's environmental preferences will be taken as data.

Given (7.20), the firm's optimization problem must be recast in somewhat different form.[16] The net present value equation (7.2) becomes:

$$\Pi = \sum_{t=1}^{T} \left\{ [p_t \cdot {}_tf(L_t, K_0, E_t) - {}_tG(E_t) \cdot L_t] \cdot \Psi_t \right\}$$

$$- Z_0 K_0 \qquad t = 1, 2, \ldots, T \qquad (7.21)$$

The variables in (7.21) and K_0, L_t, and E_t ($t = 1, 2, \ldots, T$); and the firm's objective is to determine the values of these variables that make net present value a maximum. Moreover, assuming that the wage-environment tradeoff curves (7.20) are positioned so that the desired environment is always greater than E^*,[17] the optimization problem is one of unconstrained maximization. Thus, differentiating (7.21) partially, the first-order conditions emerge as:

$$\sum_{t=1}^{T} \left(p_t \, \frac{\partial q_t}{\partial K_0} \, \Psi_t \right) = Z_0 \qquad (7.22)$$

$$p_t \, \frac{\partial q_t}{\partial L_t} \, \Psi_t = {}_tG(E_t) \cdot \Psi_t \qquad t = 1, 2, \ldots, T \qquad (7.23)$$

$$p_t \, \frac{\partial q_t}{\partial E_t} \, \Psi_t = L_t \cdot \frac{\partial \, {}_tG}{\partial E_t} \, \Psi_t \qquad t = 1, 2, \ldots, T \qquad (7.24)$$

As can be seen, (7.22) and (7.23) are parallel to conditions (7.11) and (7.12) derived from the earlier codetermination model. The essential difference between the two is that the new requirements, (7.22) and (7.23), are based on the market tradeoff curves (7.20) rather than the worker-imposed reward constraints (7.3). Both sets demand the efficient use of resources in accordance with standard marginal productivity rules.

Condition (7.24) is analogous to (7.16); the relation is clear since the structure of the "free market" model implies that $\partial q_t/\partial E_t < 0$, $\partial w_t/\partial E_t < 0$. At equilibrium, then, the decrement in revenue $p_t(\partial q_t/\partial E_t)$ must equal the decrement in the wage bill $(\partial w_t/\partial E_t)L_t$. Just as in the case of the codetermination model, it is advantageous to the firm to increase E_t (improve the work environment) as long as the diminution of the wage bill exceeds the diminution of total revenue. The second-order conditions, however, suggest that the increase in E_t must always come to an end. Intuitively, the reasons are simple. Any tradeoff curve, such as MM in Figure 7-1, is negatively sloped and approaches a minimum wage limit (w') with absolutely diminishing slope. At the same time, physical productivity falls more and more rapidly as "improvements" are made in the environment. Hence, the equilibrium value of E_t must be finite. In effect, at each cross-section of time, the firm will explore the various labor markets in existence and discover the one in which it is most advantageous to operate. That is, the firm must select the market, or the particular wage-environment pair, that is consistent with the goal of maximizing net present value.

Assuming that a unique maximum position can be reached by the "free market" model, simultaneous solution of the first-order conditions (7.22) through (7.24) will yield the optimal values for the factor inputs (K_0^{**}, L_t^{**}), the respective work environments (E_t^{**}), and the commodity outputs (q_t^{**}) over periods 1, 2, . . . , T. At each period, the firm will be purchasing labor services from a certain labor market where the given wage rate (w_t^{**}) is regarded as acceptable by the workers because they understand that the firm's production environment will be maintained at a stipulated quality (E_t^{**}). It should be emphasized that a firm does not provide the environment E_t^{**} because of altruism but because such policy serves the ends of the owners. If working conditions were less attractive than E_t^{**}, net present value would be less than its maximum of π^{**}. Equally, no attempt will be made to improve the environment beyond the level of E_t^{**}. This is so because if E_t^{**} were exceeded, value productivity would fall relatively more than wage costs, and, again, net present value would be less than π^{**}. The conclusion that emerges here, then, is that the market system is able to provide for a fine adjustment of the firm's production environment to the preferences of the labor force. According to the "free market" model, the equilibrium solution E_t^{**} can be greater than the limiting value E^* at each period through T. There is no need for labor to be confined to the relatively harsh and unpleasant conditions of work implied by E^*, provided transactions costs are not so high as to preclude the differentiation of labor markets, and provided workers are willing to sacrifice some pecuniary income for nonpecuniary rewards.[18]

The optimal values L_t^{**}, K_0^{**}, E_t^{**} determined from the solution of conditions (7.22) through (7.24) establish the maximum level for net present value (π^{**}). The latter magnitude has general interest, but from the standpoint of the firm contemplating investment in the industry, π^{**} must be greater than or equal to zero if any action is to be taken. Assuming, then, that $\pi^{**} \geqslant 0$, the solution generated by the "free market" model calls for a volume of capital investment equal to $Z_0 K_0^{**}$. And the question that arises is how this invest-ment plan compares with the one that emerges from the firm under conditions of codetermination ($Z_0 K_0$). Given the similarity of the two models based on (7.2) through (7.4) and (7.20) through (7.21) respectively, it is clear that the difference in the investment result must turn, ultimately, on the difference between systems (7.3) and (7.20). That is, the free market and codetermina-tion models are alike in all respects but one; at each period, the reward constraint:

$$U_t^0 = {}_t\phi(w_t, E_t) \qquad (7.3')$$

is virtually certain to be quite different from the corresponding market trade-off curve:

$$w_t = {}_tG(E_t) \qquad (7.20')$$

Then, since these two curves contrast with one another in respect to shape and position, systematic differences inevitably appear in the investment solutions obtained.

The problem of capital accumulation can be discussed more easily in terms of Figure 7-1. The latter depicts the situation of the firm at one particular period of time ($t = \tau$); but, assuming that the configurations at τ are typical of all periods, the argument to be developed is general. In the diagram, the ideal wage-environment solution for the firm operating in a free market system is shown as C. At this point, the equilibrium wage rate is w_τ^{**}, the environmental level is E_τ^{**}, and net present value ($\pi^{**} = \pi_2$) is a maximum. More accurately, net pres-ent value is a maximum on the assumption that optimizing adjustments, com-parable to the ones shown, have been made in the variables at all other periods through T. It should be noted that $\pi_2\pi_2$ is the highest present value contour attainable when the tradeoff curve (7.20'), or MM, is effective. By contrast, the codetermination solution is indicated at point A where the reward constraint (7.3'), or $U_a^0 U_a^0$, is tangent to the net present value contour $\pi_1\pi_1$. Given the orientation of the present value contours, $\pi_1\pi_1$ represents a lesser magnitude than $\pi_2\pi_2$; and, consequently, the codetermination case, with equilibrium wage $\hat{w}_\tau$ and equilibrium environment $\hat{E}_\tau$, implies less attractive investment prospects.

If the reasoning advanced earlier is accepted, it is obvious that when $\hat{w}_\tau > w_\tau^{**}$ and $\hat{E}_\tau > E_\tau^{**}$, the incentives for capital investment can easily be less in the codetermination case than in the free market case.[19] The first-order conditions (7.11) through (7.12) can be compared with (7.22) through (7.23).

Whether the advantage conveyed by the free market organization is large or slight depends on the character of the production function. If the capital and labor inputs are strongly complementary, and if capital productivity falls sharply as the work environment index becomes larger, the capitalist firm will be in a position to undertake significantly more investment than the codeterminationist firm ($Z_0 \dot{K}_0^{**} > \dot{Z}_0 \dot{K}_0$). Of course, as pointed out earlier, the two types of firms cannot coexist in the same industry over the long run. To survive, a given co-determination plan must extend to all firms in the industry, and the industry must secure a price for its product that is higher than the price a normal competitive industry would require.

What the free market model suggests is that the general institutional arrangements of a capitalist economy allow each worker to choose the type of production environment he finds most congenial ($E_t^{**} > E^*$) and, at the same time, permit the continuing existence of conditions favorable to investment ($\dot{K}_0^{**} > \dot{K}_0$). As long as competition rules and transactions costs are not essessive, a set of distinct labor markets is feasible, and there is no need to provide for improved working environments through codetermination legislation. Indeed, if labor participation in management is imposed by law, the situation is likely to worsen. That is, insofar as participation results in the setting of the firm's environmental level at an arbitrary value ($\dot{E}_t$) larger than the equilibrium level dictated by markets (E_t^{**}), the welfare of the system must become less than its potential. Assuming no special distributional problems have to be considered, the gain from increased nonpecuniary income, as valued by worker-consumers generally, is less than the loss from diminished commodity output, as valued by the same group. The movement toward improved working conditions can go too far and reduce the productive capacity of the industry excessively. In addition, of course, the policies that emerge under codetermination will tend to retard the rate of capital accumulation and, thus, ensure relatively reduced incomes in the future as well as the present.

Up to this point the discussion of codetermination has been conducted on the assumption that labor-participation programs are functioning in only one or a few industries in the economy. Moreover, a basic presumption has been that the underlying motive for codetermination is a desire to bring about improvements in the firm's working environment—improvements that would not otherwise be initiated in a conventional market system. But if the latter interpretation is correct, it appears that a case can be made for codetermination legislation only when some rather special conditions hold. Specifically, if transactions costs are so high as to preclude the use of multiple labor markets, it may be advantageous to accept labor participation as a means for improving production environments (which capitalists tend to fix at E^*). Even here, however, the welfare gains achieved because $\dot{E}_t$ is larger than E^* ($t = 1, 2, \ldots, T$) must be judged greater than the welfare losses that arise because capital accumulation is retarded in the codeterminationist industries. And capital accumulation will be retarded unless the workers show unusual restraint in the use of the power they obtain under codetermination. In other words, the codetermination solution $(\hat{E}_t, \hat{w}_t)$ will lead to less industrial investment than the free market solution (E_t^{**}, w_t^{**}) in all cases except those where the reward constraint $U_a^0 U_a^0$ lies on or below the market curve MM (at each period, 1, 2, . . . , T). Ideally, of course, the decision process under codetermination should be such as to duplicate the results that would arise in a system of perfect markets and zero transactions cost.[20] The possibility that this optimum will be realized, however, seems remote.

Unfortunately, the problems of codetermination go much deeper than the preceding remarks suggest. Proponents of industrial democracy will certainly not be content to see codetermination implemented in only a few industries; the plan is to have the program embrace virtually all firms and all sectors of the economy. More important, codetermination seems to be advanced not merely as a device for upgrading the firm's production environment but, rather, as a means for generating a fundamental *redistribution* of income and wealth. What is contemplated is a permanent reduction of the share of income going to the owners of capital assets. Against this background, the whole movement for industrial democracy must be viewed in a new light. Pursuit of the redistribution goal through an extensive network of codetermination firms will almost certainly have the effect of altering radically the character of a capitalist system. The operation of the economy will depend more on administrative controls than on market forces, and the long-term development of the system will be in doubt.

When government intervention in the economic process is minimal, private enterpreneurs are able to adjust to changing price-cost relations in the system by shifting capital from areas of low productivity and return to areas that are more promising. In this way, the reward secured by capital in any firm tends to be brought into equality with the general opportunity cost of capital in the economy as a whole (after allowance is made for differential risk). Thus, in the case of codetermination, if the wage rate and the environmental index are raised in one particular industry as a result of the increased bargaining strength of labor, this condition, of itself, does not mean that profit in the industry will suffer permanent reduction. Entrepreneurs can protect their interests by changing the input mix used for production, reducing industry output, and shifting capital to other sectors. At long-run equilibrium the industry price will be higher than it was before codetermination, but those firms remaining in the industry should be making normal profits.

This market-adjustment process can work relatively smoothly when only one or a few industires are involved in large-scale reorganization. Serious trouble is to be expected, however, when the economic environment suddenly undergoes major institutional change and massive reallocation of resources must be carried out over a wide front. Thus, if codetermination is introduced in many industries simultaneously, as is likely to be the case in practice, a crisis can be created. That is, the efforts of entrepreneurs to protect profit rates will tend to produce unacceptably high levels of unemployment in the affected industries, the flight of capital to sectors untouched by codetermination, the reduction of output, and the increase of prices in most key industries of the economy. Moreover, the redistribution of income that takes place under these circumstances will not favor labor as a class.[21] To the extent that capital owners can adjust to the new cost and productivity conditions, profits will be sustained. At the same time, workers who are able to maintain their jobs in codeterminationist industries will experience higher real incomes. But losers will also exist; for example, those workers who are forced to work in the overcrowded free sector will tend to receive lower real wages, and in the short-run, many workers may simply be unemployed.

How well capitalists are able to offset the effects of the codetermination program depends on the freedom of action allowed them. Obviously, if capital owners are able to shut down existing plants for long periods rather than meet the demands of their employees, redistributive gains to labor can probably be held to modest levels. Similarly, if product prices can be raised significantly while inflationary monetary-fiscal policies generate sufficient aggregate demand to justify ever higher price structures, redistribution will not take the course desired by codetermination advocates. What is implied by this fluid situation, however, is something approaching economic and political chaos. Thus, if there is insistence on the use of codetermination as a redistributive device, government intervention and controls would seem to be inevitable. In one fashion or another, the legal-institutional arrangements would have to be altered so that the owners of capital assets could not freely change an existing firm's output or employment beyond certain narrowly prescribed limits. In addition, administrative controls over product prices and the flow of investment funds would have to be established. While the details of any control scheme may vary, it is clear that free choice must be curtailed in the codetermination sector and, indeed, restrictions are likely to spread to all parts of the system as unexpected developments occur that require attention.

Given a favorable political climate, there is no doubt that a government can devise a comprehensive network of controls that will have the effect of reducing the return to capital invested in the codetermination sector. Transfer of capital from the controlled industries will be difficult, but, in any event, the incentives for movement to the free sector are likely to be limited if the latter is small relative to the former. In other words, continuing capital flows to a relatively small free sector must drive down the profit rate there and end the sector's attractiveness. Then, assuming other alternatives such as foreign investment are cut off, it follows that the owners of capital will have to accept the existence of a changed economic environment in which the effective profit rate has been permanently reduced. In such a world, the firms operating within the codeterminationist sector may carry on as quasi-capitalistic entities, but the future of the system is not promising.

While state policy can bring about the attenuation of private property rights in capital and influence the way in which existing capital assets are used in production, the state faces greater difficulty in providing for the growth of the industrial capital stock over time. Indeed, even the maintenance of the original stock presents serious problems. Private individuals whose capital assets have been reduced in value by government intervention must have limited interest in accumulating additional capital that will be subject to the same oppressive restrictions. Rather, more remunerative alternatives will be sought (.e.g., human capital), or, as is likely, the voluntary savings rate will be lowered. At the same time, the incentives of the system militate against adequate allowances being made for the maintenance of fixed capital. In general, capital owners can be expected to try to translate capital that is yielding relatively low pecuniary returns into a stream of nonpecuniary benefits that can be appropriated. As the future of private ownership becomes more uncertain, it is rational to slight depreciation and maintenance while extracting current real income. The extent to which such a policy can be effectuated depends, of course, on the cooperation (or ignorance) of the worker-directors who are monitoring the operation of the firm. Workers, however, can also benefit from a program that shifts costs to the future and increases current real income; this is so because workers have relatively short planning horizons and hold no permanent or transferable claims on the firm's capital assets.

The result implied by the behavioral patterns just described is clear; in the long run, private investors will tend to reduce their initial holdings in the co-determinationist sector of the economy and be generally unwilling to make new investments in it.[22] Thus either production and employment will fall over time or, as seems highly probably, the government will step in and take over the task of financing industry. But if this reorganization takes place, the system is irrevocably altered. In effect, the last stage in the evolution of a codetermina-tionist economy is a transition to socialist labor management. With government financing of investment, industrial capital becomes communal property. Thus, while the employees of the firm may still elect representatives to guide the organization's policies, the ultimate decision maker is now the state or the bureaucracy controlling the apparatus of the state. In a fundamental sense, cap-italism is dead.

It is true, of course, that under the new system of communally owned capital, there is greater scope for the state to manipulate the distribution of income. This is not to say that distributional "equity," however, defined, will be achieved. A decentralized socialist system based on labor management has its own special problems relative to distribution. Not only can the results be arbitrary, but the total income to be distributed is likely to be less than that in a capitalistic system because of the inherent inefficiency of labor-managed firms. Discussion of the limitations of labor management, however, constitutes a major undertaking in itself and one that lies beyond the objectives of this chapter.

Property Rights and the Method of Financing
Capital Investment

If it were true that labor's preference function at each period, $U_t^0 = {}_t\phi\,(w_t, E_t)$, was so constituted as to produce results equivalent to those given by the corresponding market tradeoff curve, $w_t = {}_tG(E_t)$, a codetermination scheme would merely mimic the operation of free markets and leave a capitalist economy essentially unchanged.[23] For example, assuming the relations depicted in Figure 7-1 are characteristic of all periods, it follows that when a curve such as $U_a^0 U_a^0$ is coextensive with MM, the solution for the wage rates (w_t^{**}) and the environmental levels (E_t^{**}) will be the same in both the codetermination and free market models. Moreover, the incentives for private capital investment will be the same in both cases; and if labor's attitudes toward reward are regarded as stable by the firm's owners, the existence of codetermination should not influence the methods used to finance the investment. Under these extreme assumptions about workers' behavior, codetermination represents a neutral policy and, certainly, poses no threat to the normal functioning of a capitalist system.

From a technical standpoint, it can be said that codetermination becomes a problem for capitalism only when the reward constraint ${}_t\phi$ lies above the tradeoff curve ${}_tG$. But, unfortunately, such an outcome would seem to be precisely the one that must emerge. There is no reason whatsoever to believe that representation on the firm's board of directors will cause workers to demand *lower* wages or *lesser* environmental levels than would be forthcoming under free markets. Quite the contrary, workers who have substantial decision-making power but no equity holdings in the firm are almost certain to insist upon higher rewards than those that markets would provide. The explanation of why this bias toward higher rewards exists is easily understood and rests on the following points.

First, it should be recognized that under a codetermination scheme, workers have no permanent or transferable claims on the capital assets of the firm. Workers receive payment for their services on a current basis as labor is performed; thus whatever pecuniary or nonpecuniary benefits employees secure must be obtained during their (relatively brief) period of tenure with the enterprise. It is reasonable to believe that these institutional arrangements affect behavior. In particular, we should expect that the demands made on the owners of the firm by labor's representatives on the board will reflect the special interests and perspectives of the group represented. The key consideration is the appropriability of rewards. At any cross-section of time, certain workers have influence on the firm's decision-making process by virtue of the powers conveyed by codetermination, and these workers have incentive to push for policies that yield them the greatest possible pecuniary and nonpecuniary income over the planning interval they have established for themselves.

To say this does not mean that the labor group possessing power can act without restraint in seeking its own narrow, short-term objectives. The interests of capital owners and the interests of, for example, those workers who might join the firm in the future must be given some attention. For clearly, if the ruling labor group within the firm were to disregard completely the welfare of all other parties, a crisis might be created; the group would tend to lose public support, the firm would be driven into bankruptcy, and the continued existence of codetermination could even be imperiled. Nevertheless, it remains true that an inherent conflict of interest exists between society as a whole and the particular group of workers that has effective representation on the firm's board of directors at any given period. The problem can be seen with special clarity when the opposing positions of the firm's owners and its current employees are considered. Since the latter have no long-term claims on capital, they have no real incentive to preserve the capital stock. Thus policies that increase the wealth of the firm over some interval of time but do not enlarge the appropriate real incomes of the employees during this same period are not likely to be regarded as desirable by the existing labor representatives and will be opposed. By contrast, the policies that will tend to find approval are those which dissipate capital and shift current costs to future periods. The reason is obvious. The optimal strategy for workers who plan to leave the firm at some date in the not too distant future is to secure large current benefits (w_t, E_t) while neglecting the firm's longer-run requirements.

In discussions of codetermination, the argument is sometimes made that the interest of labor and capital are much the same and that the new institutional structure can be helpful in promoting greater cooperation between the two parties. This view is not wholly wrong; productivity and mutual gain may be enhanced by improved communications, more tranquil labor-management relations, etc. Despite the potential advantages of codetermination, however, it is dangerous to believe that the scheme will suddenly change the traditional adversary roles of labor and capital as they have been established by years of union-management conflict. Moreover, it is important to understand that there is a major difference between what can be termed the interests of labor in general and the interest of particular group of workers having effective representation on the firm's board at any moment of time. Presumably, the workers who actually elect representatives will insist upon the implementation of policies that will benefit them, not other groups. The policies advanced, therefore, need not even be pleasing to all members of the firm's current labor force to say nothing of future workers, capital owners, or society in general.

As model (7.2) through (7.4) was constructed, the firm's owners were assumed to estimate the preference functions (7.3) that specify the reward requirements of the labor force over periods $1, 2, \ldots, T$. More concretely, the owners were supposed to decide the shape and position of the wage-environment indifference curve (as $U_a^0 U_a^0$) that is relevant for decision making at each period to T. The estimation problem is extremely complicated, however, because workers are not homogeneous and the demands on the firm must take one pattern or another depending on the particular group of workers involved in negotiation. At each period of time, the workers whose opinions count in the firm's calculations are those who constitute the majority voting bloc (or coalition) within the firm, for it is they who elect representatives to the governing board. In effect, the majority workers can impress their own special policy line on the firm whether or not all employees approve. But it is clear that as time elapses different "political" groups within the organization may gain control of policy.[24] This is so because the size and internal composition of the firm's labor force can be expected to change over time and such change can lead to shifts in political power among the contending groups of employees. Thus, from the standpoint of the firm's owners, major change in worker preferences can occur from one period to the next as new representatives, pledged to carry out new and different programs, are elected to the governing board. If participatory democracy is real, the operation of the firm cannot be understood independently of the internal political process.

There is nothing in the preceding sketch of the codetermination process that suggests workers will be moderate in their demands and seek rewards no greater than those offered by the market. Indeed, the existence of political uncertainties within the firm seems likely to cause short planning horizons to become even shorter. Quite simply, incentives are created for each dominant labor bloc to use its power while it has political influence in the firm. The trick must be to obtain the greatest possible benefits in the short run before conditions change and the opportunities for achieving specialized objectives vanish.[25] It is true, of course, that the codetermination system gives support to the fundamental idea of labor reaching its goals on the basis of coercive power rather than through the use of contracts and markets. Thus, for example, the presumption is that the firm's environment (E_t) will be shaped to suit the ruling labor majority; there is no serious expectation that individual workers will move from market to market in search of an ideal mix of pecuniary and nonpecuniary rewards. The market tradeoff curve $w_t = {}_tG\,(E_t)$ is, in effect, rendered inconsequential because the firm rather than labor has to make whatever adjustments are deemed necessary.

Under these circumstances, with the economy's labor force broken down into noncompeting groups, each firm will tend to find that both the wage rate and the environmental index are set at higher levels than they would be in a true market system.[26] The core problem is obvious; once discussion turns to what is "just" rather than to what is economic, the door is open to any claim. Decisions then turn on political strength or bargaining power. But political solutions are less efficient than market solutions. By shifting attention from the real determinants of compensation, and implying that rewards can be set at arbitrarily chosen levels, unrealistic anticipations tend to be generated. The role of capital in production is played down while, at the same time, the impression is created that institutional arrangements alone can offer major protection against risk and the costs of readjustment.

Ultimately, the extent to which effective economic power is transferred from shareholders and management to labor depends on how the basic codetermination legislation is extended. There seems little doubt that implementation of the scheme will require the growth of an ancillary legal structure if only to determine how policy impasses will be settled. A divided governing board for the firm would imply serious problems for the day-to-day operation of the enterprise. But the failure to establish clear lines of authority and responsibility would have even graver consequences for the long run. To ensure that needed investment will take place and that the firm will continue to function as a tolerably efficient economic entity under codetermination, it is necessary to give the owners of capital some confidence that competitive returns can be made on their investments and that reasonable control over productive activities will be preserved. A balance must be struck between the enlarged rights of labor and the essential requirements of capital. There is a real question, however, as to whether a workable compromise can be effected. Codetermination may represent an *unstable system* in the sense that the traditional capitalist corporation may not be able to survive the desired enlargement of labor power. In other words, if the codeterminist firm is to function as an acceptable production unit, it may be necessary to bring about changes in the legal-institutional structure that will transform the firm into something other than a true capitalist enterprise. Indeed, what seems quite possible is that in the codeterminist world, the standard corporation will become a regulated firm or a nationalized labor-managed firm.

To understand how codetermination can lead to a fundamental change in capitalist organization, it is only necessary to consider the way in which the financing of investment is likely to occur under the new plan. As has been argued, the incentives for private capital accumulation will be reduced when the decision-making power of labor is increased; but, to the extent that investment is undertaken, there is reason for entrepreneurs to minimize the commitment of their own funds. *Ceteris paribus,* the optimal strategy is to make the debt-equity ratio as large as possible. For by substituting debt capital for equity capital in the financing of investment, the owners of the firm are able to minimize the risk of capital loss and, at the same time, create a situation in which economic relations between labor and capital have greater stability. In the case of codetermination, where contractual agreements involving labor are more flexible than those generated in a true market system, other types of contracts take on greater importance.

In deciding on the investment plan, the owners of the firm have to estimate the reward preferences of labor. That is, constraint relations such as those in (7.3) are required; but the latter can be quite volatile because the same group of employees need not be in command of policy over the whole planning interval 1, 2, . . . , T. Moreover, even if there is some preference constancy over time, any agreements that may be reached between owners and workers will not find their expression in rigid contracts. Given the basic objectives of codetermination, the wage rate and the conditions of production must always be open for renegotiation. Within limits, at least, labor can participate in windfalls and can react to changing circumstances in the firm and in the economy as a whole. No matter what the particular group of workers that has influence on the firm's policies, its behavior will presumably be dictated, in large measure, by self-interest. Thus, while the group in control will normally find it advantageous to sustain the firm as a functioning organization over moderate periods of time, there is no necessary reason why workers having limited tenure must show concern for the long run survival of the firm. As noted earlier, they may well take policy stands that yield present gains but shift costs to the future and endanger the firm. The question that arises, then, is: What can the owners do about this inefficient pattern of incentives in order to protect their own interests?

If it is assumed that labor wishes to avoid actions that will result in the imminent destruction of the firm, the owners can improve their economic position by financing the firm's capital stock through borrowed funds. In other words, by making financial contracts that call for the repayment of principal and interest on some strict, long-term schedule, the owners will be able to exert pressure on workers to limit their demands (w_t, E_t) to levels that the firm can meet and still remain in business. A measure of stability is achieved through this procedure because labor's representatives on the governing board must know that the inability or failure of the firm to meet its debt obligations will lead to the bankruptcy of the firm. But such a result would tend to reduce the welfare of the firm's current employees by putting jobs in jeopardy and threatening existing levels of pecuniary and nonpecuniary income. In effect, then, the use of debt financing has the desirable consequence of reshaping the structure of incentives and of bringing the interests of owners and workers more closely into harmony.

Of course, serious problems exist with this approach. In the first place, it is by no means clear that private lenders can be found who will be willing to place large sums of money at the disposal of codeterminationist firms. The risks involved in the procedure are obvious; and, even under more normal circumstances, 100 percent financing would tend to be resisted by financial intermediaries. Moreover, the worker-directors on the board may not acquiesce to heavy debt financing of the firm's capital stock. If the firm is not being organized de novo, assent is, in fact, far from assured. And should labor fight hard to retain maximum policy flexibility for the future, the finance plan favorable to the owners could easily be defeated. Then the inefficient incentive structure discussed previously will rule. It is difficult to say a priori how the issue will be settled, but there is at least some chance that debt financing will be accepted. Labor cannot make the strongest case against the use of debt without appearing to be completely cynical and indifferent to the welfare of other parties. In any event, if a rigid debt-service program can be established over the firm's planning interval, the owners can point to objective requirements that must be met at each period 1, 2, . . . , T and the reward constraints $U_t^0 = {}_t\phi (w_t, E_t)$, $t = 1, 2, . . . , T$ can be held to lower levels.

Under codetermination, the effective reward going to labor is not decided by the operation of the labor market alone, and because this is so, it is in the interest of the firm's owners to keep equity capital to a minimum. Depending on the influence workers can exercise on the firm's decision making process through their representation on the governing board, equity capital lies in greater or lesser danger. When labor possesses substantial coercive power, as seems inevitable if codetermination is pushed as a serious national policy, actions can be taken that reduce the return on capital invested in the firm to very low levels. Indeed, even the principal may be eroded significantly by workers seeking short-term objectives. In theory, of course, entrepreneurs are free to protect themselves by using borrowed funds exclusively in financing the firm's capital stock. As a practical matter, however, some equity capital will always be required, and thus the firm's owners must always be concerned with a basic capital sum that is subject to loss.[27] To the extent that such capital bears high risk and can be expected to earn low or negative returns, it follows that other private investment alternatives will be sought.

Effectively, the situation means that investors will tend to avoid undertakings in the sector of the economy where codetermination is enforced. Since there will always be some investment opportunities that are unaffected by the codetermination scheme, the flow of funds will be shifted accordingly. For example, if small firms and partnerships are not covered by the participatory legislation, capital accumulation will be accelerated in these areas.[28] Similarly, investment in human capital, in foreign ventures, in government securities, etc. may be encouraged. But regardless of the specifics of the reorganization, it is clear that the overall pattern of investment in the economy will be distorted by codetermination and that the allocation of resources will not be Pareto optimal.

The preceding discussion suggests that complete understanding of the effects of codetermination can be achieved only when the background conditions of the system are specified in great detail. Obviously, the coverage of the program is important but the problem goes beyond this consideration. The way in which codetermination actually functions must depend on the nature of the political process in the state and on the general legal and institutional structure that is developed. If there is determination to effect fundamental changes in income and wealth distribution, and if codetermination is seen as one instrument of such reform, continuing governmental intervention and economic adjustment can be anticipated. Then no strategy that capital can pursue will prevent a trend toward diminished opportunities for remunerative corporate investment. For example, even if it were possible to move to 100 percent debt financing of the firm's capital stock, the move would be unavailing. From the standpoint of labor, forcing the firm into bankruptcy could be justified as a way of dramatizing the inherent "inefficiency" of traditional capitalist organization. That is, as long as confidence existed that the government would intervene and not only maintain production but establish a favorable income policy, all would be well. Codetermination could, in effect, be used by labor as the means for bringing about a shift to a "superior" system. In the new scheme, the private corporation would, presumably, be transformed into a regulated firm or a type of labor-managed socialist firm, and the traditional market system would be relegated to a role of secondary importance.

Viewed in this light, codetermination represents a good deal more than a program to encourage the spread of industrial democracy. No matter what the motivations for the implementation of the policy, it seems clear that if significant decision-making power is conferred on employees, profound changes can be expected in the capitalist system. And, unfortunately, the changes do not promise to be for the better. At base, there is a problem because an inefficient incentive structure is created. Workers are granted rights to make decisions affecting the capital assets of the firm but have no responsibility for supplying this capital, and no long-term claim on the income derived from it. In consequence, the owners of capital, and ultimately society, are forced to assume the risk of decisions made each period by a group of individuals not primarily interested in the preservation of capital. With these institutional arrangements, it follows that the stage is set for economic difficulties and the demand for further regulation and control. The argument here is simple but nonetheless valid; certainly, the basic deficiencies of codetermination should be recognized and faced squarely before a potentially harmful public program is set in motion.

Notes

1. By assumption, the industry is not in long-run equilibrium; existing firms are securing extranormal profits.

2. To simplify the analysis, no consideration is given to the possibility of increasing or reducing the capital stock K_0 over the planning interval $1, 2, \ldots, T$ through further investment or disinvestment.

3. The size of the firm and the magnitude of the firm's labor force may also be important influences on the level of E_t.

4. Of course, in the absence of forward markets, the prices ruling at future time periods have to be estimated.

5. The production function is usually defined in such way as to preclude variation in E. The organizational form (say E^*) consistent with the greatest output of the commodity for any input pair (L_t, K_0) is taken as the appropriate form to use. Then, the function is given as: $q_t = {}_t f(L_t, K_0, E^*)$, where E^* is a parameter. The latter tends to be regarded as fixed except insofar as technological change occurs.

6. G. Tullock, "The General Irrelevance of the General Impossibility Theorem", *Quarterly Journal of Economics,* May 1976, 81, 256-70. See section IV below for a discussion of whose preferences count in policy determinations.

7. It is conceivable that productivity does not decline monotonically as E_t is made larger than E^*. Then, over a certain range, lessening worker alienation could result in greater productivity. In practice, there may well be substantial ignorance of the relation between E_t and the productivity of inputs. *Mutatis mutandis,* the analysis of the chapter could be adapted to deal with more complex cases of the type just suggested.

8. Nonnegativity conditions hold on the variables: K_0, L_t, w_t, $t = 1, 2,$ $\dots, T$.

9. The rule may, of course, be ambiguous if, for example, the cash flow stream is irregular, etc. See W.H. Jean, *The Analytical Theory of Finance* (New York: Holt, Rinehart and Winston, Inc. 1970), pp. 6-65.

10. If there is very little worker interest in improving the production environment, the whole alienation argument is called into question. At another level, it can be pointed out that if progressive income taxes are in effect, workers may find it desirable to secure greater real income in (untaxable) nonpecuniary form.

11. The properties of ${}_t\phi$ and ${}_t f$ are such that the second-order conditions for the maximum can be expected to hold. By assumption, the system (7.2) through (7.3) is well behaved; the welfare and production functions possess the mathematical properties usually ascribed to them in the literature. In particular, the welfare functions ${}_t\phi$ are taken to be globally strictly quasiconcave, while the effective production function at any period t is globally strictly concave. The latter reflects varying returns to scale—with diseconomies ultimately overcoming economies.

12. The model assumes that all of the constraints in (7.15) are binding. In other words, workers always demand a welfare level of U^0 to be provided by the firm.

13. As a special case, it is possible for $U_b^0 U_b^0$ to be tangent to an isoyield curve at $E_t = E^*$.

14. C.E. Ferguson, *The Neoclassical Theory of Production and Distribution* (Cambridge: Cambridge Univ. Press, 1969), p. 71, pp. 109-110.

15. The argument is also made by radical critics of capitalism that the objective of those in control of the production process is not profit making per se,

but maintenance of their class position in production. Thus, while profit making may be a crucial instrument toward this end, when profit making conflicts with capitalist control of the system, the option is always for the maintenance of control. Effectively, certain types of less-alienating work environments are ruled out because of their presumed long-term consequences for the economic and political organization of society. See H. Gintis, "Consumer Behavior and the concept of Sovereignty: Explanations of Social Decay," *American Economic Review* (May 1972): 62, 270.

16. In general, the problem can be conceived as one of maximizing the net present value function (7.2) subject to: (7.4) $E_t \geqslant E^*$ and (7.20) $w_t = {}_tG(E_t)$, $t = 1, 2, \ldots, T$.

17. In other words, at each time period, the curve is analogous to MM in Figure 7-1.

18. Obviously, workers would like to secure constant or greater wages and, at the same time, be granted improved working conditions. To some extent, labor participation legislation seems to provide this kind of outcome and, thus, has political appeal. But, realistically, an economic choice must be made. A tradeoff is always necessary; wages must be reduced sufficiently to justify the use of technically inferior methods of production.

19. Again, it is assumed that what is true in period τ is true in all periods.

20. If $U_a^0 U_a^0$ lies below curve MM, the (w_t, E_t) solution will be suoptimal relative to the market determined ideal. That is, the level of E_t will be too low and the volume of capital investment encouraged will be too large because the firm will have a false impression of the true opportunity costs in the system.

21. The way in which this problem can be analyzed is suggested by J.G. Ballentine and W.R. Thirsk, "Labour Unions and Income Distribution Reconsidered," *Canadian Journal of Economics* 10 (February 1977): 141-148.

22. If labor's demands are not excessive and the rate of return to capital in the codetermination sector is merely reduced to a lower, but positive, level, private investment may continue there. In other words, with no superior alternatives available, entrepreneuers may be willing to accept a low profit rate rather than not invest at all.

23. It might be argued that codetermination can approximate the results of differentiated labor markets while avoiding the high transactions costs associated with these markets. Then codetermination would represent the superior alternative.

24. It is also true, of course, that labor unions may influence the opinions of the worker-directors concerning policy and that the objectives of unions can change over time.

25. The group of workers holding effective political power in the firm at any time has incentive to perpetuate its power by establishing limits on the size and composition of the firm's labor force. Ideally, the group would prevent any of its own members from being fired and, at the same time, deny employment

to any new workers who might have policy disagreements with the dominant group.

26. Since labor mobility is reduced, the reward solution tends to reflect "average" preferences and leave most individuals at second-best positions.

27. Conceivably, some type of preferred stock might be used as an alternative means for financing the firm's capital stock.

28. Tax incentives could be introduced to help channel funds to the co-determination sector.

8

The Economic Consequences of Codetermination on Employment and Income Distribution

Lowell Gallaway

The various resource papers that have been presented indicate rather clearly the burgeoning interest in the Western world in some form of worker participation in business decision making beyond that encompassed in the concept of collective bargaining. As justification for the extension of worker participation, it is frequently observed that workers have a very important stake in the operation of the businesses that provide their livelihoods. For example, in the Green Paper issued by the European Communities Commission it is flatly asserted that:

> . . . employees are increasingly seen to have interests in the functioning of enterprises which can be as substantial as those of shareholders, and sometimes more so. Employees not only derive their income from enterprises which employ them, but they devote a large proportion of their daily lives to the enterprise. Decisions taken by or in the enterprise can have a substantial effect on their economic circumstances, both immediately and in the longer term; the satisfaction which they derive from work; their health and physical condition; the time and energy which they can devote to their families and to activities other than work; and even their sense of dignity and autonomy as human beings.[1]

This pronouncement suggests that worker participation in business decisions is necessary in order to satisfy individual's desires for some degree of control over both the direct economic conditions, i.e., wages and employment, surrounding the act of work as well as the conditions that shape what is best thought of as the work environment. Thus we may conceive of two broad classes of phenomena that worker participation in decision making attempts to control, (1) wage-employment conditions and (2) the "quality of life" in the workplace.

Superficially, these appear to be quite different problems. However, on closer examination they merge into one another. This has been ably demonstrated by Eirik Furubotn who notes first that, "In practice, the work environment can be improved only by sacrificing marketable output."[2] In turn, this implies a lower marginal product for labor and, in a competitive set of labor markets, a lower wage. Thus monetary compensation for deficiencies in the work environment is already incorporated in the observed wage rate. Therefore, for the purpose of analyzing the economic effects of worker participation in

169

enterprise decisions we may focus on just the basic wage and employment dimensions of the problem. In effect, hereafter, the term *wages* will be taken to include the monetary equivalents of any quality of life advantages or disadvantages associated with the workplace.

The standard arguments for a greater worker voice in business decisions that affect wage and employment conditions are that it is necessary in order (1) "to bring about an important condition for economic democracy through a more equitable division of wealth, income, and influence,"[3] and (2) to protect employees from the employment effects, both short and long term, of arbitrary investment and marketing decisions made by the enterprise. These suggest two distinct dimensions to the employees' interest in the economic decisions of a firm, one concerned with exercising greater control over the amount of remuneration per unit of work effort and the other with the determination of the number of units of work effort that will be hired by the enterprise. The economic impact of increased worker control over these two phenomena is the subject of my analysis.

The Wage Decision: The Case of the Individual Firm with Income-Mixing Arrangements

We turn first to the question of the basic issue of the wage decision made by the business enterprise. Assume a situation in which employers and workers participate in essentially competitive labor markets and, consequently, a wage rate that is equated with the marginal product of labor.[4] Now introduce some form of workers participation in the enterprise decision-making process with respect to wage levels. As has been clearly indicated in the previous chapters, this participation can take a variety of forms. Borrowing Arthur Shenfield's taxonomy, we have (1) codetermination, (2) copartnership, (3) profit-sharing, (4) consultation, or (5) collective bargaining. My interest is in the first four of these, and they can be further grouped into two broad categories, (1) arrangements that "mix" wage and profit income, and (2) those which do not. The income "mixing" forms of worker participation are, of course, copartnership, which provides workers with partial "ownership" of the enterprise and, therefore, entitlement to a share of profits, and straightforward profit-sharing, which does not include any transfer of ownership.

To analyze the impact of income-mixing types of arrangements at the level of the individual firm, consider a competitive situation in which factor prices and the price of the product being produced are determined exogenously from the firm. Now profit-maximizing behavior by the firm implies that the ratio of the marginal products of the factors will be brought into equality with the ratio of the factor prices. If the firm's production function is assumed to be of the form

$$0 = a(k)^\alpha L \qquad \alpha < 1 \qquad\qquad (8.1)$$

where 0 denotes physical output, k represents the capital-labor ratio, and L the total labor input,[5] this implies

$$k = (\alpha)/(1 - \alpha) \delta \qquad\qquad (8.2)$$

where δ is the ratio of the wage rate to the unit cost of capital.

Introducing some form of income-mixing worker representation scheme into the enterprise's decision-making process will increase the cost per unit of labor by some fraction of the share of the firm's income that would ordinarily be claimed by the owners of capital. Let this fraction be symbolized by λ. Assuming that the enterprise would adjust its factor mix so that the marginal product of capital would remain equal to the exogenously given cost of capital, labor's claiming a fraction of the reward to capital would have the effect of changing the firm's perception of the relationship between factor prices from the ratio of the wage rate (w) to the unit cost of capital (c) to

$$w/c + \lambda k \qquad\qquad (8.3)$$

This would have the effect of changing to the equilibrium capital-labor ratio to

$$k' = (\alpha\delta)/(1 - \alpha)\left\{1 - \lambda[\alpha/(1 - \alpha)]\right\} \qquad\qquad (8.4)$$

Dividing (8.4) by (8.2) gives

$$k'/k = 1/\left\{1 - \lambda[\alpha/(1 - \alpha)]\right\} \qquad\qquad (8.5)$$

which indicates that the end result of workers' claiming a share of profits would be an increase in the capital-labor ratio or, put conversely, a decrease in the labor-capital ratio.

This still does not reveal how the adjustment to a higher capital-labor ratio will be made. In the short run, where no adjustment in the capital stock is possible, it obviously would require a reduction in the quantity of labor employed and, in all likelihood, operation of the firm with a factor mix that is nonoptimal. This is illustrated by the production isoquant map shown in Figure 8-1. The locus $K_0^* L_1^*$ reflects relative factor prices for capital and labor prior to the imposition of an income-mixing worker-participation scheme, and $K_0^* L_1^*$ is based on those prices after it is adopted. In the initial situation K_0 of capital and L_0 of labor are employed at a point on the firm's expansion path. This is assumed to be the profit-maximizing level of output. In the worker-participation regime, K_0 of capital is still employed but only L_1 of labor may be hired for the same

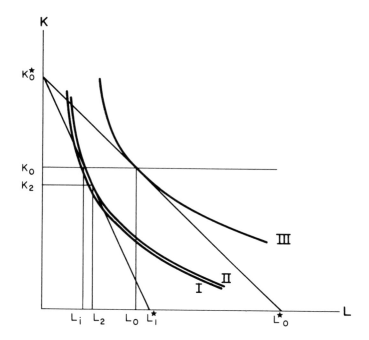

Figure 8-1. The Production-Isoquant

level of factor expenditures involved in the initial case. Thus output is reduced (from that implied in isoquant III to the output associated with isoquant I). Further, there is no guarantee that this is an optimal factor mix. In the case illustrated, the optimal combination with this level of factor costs is K_0 of capital and L_2 of labor.

To further complicate matters in the short run, it is obvious that the increased costs incurred by the firm will place it in a position in which it will continue to operate only if its revenues exceed its variable costs. Within this framework, the source of the cost increases becomes clear. The firm must incur both the exogenously determined market costs for capital plus a wage cost that is increased by some fraction of the market cost of capital. Thus the single firm with an income-mixing worker-participation scheme is placed at a competitive disadvantage with respect to other firms.

The long-run adjustment for a single firm under competitive conditions is really quite simple. Even if it moved to the optimal factor combination K_2L_2, it would still be operating with higher unit costs than its competitors, and therefore the long-run adjustment would be for the enterprise to cease doing business under these conditions and permit the capital it was using to be shifted into other areas of economic activity. Thus the clear implication is that profit-sharing of the type we have discussed here, i.e., practiced by a single firm, is not a viable economic arrangement and will lead to some degree of nonemployment of labor.

An obvious reaction at this point is to be suspicious of such a conclusion since there are recorded instances of individual firm profit-sharing arrangements of a voluntary character of long standing. This is quite possible if we modify one of our assumptions, namely, the proposition that in addition to any profit-sharing income that accrues to a firm's workers they also receive the exogenously determined market wage. Assume instead a situation in which both workers and the business enterprise regard profit-related worker remuneration as an imperfect substitute for direct wage payments. Such a situation can be illustrated by an Edgeworth box type diagram such as that shown in Figure 8-2.

The firm's preference function (broken indifference curves) with respect to the two different forms of worker remuneration is oriented to the origin $0'$ and the workers' preference function (solid indifference curves) to the origin 0. The contract curve is CC'. Now an opportunity constraint W^*P^* representing the amount of income to be distributed is introduced that determines the optimum allocation of worker income between direct wage payments and profit-related income. This may be an eminently sound economic arrangement since profit-

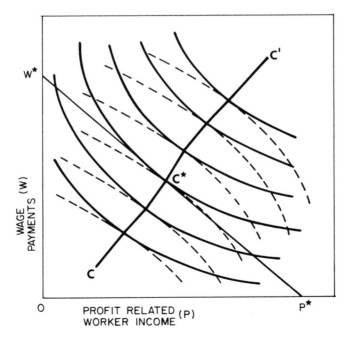

Figure 8-2. An Edgeworth Type Diagram

related worker income *is viewed by both workers and the firm as a substitute for direct wage payments.* However, this is quite a different situation from that we have assumed in our analysis. To the extent that income-mixing arrangements are of the type shown in Figure 8-2, they are of relatively little consequence economically since they should not produce relative factor costs that are markedly different from those which would exist in a competitive market. In fact, under these circumstances a situation can be evisioned in which the enterprise might face a more favorable set of factor costs than its competitors. This would seem to be a relatively rare case, though. Otherwise, arrangements of this sort would be much more numerous in areas that did not legally mandate them.

The Wage Decision: The Case of the Individual Firm with Non-Income Mixing Arrangements

We turn now to the instance in which the individual firm is confronted with increased worker participation in the form of non-income-mixing forms of inclusion in the enterprise's decision-making process. Assume that workers will use this power to impose an additional wage cost on employers, either in the form of improvements in the quality of the work environment or in the form of direct wage payments. This increment to wage costs will have the effect of multiplying the market wage faced by the firm by a factor $(1 + \beta)$. Now, replicating the earlier analysis, the equilibrium capital-labor ratio for a firm faced with this situation is given by

$$k' = (\alpha/1 - \alpha)\delta(1 + \beta) \tag{8.6}$$

and the ratio of this to the equilibrium capital-labor ratio in the absence of the worker-participation arrangement is

$$k'/k = 1 + \beta \tag{8.7}$$

Thus we again have the predictable effect of an increase in the capital-labor ratio with all the implications this has for the competitive position of an individual firm. Actually, there are only minor differences between these two situations at this point, although in a later section of the chapter I will point out some significant differences in the behavioral implications of the two cases. For now, though, I merely note that the parameter β can be transformed directly into an equivalent λ (denoted as $\hat{\lambda}$) as follows:

$$\hat{\lambda} = \beta(1 - \alpha)/\alpha \tag{8.8}$$

Substituting (8.8) into (8.7) produces

$$k'/k = 1 + [\alpha/(1 - \alpha)]\lambda$$

which is conceptually quite similar to expression (8.5).

The Wage Decision in the Income-Mixing Case: A More Macro View

To now I have focused exclusively on the case of a single firm that is faced with a worker-participation scheme in the context of generalized competitive markets in which there typically are no such arrangements. While the results are enlightening and suggestive, they merely set the stage for a more generalized analysis in which it will be assumed that worker-participation plans are the rule rather than the exception. Again the income-mixing-type arrangement will be considered first.

When worker participation in enterprise decision making becomes widespread, the major change is that factor prices can no longer be regarded as being determined exogenously. Rather, they must now be viewed as being directly affected by the presence of participatory mechanisms. Consequently, when income-mixing-type institutional arrangements are adopted they, produce a general increase in the price of labor and a reduction in the rewards to capital. This implies that unless an adjustment is made in the capital-labor ratio in the economy, labor will be receiving more than its marginal product and capital less. Obviously, the adjustment that is required calls for an increase in the amount of capital employed relative to the quantity of labor. But how much of an adjustment might be required? And what is the mechanism for making it?

To answer these questions I will apply expression (8.2), which defines the equilibrium capital-labor ratio in terms of (1) the parameter α in the production function and (2) the ratio of the wage rate to the unit cost of capital. To illustrate how the expression works, a numerical example will be given using actual data for the manufacturing segment of the American economy for 1970. First, we assume a value of 0.25 for the parameter α. This is reasonably consistent with the data that indicate that profits in the manufacturing sector of the economy in 1970 constituted between 23 and 24 percent of income originating in manufacturing.[6] All that is needed now is some estimate of relative factor costs. The 1970 Census of Manufactures data indicate that annual payroll expenditures per employee in manufacturing were $7966.[7] I will use this as a measure of wage costs. For capital costs I may use either some measure of the interest cost per dollar of capital or the opportunity cost of employing capital, as measured by the normal or average profit rate in manufacturing. Based on Census of Manufactures estimates, the value of capital in manufacturing is calculated to be $533.8 billion, while total net operating profit (before taxes) is estimated to be $51 billion.[8] This gives a profit rate of 9.55 percent, which implies an annual cost for a dollar of capital of $0.0955. Inserting these values in expression (8.5) and solving gives an estimated equilibrium capital-labor ratio of $27,805, which is almost embarrassingly similar to the official estimate of $27,800.[9]

Using these estimates as a benchmark, the impact of instituting income-mixing worker-participation arrangements in the United States can be estimated by assuming certain shifts in the ratio of relative factor costs. For example, under a system in which 10 percent of the profit share of income accrued to labor, the cost of labor for all firms would rise by $3\frac{1}{3}$ percent while the profit rate would fall by 10 percent. In the case of the American economy circa 1970, this would involve an increase in employee compensation to $8.232 and a fall in the profit rate to 8.59 percent. Under these conditions the equilibrium capital-labor ratio would rise to $31,944.

Knowing the capital-labor ratio that would result from a given degree of profit-sharing, it is possible to estimate the employment effects implicit in the adjustment to the new capital-labor ratio under differing sets of assumptions. At one extreme, it might be assumed that there would be no change in the total capital stock. With such an assumption, employment under income-mixing arrangements is given by

$$L_1 = (k_0/k_1)L_0 \qquad (8.10)$$

where the subscripts 0 and 1 denote, respectively, before and after values for the variables. In the example of 10 percent profit-sharing for the United States, this would imply a decrease in employment of 13 percent, which would also involve a decline in output of 9.7 percent.

An alternative assumption would be that output would remain unchanged. In such a case, expression (8.10) becomes

$$L_1 = (k_0/k_1)^{\alpha}L_0 \qquad (8.11)$$

and the employment effect for the example under consideration is reduced to 3.4 percent. This would appear to be the lower limit on direct employment effects since it assumes that despite the lower returns to capital it will be possible to expand the capital stock sufficiently to exactly compensate in an output sense for the diminution in the labor input into the productive process This may involve some heroic assumptions about capital markets.

Table 8-1 contains estimates of the employment effects of income-mixing worker-participation schemes based on the economy of the United States

Table 8-1
Tradeoff between Share of Profit Income Diverted to Workers and Reductions in Employment (Based on United States, 1970)

Share of Profit Income Diverted (λ)	Reduction in Employment	
	No Change in Capital Stock	No Change in Output
.05	6.6%	1.7%
.10	13.0	3.4
.15	19.0	5.2
.20	25.0	7.0
.25	30.8	8.9
.30	36.4	10.8
.33	40.0	12.1

Source: Calculations from data described in text.

similar to those already discussed for value of λ ranging from 0.05 upward. If we focus on the lower bound estimates of employment effects, they vary from 1.7 percent with $\lambda = 0.05$ to 12.1 percent for $\lambda = {}^1/_3$. The implication of the calculations shown in Table 8-1 is that moving toward income-mixing worker-participation arrangements very likely involves some fairly substantial reduction in employment levels unless some action external to the markets involved is taken to vitiate these effects. This possibility will be treated later in the chapter.

The Wage Decision in the Non-Income-Mixing Case: A More Macro View

Turning to the situation in which non-income-mixing forms of worker participation in business decision making are invoked, similar lower-bound calculations of the impact of various values for the parameter β are shown in Table 8-2. Predictably, they show employment effects similar to those found in the case of income-mixing participation. As a rough rule of thumb, every 1 percent increase in the level of wage remuneration results in a 1 percent reduction in employment. These are certainly significant employment effects and confirm the proposition that I have frequently advanced to the effect that to the extent worker-participation arrangements results in higher remuneration (either direct or indirect) for workers and at the expense of some reduction in employment. This suggests the next topic for discussion, namely, the types of response that might be expected to these employment effects.

Table 8-2

Tradeoff between Increases in Wage Rate at Expense of Profits (Based on United States, 1970)

Proportion by which Wage Rate is Increased (β)	Reduction in Employment Assuming No Change in Output
.0167	1.8%
.0333	3.4
.0500	5.2
.0667	7.0
.0833	8.9
.1000	10.8
.1111	12.1

Source: Calculations from data described in text.

Adjustment to Employment Effects at the Private Level

The potential for worker participation in business decision making to have negative employment effects if the increase in worker control is used to increase the levels of individual remuneration within the firm raises the possibility that the threat of unemployment will serve to moderate the wage demands of workers. I illustrate the way in which this might happen in Figure 8-3, which depicts a worker-preference function for differing combinations of employment and λ, the profit-sharing parameter in the income-mixing case. Employment (L) and λ are presumed to be imperfect substitutes for one another, and maximum employment possible is indicated by L_0, the level of employment prior to the substitution of some form of worker sharing in the nonwage income generated by the business enterprise. Similarly, the maximum λ to be considered is one.

All that is needed to determine what worker response will be to the possibility of unemployment resulting from profit-sharing is an opportunity constraint. If workers believe that the choice of λ will affect only employment while leaving output unchanged, the appropriate opportunity constraint is given by the lower bound estimates of employment effects presented in Table 8-1. Since this constraint is convex with respect to the origin, it will generate the normal tangency solution to the decision-making problem facing workers. This is shown in Figure 8-3, and it indicates that the expected worker response to the employment effects implicit in any particular value of λ will be to prefer a λ somewhere intermediate between zero and one. The optimum λ for workers will depend, of course, on the nature of their preference function. In fact, a preference function can be constructed with rates of substitution between λ and L that will yield a boundary solution at the employment end of the oppor-

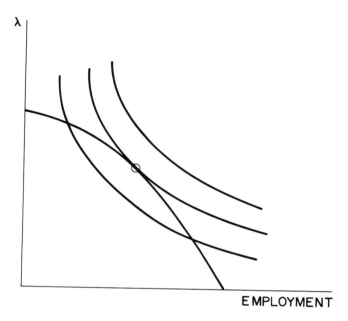

Figure 8-3. A Worker Preference Function

tunity constraint.[10] However, the case of a nonboundary solution would seem to be the more likely situation.

The tangency solution shown in Figure 8-3 provides the upper limit on the value of λ that will result in fact. Whether that limit will be reached depends upon the extent of the power to influence business decisions that is obtained by workers through the worker-participation arrangements that are developed. If they do not have sufficient influence to enforce what is to them the optimal λ, the outcome will be a value of λ falling between 0 and the workers' optimum. Of course, if they have the power to choose a λ higher than the optimal one, they will refrain from doing so.

From this analysis it seems that while there might be some tendency for a private (i.e., worker) response to mitigate the employment effects of worker participation in enterprise decision making, it will be of a limited scope. This is particularly the case in that the preference functions of worker decision makers are likely to be dominated by concern for the welfare of the members of a firm's labor force who remain employed.[11] Remember, even at a value of λ of $1/3$, the employed still outnumber the unemployed by seven to one according to the lower-bound employment-effect estimates shown in Table 8-1. Therefore, it would appear likely that the private response to the presence of the negative employment effects I have postulated will be minimal.

The foregoing analysis has been couched solely in terms of income-mixing-type worker-participation schemes. What about non-income-mixing types? At first glance, they might seem to have virtually the same effects as income-mixing devices since the parameter β may be transformed directly into an equivalent λ. However, there is an additional complication here, namely, the differential uncertainty involved in the receipt of wage and nonwage income. Ordinarily, profit income will show more variability and unpredictability than wage income. Consequently, if workers are risk averse, the same average amounts of profit and wage income will not be regarded as being equivalent. Rather, more profit income than wage income will be required to provide workers with the same amount of satisfaction. Therefore, an additional transformation beyond the simple arithmetic one shown earlier is necessary in order to show equivalencies between λ and β. What this means in terms of our analysis is that for workers to achieve the same amount of satisfaction from increasing their individual income levels through worker participation requires a large shift in income (and a greater employment effect) under income-mixing-type arrangements than under non-income-mixing. However, this does little to alter the basic conclusion that the private response to ameliorating employment effects will be minimal.

Adjustment to Employment Effects at the Social Level

If the private response to employment effects is weak, all that remains as a mechanism for adjusting to these problems is some form of concerted social action, such as an attempt to stimulate economic activity through devices such as monetary and/or fiscal policy. Assume, for example, that worker-participation schemes have created a given amount of unemployment. Why not simply increase aggregate money demand sufficiently to absorb the existing unemployment? Unfortunately, life is not that simple. The linkage between increases in aggregate money demand and increases in output and employment presents problems. Raising levels of aggregate money demand shifts commodity demand curves positively and, *ceteris paribus,* increases commodity prices. At these higher commodity prices producers are willing to supply greater quantities of goods and services, and output and employment will expand *provided* there are no changes in the supply conditions governing the provision of those goods and services. This is the meaning of the *ceteris paribus* condition.

In our context, the *ceteris paribus* assumption means that wage rates do not rise and cause an upward shift in commodity supply curves. At least, they do not rise by enough to vitiate the output and employment effects of the demand stimulus. What this implies is that commodity prices rise more rapidly than money wage compensation (including any profit-sharing-type income) and that real wage rates fall. Consequently, for an aggregate demand stimulus to be effective in eliminating the negative employment shifts under discussion, it must result in an erosion of the real gains that workers have achieved through the device of worker-participation arrangements.

What I am describing here is, of course, the familiar case of money illusion operating in the labor market. Output and employment are stimulated precisely because workers do not sense the losses to them implicit in commodity price increases and the rise in the nonwage share of income that accompanies it. Thus for aggregate-demand-type stimulation of the economy to be effective in negating the unemployment effects of worker participation it must undo and reverse the gains workers achieve under such arrangements. In fact, if this type approach to dealing with employment effects were completely successful, the following equality would hold:

$$w_0/p_1 + \lambda\pi/p_1 = w_0/p_0 \qquad (8.12)$$

where w_0 and p_0 denote, respectively, the money wage rate and price level prior to the institution of worker participation, π is the profit per worker employed, and p_1 is the price level after demand stimulation. From (8.12) it is clear that elimination of employment effects through demand stimulation means returning the real wage to its preworker-participation level. Of course, throughout this analysis I am assuming a stationary economy from the growth standpoint.[12]

What is the likelihood of success in eliminating the employment effects implicit in meaningful worker participation if an aggregate demand stimulation approach is used? The answer to that question turns on the extent to which workers are the victims of money illusion in the labor market. In the United States, at least, the record in this respect suggests that one could only hope for transitory improvements in the unemployment situation using this form of social policy. It does not appear that American workers can be "fooled" in this fashion for any protracted period of time. For the most part, the unemployment problems of the 1970s in the United States are the product of workers (1) recognizing the impact of price increases on their real wage position during the 1960s and (2) beginning to anticipate inflation in their wage demands.[13] As a result, conventional methods of aggregate economic stimulation have proven relatively unfruitful because of their being anticipated and discounted. Therefore, if our present experience in the United States is considered, it does not seem that the use of the usual tools of monetary and/or fiscal policy afford much prospect of providing any permanent amelioration of the employment effects implicit in worker participation.

The reason for this is simple. If through worker participation in the decision-making processes of enterprises they acquire the power to substantially alter the structure of relative factor prices in favor of workers, the end result will be an increase in the "natural" or "normal" rate of unemployment in the system. In effect, what is involved is a shift to a higher full-employment unemployment rate than that which previously existed. The significance of this lies in the inability of standard demand stimulation techniques to produce anything other than minor and temporary deviations below this normal unemployment rate. Further, if a society persists in believing that it is possible to play the "money illusion" shell game on workers on a permanent basis, it is merely deluding itself and imparting a substantial inflationary bias to the economy.

Given the improbability of social intervention being able to compensate successfully for the unemployment effects of worker participation through the indirect means of increasing aggregate money demand for goods and services, is there any alternative policy approach that might achieve the same end? The answer is affirmative. If it is not possible to adjust, after the fact, to change in capital-labor ratios, why not prevent the substitution of capital for labor that would normally follow in the wake of a worker-participation-induced increase in the wage rate? In short, another way to deal with the problem of employment effects is to require some sort of public approval before dismissals of employees could occur. A step in this direction was taken by the European Community in September 1975 when it required that "projected collective redundancies are to be notified in advance to a competent public authority, and will not normally take effect until a period of thirty days has expired during which time the public authority is to seek solutions to the problems raised by the projected redundancies."[14]

What this implies is a transferral of decisions regarding optimal factor mixes out of the market place and into the political arena. The likely upshot of this would seem to be the introduction of some substantial inefficiencies into the economy. After all, it is an economic commonplace that given a particular factor price structure, providing a level of output with a capital-labor ratio other than the optimal one will result in higher costs of production. Therefore, this solution to the employment problems generated by worker participation involves some cost in terms of productive efficiency. Beyond that, the substitution of political decision-making apparatuses for economic will probably serve to cause workers to be more aggressive in terms of their use of the power that worker participation has permitted them. In effect, consistent use of social mechanisms to eliminate employment effects will cause the workers' preference function to shift in a fashion that will increase the value of λ they regard as optimal. Thus direct interference in the form of limiting the extent to which capital-labor ratios may be altered will actually cause workers to pursue a course of activity that will result in even greater distortions of actual capital-labor ratios away from optimal.

Distributional Impacts of
Worker Participation

Let us assume at this point that I am considering an economy that has wide-spread worker participation that has been effective in increasing the real wage rate received by the employed members of the population. Any employment effects implicit in this arrangement are included in the "natural" rate of unemployment for the system, and full employment is defined as that level which is consistent with the existence of the natural rate of unemployment. The question I ask is, "What are the long-term impacts of this situation on the distribution of income between capital and labor?"

I will approach the problem within the context of a Solow-type neoclassical growth model.[15] It is well known that in such a model equilibrium output per head is some function of the equilibrium capital-labor ratio (k^*) and the equilibrium condition is

$$f(k^*) = [(\dot{L} + \tau)/s] k^* \qquad (8.13)$$

where $\dot{L}$ denotes the rate of growth in the labor force, τ is a technological progress parameter that measures the rate of increase in labor productivity attributable to technological progress, and s is a parameter that measures the ratio of saving to income in the economy. A graphic representation of the equilibrium condition is useful and is shown in Figure 8-4.

It is also well known that the distribution of income between capital and labor at any equilibrium point on the per worker production function $f(k)$ is given by extending a line tangent to the equilibrium point to the output per head axis, with the distance along this axis from the origin to the point of intersection being the wage rate and the distance from the point of intersection to the equilibrium output per man representing profits per worker employed. Consequently, a distributional locus (denoted as $\phi(k)$) may be traced that defines the relative shares of capital and labor in the income generated by the productive process.

To assess the impact of worker participation I assume an increase in the wage rate per man from w to w_1. This involves a movement to a higher equilibrium capital-labor ratio, k_1^*, a higher output per employed worker, q_1^*, and a movement to a new point on the distributional locus $\phi(k)$. The effect of the shift to a different point on $\phi(k)$ depends on the characteristics of the production function. If it is a constant returns-to-scale function with an elasticity of substitution of unity, a 1 percent increase in the price of labor relative to the price of capital will produce a 1 percent increase in the capital-labor ratio and no change in the fraction of income accruing to either labor or capital. An

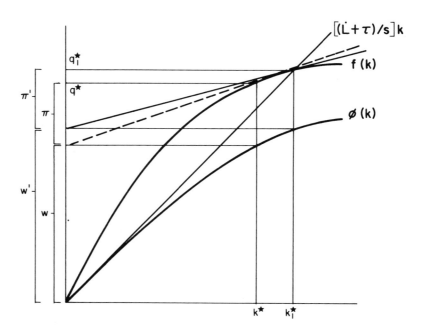

Figure 8–4. The Equilibrium Situation

example of such a function is the familiar Cobb-Douglas one in which the parameter α defines the distribution of income between capital and labor. Therefore, for the rise in the wage rate from w to w_1 to have any effect on the distribution of income between capital and labor, the elasticity of substitution in the production function must differ from unity. More precisely, to shift the distribution in favor of workers as a group, the elasticity of substitution must be less than unity.

While the available empirical evidence with respect to the character of production functions is mixed, for the most part it points in the direction of their having an elasticity of substitution not significantly different from unity.[16] If this is the case, the conclusion is clear that worker participation will not have any effect on the functional distribution of income as long as employers are left free to adjust their capital-labor ratios to reflect the relative factor price structure that will emerge from worker-participation-type arrangements. However, if employers are constrained in their ability to vary factor combinations, the functional distribution of income can be altered in the direction of increasing the labor share and reducing the capital share of income. All that such constraints would amount to is a political decision to make the elasticity of substitution less than unity.

While there will be virtually no change in the functional distribution of income in a world in which employers are free to adjust capital-labor ratios, there will be some impact on the personal distribution of income. Specifically, through the mechanism of employment effects there will be a redistribution of income away from the nonemployed portion of the labor force toward those who remain employed. Of course, we are talking here of the income distribution before taxes are levied and transfer payments made. To the extent the social impacts of employment effects are ameliorated through social transfer payments, it is possible for the after-tax functional distribution of income to be altered. For example, if nonwage income is taxed more heavily to finance transfers to the nonemployed, the after-tax distribution will be shifted in favor of the labor component. Therefore, there may be indirect redistributional effects at the functional level, even though direct ones are lacking.

Some Observations on Worker Participation and Economic Growth

The analytical framework employing a Solow-type neoclassical growth model is also useful in shedding some light on the likely impact of worker-participation arrangements on long-term economic growth in a market economy. In such a model the equilibrium growth rate in output per employed member of the population is

$$\dot{q} = \dot{L} + \tau \tag{8.14}$$

Now, since a generalized increase in the wage rate relative to the profit rate requires that the magnitude $(\dot{L} + \tau)/s$ fall, the possibility of worker participation impacting on the growth rate is obvious. Whether it does, depends on the behavior of s, the savings ratio. Unless s rises, $\dot{L} + \tau$ must fall in order for the quantity $(\dot{L} + \tau)/s$ to decrease. What is the likelihood of this? Remote, apparently. For example, Peovich has argued that in the worker-managed firm, à la Yugoslavia, there will be a decline in the savings ratio.[17] In addition, two different versions of an aggregate savings function suggest that s will, in reality, either remain unchanged or decline. First, consider the Kaldor savings function:[18]

$$s = s_w W/0 + s_p P/0 \tag{8.15}$$

where s_w and s_p denote the savings propensities out of wage income (W) and profit income (P), respectively. Now, if the aggregate production function is of the Cobb-Douglas type, (8.15) becomes

$$s = s_w(1 - \alpha) + s_p \alpha \tag{8.16}$$

and it is apparent that s will remain constant unless s_w and s_p change. Or, as an alternative, take the standard classical savings function in which

$$s = f(r) \qquad ds/dr > 0 \qquad\qquad (8.17)$$

where r denotes the profit rate.

Since the profit rate is given by the slope of the production function at the point associated with the equilibrium capital-labor ratio, it is obvious that the lower profit rate associated with worker participation will result in a lower savings ratio. If this is the case, $\dot{L} + \tau$ must fall even more substantially than was required in the case of the Kaldor savings function to accommodate the changed relative factor price structure imposed by worker participation.

The implications of this argument would seem to be clear. Unless one postulates a savings function in which the savings rate is *negatively* associated with the profit rate, worker participation implies a reduction in $\dot{L} + \tau$ and a reduction in the growth rate at equilibrium. This can be accomplished either through a slowing in the rate of technical progress or a decline in the rate of growth in the size of the labor force associated with the "natural" rate of unemployment. If we assume the population growth rate to be an exogenously given constant, the latter implies a consistent increase in the "natural" rate of unemployment. Either way, the prospects are not encouraging if growth is taken to be a desirable objective. However, if one desires less economic growth, shifting to a decision-making mechanism involving a greater degree of worker participation would seem to be a viable policy approach.

Concluding Remarks

In an effort to integrate in a meaningful fashion the rather diverse strands of analysis presented in this chapter, a descriptive sketch will be provided of the likely course of events that would ensue following the conversion of a capitalistic, market-oriented economy, say, at the risk of being parochial, the United States, to a full-blown system of substantial and meaningful worker impact on the decisions made by business enterprises. I would anticipate that workers would use their additional power to increase money wage rates at the expense of profit rates. If successful in this respect, the predicted outcome is a rise in the natural unemployment rate in the economy. Undoubtedly, this would trigger a round of the standard policies for stimulating money aggregate demand. However, unless workers are the victim of money illusion in the labor market, all this will accomplish is an inflation of price and wage levels in the economy with no permanent reduction in unemployment.[19] Further complicating the situation will be a decline in the overall growth rate, either as the result of a slowing in the rate of technical progress or a tendency for the natural rate of unemployment to grow through time.

Faced with the triple dilemma of price inflation, high unemployment, and a retardation in the growth rate, the likely diagnosis by policy makers will be that the capitalistic system of free markets is incapable of making the necessary adjustments in the economy and, consequently, some form of systematic intervention by a central authority is required. At first, it is likely to take the form of wage and price controls to temporarily stabilize the system. This is apt to be followed by some sort of incomes policy, i.e., substitution of political for economic judgments in the arena where the functional distribution of income is determined, as well as direct interference with the employment decisions made by business enterprises.

Ultimately, this system will bog down in a morass of bureaucratic rigidity and inefficiency, and the misallocation of resources it has introduced into the system will reach what will be regarded by the implementers of public policy as "crisis proportions." At this point, they will recognize the futility of their piecemeal tinkering with the economy. Unfortunately, though, their conclusion will not be that it is appropriate to retreat from these policies in the direction of freer markets and a more automatic system of making economic adjustments. Rather, they will interpret the failures of partial interference in the system as being a measure of the true extent of the malaise that besets capitalism. In short, they will conclude that the system is really sicker than anyone thought and that the only cure is full-blown central planning.

A distorted view of the potential long-term impact of worker participation in enterprise decision making? Perhaps. However, I suspect it is more accurate than the notion that is the basic foundation of the argument for direct worker participation, namely, that workers do not have any meaningful input into the decision-making processes of enterprises unless there be some form of inclusion of worker representatives in enterprise decision making bodies. This simply ignores the manner in which labor markets function to limit the range of discretionary alternatives available to a business enterprise. If an employer arbitrarily chooses to offer a wage rate that is substantially less than the prevailing one, there will be a systematic withdrawal of labor from that employer; and conversely, if he offers a wage substantially greater than normal, he would have an excess of applications for jobs. This is merely the familiar notion of workers moving between jobs in response to differential economic opportunities. To the extent that workers behave in this fashion, they already possess a democratic input into the decision-making process, an input that is often characterized as "voting with one's feet." But, critics will say, this opportunity is so limited that it is really of little significance. Not so, at least according to data for the United States. In 1973, for example, the quit rate in American manufacturing was 2.7 percent *a month.*[20] This translates into 32.4 percent a year, almost one-third of the labor force engaged in this type employment. And this is a voluntary movement. It is a *quit* rate and does not include dismissals.[21] This is a substantial amount of movement, more than enough to permit workers to register, at the margin, their likes and dislikes with respect to the wage–employment conditions packages offered by various employers.[22] This is certainly worker participation in the decisions that affect their lives; worker participation, incidentally, that does not carry with it all the disruptive economic consequences that attend the more obvious forms of worker control over enterprise decision making that we have been discussing.

Notes

1. European Communities Commission, *Employee Participation and Company Structure in the European Community,* Bulletin of the European Communities, Supplement (August 1975): 9. Hereafter referred to as the Green Paper.

2. Eirik Furubotn, "Worker Alienation and the Structure of the Firm," in Svetozar Pejovich, ed., *Governmental Controls and the Free Market, The U.S. Economy in the 1970s* (College Station, Texas: Texas A&M Univ. Press, 1976), p. 203.

3. Green Paper, p. 56.

4. These assumptions would have to be modified only slightly to fit the case in which there is a substantial amount of collective bargaining in the society. In such a case, all that is critical is that employers be free to adjust the quantity of labor they hire so that the wage rate is equal to the marginal product of labor.

5. This is, of course, the simple Cobb-Douglas production function of the form.

$$0 = aK^{\alpha}L^{1-\alpha}$$

where K denotes the total amount of capital employed.

6. Data from the *U.S. Statistical Abstract, 1974* indicate that in 1970 national income originating in manufacturing was 218 billion dollars (Table 1219). Net operating profit (before taxes) of manufacturing corporations was 50 billion dollars (Table 1220). It is further estimated (from Table 776) that profits in manufacturing attributable to noncorporate forms of business amount to another one billion dollars. This gives the estimate of the profit share at between 23 and 24 percent.

7. Ibid., Table 1217.

8. The estimate of total capital stock in manufacturing is derived by multiplying the capital invested per employee in manufacturing (from Table 1226, *Statistical Abstract, 1974*) by the number of employees in manufacturing (Table 1217).

9. Ibid., Table 1226.

10. No boundary solution is possible at the λ end of the constraint since the factor-price ratio (and capital-labor ratio) becomes infinite for a value of λ equal to unity.

11. This is a phenomenon that is widely recognized in the literature dealing with trade union behavior. See, for example, William Fellner, *Competition Among the Few* (New York: Knopf, 1949), pp. 252-276; and Allan Cartter, *Theory of Wages and Employment* (Homewood, Illinois: Irwin, 1959), pp. 82-83.

12. Modifying the discussion to incorporate a growth factor would merely entail multiplying both sides of equation (8.12) by the growth rate.

13. For details of the operation of this mechanism, see Lowell E. Gallaway, "The Folklore of Unemployment and Poverty," in Pejovich, *Government Controls,* pp. 41-47.

14. Green Paper, pp. 12-13.

15. Robert M. Solow, "A Contribution to the Theory of Economic Growth," *Quarterly Journal of Economics* (February 1956): 65-94.

16. For a thorough discussion of this question, see Zvi Griliches, "Production Functions in Manufacturing: Some Preliminary Results," in Murray Brown, ed., *The Theory and Empirical Analysis of Production,* Studies in Income and Wealth, vol. 31 (New York: National Bureau of Economic Research, 1967), pp. 275-322.

17. Svetozar Pejovich, "The Firm, Monetary Policy and Property Rights in a Planned Economy," *Western Economic Journal* (September 1968): 193-200.

18. Nicholas Kaldor, "Alternative Theories of Distribution," *Review of Economic Studies* 2 (1956): 83-100.

19. It is worth noting that if workers are victims of money illusion to a sufficient extent to eliminate the employment effects of worker participation, then nothing has really changed as the result of worker participation and the whole issue is trivial.

20. *Statistical Abstract, 1974,* Table 561.

21. On the other side of the market, it is worth noting that the accession rate was 4.8 percent a month in 1973, or over one-half the total labor force through the course of a year.

22. For a summary of some of the evidence on this point for industrial, occupational, and geographic labor markets, see Lowell E. Gallaway, *Manpower Economics* (Homewood, Illinois: Irwin, 1971), chaps. 3, 4, and 5.

Index

Index

About the Contributors

Arthur Shenfield, a British economist and barrister-at-law, has taught at a number of American universities. In 1977 he was Regent's Professor of Economics at the University of California and a visiting professor of economics at the University of Dallas. He is currently visiting professor at the University of San Diego Law School.

Malcolm R. Fisher is a professor at the Australian Graduate School of Management, University of New South Wales. Until recently Professor Fisher was a university lecturer at Downing College, Cambridge University.

Hans G. Monissen has a chair in monetary economics at the University of Giesen, Germany. Professor Monissen has published numerous articles in prominent European journals.

Rune Ryden was formerly a professor of economic history at the University of London. He is a member of the Swedish Parliament. Professor Ryden was a visiting professor at Ohio University in the early 1970s.

Douglass C. North is chairman of the Department of Economics, University of Washington. Professor North is one of the most prominent economic historians in the country and author of many books and articles.

Eirik Furubotn is a professor of economics at Texas A & M University. Professor Furubotn is an internationally recognized author on the labor-managed firm.

Lowell Gallaway is a distinguished professor of economics at Ohio University. Professor Gallaway is widely published in the fields of labor, economics of poverty, and economic welfare.

About the Editor